Value for Money in Health Spending

OECD

ORGANISATION FOR ECONOMIC CO-OPERATION AND DEVELOPMENT

The OECD is a unique forum where governments work together to address the economic, social and environmental challenges of globalisation. The OECD is also at the forefront of efforts to understand and to help governments respond to new developments and concerns, such as corporate governance, the information economy and the challenges of an ageing population. The Organisation provides a setting where governments can compare policy experiences, seek answers to common problems, identify good practice and work to co-ordinate domestic and international policies.

The OECD member countries are: Australia, Austria, Belgium, Canada, Chile, the Czech Republic, Denmark, Finland, France, Germany, Greece, Hungary, Iceland, Ireland, Israel, Italy, Japan, Korea, Luxembourg, Mexico, the Netherlands, New Zealand, Norway, Poland, Portugal, the Slovak Republic, Slovenia, Spain, Sweden, Switzerland, Turkey, the United Kingdom and the United States. The Commission of the European Communities takes part in the work of the OECD.

OECD Publishing disseminates widely the results of the Organisation's statistics gathering and research on economic, social and environmental issues, as well as the conventions, guidelines and standards agreed by its members.

> *This work is published on the responsibility of the Secretary-General of the OECD. The opinions expressed and arguments employed herein do not necessarily reflect the official views of the Organisation or of the governments of its member countries.*

ISBN 978-92-64-08880-1 (print)
ISBN 978-92-64-08881-8 (PDF)

Series:
ISSN: 2074-3181 (print)
ISSN: 2074-319X (PDF)

Also available in French: *Optimiser les dépenses de santé*

Photo credits: Cover © skodonnell/lstockphoto
© Scott Hales/Shutterstock.com.

Corrigenda to OECD publications may be found on line at: *www.oecd.org/publishing/corrigenda*.

Foreword

OECD health ministers met in Paris on 7th-8th October 2010 to reflect on the tremendous progress made in the health of the populations of their countries, due in no small part to the improvements that have been made in health systems. But they also considered the difficult path they must walk in the future. Countries have to improve the value they get from the large and increasing investment they are making in health care. This is now all the more difficult – and urgent – in light of the difficult fiscal situation facing many countries in the aftermath of the economic crisis.

OECD countries have made tremendous strides in improving population health over recent decades. Life expectancy at birth has increased, rising on average by ten years between 1960 and 2008. Almost all countries have some form of public or private insurance covering the risk of ill health and high medical costs and access to basic health care has also improved. However, these achievements have not come cheaply – countries have confronted steady increases in the cost of health care spending over recent decades. Looking to the future, OECD countries will continue to face upward pressures on health spending from a number of factors including demographic change, advances in medical care technology and the growing expectations from patients and the electorate at large. What can countries do to get the most value for money while maintaining the goals of quality and access that people have come to expect? This report explores the different tools available to countries to increase the value of their health care investments.

This report reflects the contribution of colleagues from in and outside of the OECD. Michael Borowitz co-ordinated the report. Chapter 1 was prepared by David Morgan with assistance of Eva Orosz; Chapter 2 by Howard Oxley; Chapter 3 by Valérie Paris; Chapter 4 by Michael Borowitz, Professor Richard Scheffler and Brent Fulton from the University of California at Berkeley; Chapter 5 by Michael Borowitz and Maria M. Hofmarcher at Gesundheit Österreich GmbH; Chapter 6 by Valérie Paris, with the assistance of Rita Faria; Chapter 7 by Michael Borowitz and Elettra Ronchi. Marion Devaux provided statistical assistance for several chapters, and the text was prepared for publication by Isabelle Vallard and Judy Zinnemann. Authors would like to thank Raphaëlle Bisiaux for her assistance, and Tracey Strange and Marlène Mohier for their editing work. Many members of the OECD Health Division provided comments on one or more of the chapters. Mark Pearson, head of the OECD Health Division, supervised the preparation of the report and provided useful comments on various versions. Country experts and delegates to the OECD Health Committee were particularly active in making suggestions about the issues that needed to be addressed and providing information on national policies and evaluations.

This book has...

StatLinks

**A service that delivers Excel® files
from the printed page!**

Look for the *StatLinks* at the bottom right-hand corner of the tables or graphs in this book.
To download the matching Excel® spreadsheet, just type the link into your Internet browser,
starting with the ***http://dx.doi.org*** prefix.
If you're reading the PDF e-book edition, and your PC is connected to the Internet, simply
click on the link. You'll find *StatLinks* appearing in more OECD books.

Table of Contents

Tables

Figures

Acronyms

ADR	Adverse Drug Reaction
AHRQ	Agency for Healthcare Research and Quality
AIDS	Acquired Immune Deficiency Syndrome
AIHW	Australian Institute of Health and Welfare
AMI	Acute Myocardial Infarction
BIA	Budget Impact Analysis
BMI	Body Mass Index
CAD	Canadian dollars
CAPI	Contract for Improvement of Individual Practice
CCM	Chronic Care Model
CDI	Communicable Diseases Intelligence
CDM	Chronic Disease Management
CEA	Cost-effectiveness Analysis
CED	Coverage with Evidence Development
CER	Comparative Effectiveness Research
CHD	Coronary Heart Disease
CHF	Swiss franc
CMS	Centers for Medicare and Medicaid Services
CPOE	Computerised Physician Order Entry
DDD	Defined Daily Doses
DFID	Department for International Development
DIMDI	German Institute for Medical Information and Documentation
DMP	Disease Management Programme
DOQ	Doctor's Office Quality
DRG	Diagnostic-Related Groups
EBM	Evidence-based Medicine
EGA	European Generic Medicines Association
EMR	Electronic Medical Records
EUR	Euro
FFS	Fee-for-Service
G-BA	Federal Joint Committee of Health Insurance Funds, Hospitals and Physicians (Germany)
GBP	Pound Sterling
GDP	Gross Domestic Product
GP	General Practitioner
GPII	General Practice Immunisation Incentive Scheme (Australia)
HAS	Haute Autorité de Santé (France)
HEDIS	Health Plan Employer Data and Information Set (Medicare, United States)

HER	Electronic Health Records
HIRA	Health Insurance Review Agency (Korea)
HIV	Human Immunodeficiency Virus
HMO	Health Maintenance Organisation
HTA	Health Technology Assessment
ICD	Implantable Cardioverter Defibrillator
ICER	Incremental Cost-effectiveness Ratio
ICO	Integrated Care Organisations
ICT	Information and Communication Technologies
IMS	Intercontinental Medical Statistics
INAHTA	International Network of Agencies for Health Technology Assessment
INN	International Non-proprietary Names
IOM	Institute of Medicine
IQWiG	Institute for Quality and Efficiency in Health Care (Germany)
LDL	Low Density Lipoprotein
LFN	Pharmaceutical Benefits Board (Sweden)
MCCD	Medicare Co-ordinated Care Demonstration
MPV	Medical Practice Variations
MRI	Magnetic Resonance Imaging
MRP	Maximum Reimbursement Price
NAO	National Audit Office
NEHEN	New England Healthcare Electronic Data Interchange Network
NHA	National Health Account
NHS	National Health Service
NICE	UK National Institute for Health and Clinical Excellence
NZD	New Zealand dollar
OTC	Over the Counter
P4P	Pay-for-Performance
PACS	Picture Archiving and Communications Systems
PAS	Patient Access Scheme
PBM	Performance-based Management
PBS	Pharmaceutical Benefits Scheme
PCI	Percutaneous Coronary Intervention
PEA	Pharmaco-economic Assessment
PGP	Physician Group Practice
PHO	Primary Health Organisations
PICS	Picture Archiving and Communications Systems
PIP	Practice Incentives Program
PMPRB	Patented Medicine Prices Review Board (Canada)
PPP	Purchasing Power Parity
PPRI	Pharmaceutical Pricing and Reimbursement Information
PPRS	Pharmaceutical Pricing Regulation Scheme (United Kingdom)
PROM	Patient Reported Outcomes Measurement
QALY	Quality-Adjusted Life Year
QOF	Quality and Outcomes Framework (United Kingdom)
R&D	Research and Development
RBF	Results-based Financing

RBRVS	Resource-based Relative Value Scale
RCT	Randomised Controlled Trials
SBU	Swedish National Agency for Health Technology Assessment
SVR	Council on the Assessment of Developments in Health Care (Germany)
THE	Total Health Expenditure
USAID	United States Agency for International Development
USD	US dollar
VAT	Value Added Tax
VIP	Value Incentive Programme
WADP	Weighted Average Disclosed Price
WHO	World Health Organisation

Executive Summary

Oecd countries have made tremendous strides in improving population health over recent decades. Life expectancy at birth has increased, rising on average by ten years between 1960 and 2008. Today, a woman aged 65 can expect to live another 20 years, and a man an additional 17 years. And although socio-economic inequalities in health status and access to care remain, reductions in child mortality and gains in population health have continued to improve at a steady pace. These achievements can in part be attributed to increased incomes and higher levels of education. But a good portion of these gains comes from improvements in health care itself – through technological progress and evidence-based treatment, in particular.

Health systems are now more effective and of higher quality than ever before. Access to care, too, has continued to improve. Mexico and Turkey have recently introduced reforms to provide coverage for the poor or uninsured. The United States has just passed legislation that will mandate health insurance coverage for almost everyone. OECD countries are closer than ever before to achieving universal or near universal coverage for a core set of services. Such reforms have particular importance during recessions, when incomes are lower for some families, making the costs of poor health particularly hard to bear.

The economic crisis has led to increased pressure on public finance. Given that the largest share of health spending is funded from public budgets, fiscal constraints will heighten the need for governments to control costs and improve value for money for health spending. However, these short-term objectives come in the context of longer-term trends: pressures for increased health spending will be unrelenting, fuelled by technological changes, population expectations and ageing.

Governments have available to them a wide range of policy tools to control costs. Short-term "command and control" policies can hold expenditures down in the short term, but they often have unfortunate consequences in the long term. In addition, they do little or nothing to moderate the underlying pressures which are pushing health spending up over the medium term. There are promising avenues for controlling health spending in the longer term by improving value for money, particularly the quality of health care. Moreover, to reap these potential gains often requires new investments upfront. Hence, many countries face a dilemma: short-term and long-term policy priorities sometimes point in different directions.

This publication takes on the subject of how best to structure health policies to get the best results from what is invested, providing in-depth analysis of the health expenditure patterns and policy options to improve value from health spending in both the short and long term. It reviews several promising new areas for improving value for money in health.

What does health care spending look like in the OECD?

With three-quarters of health spending funded from public budgets, concerns about the allocation of resources and the efficiency of spending come to the forefront, especially so when money is tight and governments face difficulties in financing public sector deficits. Chapter 1 shows that health spending represents 9% of OECD economies (2008). It exceeds 10% in seven OECD countries – the United States, France, Switzerland, Austria, Germany, Canada and Belgium. While the rate of increase in health spending has slowed in the period 2003-08, health expenditure growth has still exceeded economic growth in almost all OECD countries in the past 15 years. Factors exerting upward pressure on health spending (technological change, population expectations, increased incomes and, to a varied extent across countries, population ageing) will continue to drive health spending higher in the future. According to OECD projections, public health spending could increase by between 50% and 90% by 2050, depending on the assumptions made.

What are OECD countries doing in the face of financial constraints and what should they be doing next?

This review comes in the context of one of the deepest recessions on record, when OECD countries are focussing on how to enhance the efficiency and effectiveness of health care systems to ensure that goals of access to and quality of health care continue to be met. Chapter 2 looks at policy options available to governments to tackle the financial sustainability of health systems and assesses their possible impact.

In most OECD countries, governments have considerable control over the supply of health inputs and their prices. Measures that control inputs, set caps to budgets, or freeze prices, can lead to significant cost cuts or strongly moderate the rate of growth in health spending. These tools have been utilised widely, albeit with different intensity over time and across countries. Most OECD countries impose health expenditure caps, particularly in the hospital sector. They appear to be most successful particularly in single-payer systems or countries with integrated health financing and supply.

Wage controls – typically occurring in the context of broad public-sector pay restrictions – have more commonly been implemented in countries with integrated health systems and those with salary-based remuneration for health professionals (for example, Denmark, United Kingdom and Ireland for hospitals, but also Finland, Spain and Sweden). In fee-for-service environments, most OECD governments have maintained oversight over price setting or set prices administratively (e.g. Japan, Korea), sometimes in response to a break-down of negotiations with providers (e.g. Australia, Belgium, Canada, France, Luxembourg).

Policy tools addressing the demand side are also commonly used. For example, restricting the scope and depth of the benefit package of essential health services can lessen pressures on public expenditures. This includes government decisions about the benefit package (what is or is not covered) but also greater cost sharing by patients. Greater out-of-pocket spending, however, falls most heavily on the poor and may hinder access to care. Targeted programmes may be needed to help protect the most vulnerable in society.

The experience of countries which promptly reduced health expenditure after previous recessions suggests that the impact is short-lived. It is even possible that measures taken to restrict costs in the short run can increase long-run spending – if necessary investments are delayed and desirable prevention policies are not implemented. Many of the short-term policies can result in reduced access to care, less equitable provision of services, less responsive care, poorer quality, and delayed access to desirable new technologies.

Medical care: does it work and is it worth it?

Patients, providers and payers have a common interest in ensuring that health care systems do not waste resources. Many studies have observed significant variations in medical practice within and across countries that are not always fully explained by variations in epidemiological needs. According to the United States Institute of Medicine, half of health care services are still provided without any evidence about their effectiveness. In addition, where there is strong evidence of effectiveness, people do not always receive appropriate treatments. For instance, the Rand Corporation estimated in 2001 that more than half of the care received by American adults for a set of 30 acute and chronic conditions was not consistent with recommendations of evidence-based medicine.

Chapter 3 suggests that large efficiency gains could be achieved by introducing more rational decision making into clinical care. Evidence-based medicine (EBM) and health technology assessment (HTA) can be used to inform decision making at the patient level (clinical guidelines) or at the system level (to inform coverage decisions). EBM and HTA help answer two fundamental questions regarding a health care service: does it work, and is it worth it?

Though countries have been paying more attention to such issue, many have not yet realised the full potential of EBM and HTA. Only a few countries produce and actively disseminate clinical guidelines to inform decision making at the doctor and patient levels. Even in countries with advanced institutions and practice of HTA, clinical recommendations are not always diffused in an efficient manner, guaranteeing doctors' and patients' adherence. Many OECD countries have adopted explicit structures or processes to help purchasers make informed decisions on coverage of pharmaceuticals or costly new technologies, but other types of services are less scrutinised. EBM and HTA have already increased the transparency of decision making and helped to ensure that new investments are worth their cost, but there is scope to do more.

Can incentives improve performance and efficiency?

Chapter 4 looks at OECD countries which are experimenting with new methods of paying providers and sometimes patients to improve the quality of health care, often known as pay for performance (P4P) or payment for results. There are growing numbers of schemes testing new models for rewarding quality: in OECD countries like the United States, United Kingdom, and Germany; in middle-income countries like Brazil, China, and India; and in low-income countries like Rwanda. These P4P schemes are testing whether new ways of paying providers (hospitals, primary care, integrated systems) that use some type of synthetic measure of quality show improvements in the *quality* of care and also improve *value for money* in health.

P4P programmes have been widely introduced across OECD countries, yet the research designs to evaluate them are often inadequate to provide a definitive answer about the effect of P4P programmes on quality and costs. Ironically, the best evaluated P4P schemes are in low-income countries supported by the World Bank administered Health Results Innovation Trust Fund. Evidence suggests that giving incentives for priority public health interventions like cancer screening works. P4P also appears promising in getting physicians to follow evidence-based guidelines for chronic conditions like diabetes and cardiovascular diseases. But there are still challenging measurement and design issues.

Can better co-ordination of care make a difference?

Chapter 5 looks at the increasing complexity of health care systems in OECD countries – in terms of multiple layers of caregivers, a diverse range of settings and a complex combination of public and private insurance funds that handle payments. Multiple providers, lack of adherence to care protocols, inconsistencies in reimbursement and decentralised medical records are still the norm in most OECD health systems. With more patients receiving care from multiple providers for chronic conditions, there is a growing problem of fragmentation within health systems. This results in poor patient experiences, coupled with ineffective and unsafe care.

The health problems systems have to deal with have evolved too. Chronic diseases, including cardiovascular diseases, cancers, respiratory conditions, diabetes, and mental disorders, now account for the largest segment of the burden of disease and a large percentage of health care costs. The WHO estimated that 60% of deaths were due to chronic diseases worldwide (not including HIV/AIDS) and for 86% of deaths in the European region. The economic and medical progresses that have extended life spans have accompanied certain lifestyle trends that contribute to the development of chronic diseases such as diabetes, heart disease and cancer. In essence, health care has become good at keeping people alive with diseases that would in the past have killed them, and even in the recent past.

So far, the complexity of financing streams and the difficulty in transferring electronically medical records from one provider to another have proven to be barriers to greater co-ordination of care. It can also be difficult to provide the right incentives to hospital and primary care providers to co-ordinate. To overcome these barriers, a number of innovative schemes have been tried, including integrating primary care and hospitals together, and rewarding physicians if they manage to co-ordinate care more effectively. Results have been mixed, however. Some initiatives have reduced costs somewhat, but a more common finding is an improvement in the quality of care (and hence improving value for money).

Specific areas appear to be promising such as mental health care, particularly for depression and schizophrenia, and palliative care for patients with multiple disorders. The models that work in these areas include multiaxial teams linking primary and specialist care, a care co-ordinator and greater patient empowerment. Also, the use of "predictive modelling" tools to target costly disease management programmes to those who will be most likely to benefit can improve the cost effectiveness of these programmes. The failure to achieve cost savings in other areas of care reflects in part the fact that co-ordination itself is expensive, but also that it is unrealistic to expect cost savings in treating those with extensive co-morbidities.

The role of patients in the care process has also taken on much greater importance in recent years. Yet it has been very difficult to determine the best way to involve patients in their own care, not least because people vary greatly in their responsiveness to information, advice and treatment guidelines.

How to draw all the benefits from pharmaceutical spending?

Chapter 6 reviews recent developments in pharmaceutical policies in OECD countries, which generally try to achieve a balance betwen three broad objectives: make medicines accessible and affordable to patients; contain public spending growth; and provide incentives for future innovation.

Pharmaceutical spending accounts for 17% of total health spending on average in OECD countries, ranging from only 8% of total health expenditure in Norway to 32% in Hungary. In the past, pharmaceutical spending has risen at a faster pace than total health spending but this trend has now reversed: between 2003 and 2008, real pharmaceutical expenditure has grown by 3.1% per year on average in OECD countries, while total health spending has increased by 4.5%. Over this period, growth in pharmaceutical spending surpassed growth in total health expenditure in only nine OECD countries.

Policy makers have attempted to contain pharmaceutical expenditure growth via a mix of price and volume controls, as well as policies targeting specific products (e.g., through product rebates) or increasing the share of cost borne by users. Recently, reductions in drug prices for reimbursed pharmaceuticals have been announced in several countries (e.g. Ireland and Greece).

The main concern of policy makers now is that current pharmaceutical pricing and reimbursement policies may not always deliver good value for money. Several countries for instance do not exploit the full potential of off-patent markets. In 2008, the share of generics in pharmaceutical markets ranged from a low of 15% in Ireland to a high of 75% in Poland. OECD countries have implemented policies to promote generic uptake: physicians have been given the possibility to prescribe in international non-proprietary name, and pharmacists the right to substitute generics for brand-name products in almost all countries. However, OECD countries with low generic penetration may need stronger incentives for providers and patients to foster generic use. In some more mature generic markets, price competition does not always benefit consumers and payers as discounts agreed by generic manufacturers to pharmacists are not passed on. A few countries have tried to tackle this issue through tendering processes (e.g. Germany, the Netherlands) or through periodic revisions of reimbursement prices reflecting market dynamics (e.g. Australia).

Decision makers are also increasingly concerned by the introduction of new drugs with very high costs and low or uncertain clinical effectiveness. While these drugs may be important for future innovation, public payers are not always willing to pay for medicines with low cost effectiveness and/or uncertain benefits. At the same time, public pressure to cover new treatments is often high. As a response to this dilemma, public payers are now using innovative payment methods: product-specific agreements are concluded to share the risks (of negative clinical response) with manufacturers or to cap public spending. These agreements are promising, but should be subject to rigorous and public evaluation.

What can information technology do for health care in terms of cost and value?

ICT has great potential to increase value for money in health, yet the health sector lags far behind other parts of the economy in exploiting the productivity benefits of ICT. Chapter 7 shows how ICT can make significant improvements in health care delivery – reducing medical errors, improving clinical care through adherence to evidence-based guidelines, and preventing duplication and inefficiency for complex care pathways. It examines barriers to getting the maximum benefit from ICT, including privacy concerns and the lack of common standards and co-ordination across systems, as well as the reasons why the implementation of electronic health records is slow in most countries.

The most immediately promising applications are improving the co-ordination of care for managing chronic diseases where health professionals could share information to manage complex diseases; and enabling patients to have more involvement in their own care.

There is a need for new business model for ICT which allocates funds from those who benefit from ICTs to those to have to bear the costs. In the current environment, providers bear most if not all of the costs and yet receive little benefit, which are mainly improved patients outcomes and reduced acute care costs.

There are also often weaknesses in the governance of ICT. Managing complex projects is notoriously difficult, and Ministries of Health do not have a good record in this respect. The ultimate objective of transforming the way in which health care is delivered is often forgotten in face of technical design issues. Governments need to establish commonly-defined and consistently-implemented standards to ensure communication between health care providers. While health care organisations have access to an ever increasing number of information technology products, their systems often cannot speak to each other, thus preventing the gains from sharing information. "Linkages" remain a serious problem. Electronic health record systems must be interoperable, and clinical information must still be meaningful once transferred, both between systems and between versions of the same software. It must also be gathered consistently if secondary analysis is to be performed effectively. Only if information is widely shared can ICT achieve the wider benefits of improved patient outcomes at lower cost.

Conclusions

Given the state of government finances, some countries may need to restrict urgently public health spending. Past experience shows that this can be done. Past experience also shows that it can be done badly, compromising important health policy goals, but also by simply deferring spending to the future. In deciding how to tackle the short-term issue of reducing spending, countries must not lose sight of the long-term issues.

These long-term issues are in reality much more worrying than the conjunctural fiscal situation. Increases in health spending are inevitable. Health policy makers have to ensure that these increases deliver real value for money. This will not happen automatically; health systems are not a "normal" part of the economy, where market forces can, within reason, be expected to drive innovation, responsiveness, cost efficiency and quality. To ensure that health systems continue to deliver improvements in health outcomes at reasonable cost, governments have to ensure that the basic framework for health care is right, and this requires some big changes in how health systems operate. As described in this book, some of these changes may require more spending now in order to achieve bigger efficiency gains in the future. Not the least of the dilemma's facing policy makers is how to realise these gains at a time when money for health is tight.

Chapter 1

How Much is Too Much?
Value for Money in Health Spending

This chapter starts with a look at recent trends – focusing on the last decade and a half – in health spending and its components. The main drivers behind health expenditure growth are then discussed and, on the basis of this, possible future spending pressure. The chapter then presents a brief assessment of the current macroeconomic situation facing OECD countries, drawing on the latest projections of countries' fiscal positions and concludes with a discussion of recent evidence on the degree of system inefficiency, suggesting that there is scope for addressing sustainability, financial or economic, by improving the efficiency of resource use to that of the best performers.

1. Introduction

OECD countries have made tremendous strides in improving population health over recent decades. Life expectancy at birth has increased, rising on average by ten years between 1960 and 2008. Gains at older ages have been even more dramatic. Today, a woman aged 65 can expect to live a further 20 years, and a man an additional 17 years. Although socio-economic inequalities in health status and access to care remain, reductions in child mortality and gains in population health have continued to improve at a steady pace over the past few decades (OECD, 2009a). Levels of morbidity have fallen and infant mortality is now five times lower today than it was in 1960.

Part of these achievements can be put down to increased incomes and higher levels of education. But a good portion has originated in the improvements in health care itself. Technological change has brought better treatments and benefitted a wider section of the population. For example, improvements in anaesthesia combined with non-invasive surgery have meant that a greater number of older patients can be operated with less pain and faster recovery than before. Even in the past few years, huge improvements have been made in the treatment of stroke and other heart diseases, reducing mortality rates from these diseases dramatically. Public health has also improved with higher levels of immunisation which has limited the spread of communicable disease.

Health systems have also evolved such that almost all countries have some form of public or private insurance covering the risk of ill health and high medical costs and access to quality health care has also improved. Less developed OECD countries have progressed in this area: Mexico and Turkey have increased insurance cover for the poorest groups of the population. The historic health reforms in the United States pave the way towards mandated health insurance for a wider share of the population. Improvements in medical-practice standards have been accompanied by efforts to reduce the provision of inappropriate services and address shortcomings in the quality of care.

OECD health systems are more effective, provide higher quality care, and have given access to health care to a larger share of the population than ever before. However, these achievements have not come cheaply. Countries have confronted steady increases in the cost of health care spending over recent decades. Total health expenditure has now reached 9% of GDP for the average OECD country with seven countries having a ratio of over 10% (the United States, France, Switzerland, Austria, Germany, Canada and Belgium), compared with only three countries a half decade before. How much and what they consume in terms of health care, as well as the rate of growth of health spending, varies enormously between countries as do the health outcomes.

Looking to the future, OECD countries will continue to face upward pressures on health spending from a number of factors including demographic change, advances in medical care technology and the growing expectations from patients and the electorate at large. Since the public purse finances the vast majority of health-related spending in most countries, these increasing demands for health services need to be seen in the current context of increasingly constrained public finances.

This, then, is the challenge for health systems. When those who pay for health look at what they get for their money, can they be sure that they are getting value for their money?

Talking of "value for money" in health expenditure is sometimes taken as a coded way of talking about "cuts" in spending. This is *not* what is meant in this publication. It is rather used in the sense of whether the benefits of spending exceed the costs. Increased value for money can come from reduced spending, it is true, but it can come equally from delivering more of the things that we value in our health systems.

There are as many different frameworks for looking at the benefits or objectives of the health system as there are analysts looking at the topic,[1] but they are all in reality very similar. The OECD analyses health care systems on the basis of four main pillars or objectives:

- The *first pillar* is whether health care systems provide widespread access to health care services and adequate insurance against the cost of care for the population at large in an equitable manner.

- The *second pillar* relates to whether the care provided is of high quality and whether health care providers are responsive to patient/consumer needs.

- The *third pillar* considers whether the cost of the health care system can be sustained over the longer haul given political constraints and choices imposed by the total government financial resources and the other calls on the public purse such as education.

- The *fourth pillar* is whether care is provided in an efficient and effective manner.

The first two objectives concern how well health care systems are performing in terms of health care supply and whether the provision of care services are of high quality and adapted to patient needs. The third and fourth criteria consider whether resources are adequate and being put to good use.

Furthermore, though not included in most listings of the objectives of the health system, it is also true that health is a significant sector of the economy, and is one that is usually under some form of public control. This means that the health system can sometimes be used by governments as an instrument in wider economic policies. For example, in the recent recession, spending on health has acted as an automatic stabiliser to the economy, and has been a source of jobs growth when most other sectors have been in decline.

The emphasis placed on health policy goals by individual governments can of course vary in importance both over time and between countries for very good reasons. Countries may legitimately have different priorities, reflecting their own societal preferences and needs. Priorities may also change over time to respond to different economic circumstances, health care needs, population expectations and advances in medicine. Indeed, the strengthening of health systems through net increases in spending to benefit from the opportunities brought by new technology and to tackle continuing unmet needs, while at the same time seeking efficiency improvements, may be seen as an optimal dual approach.

Nonetheless, wide differences remain across countries in both the level of resources allocated to health and in the efficiency and effectiveness with which they are used. There are wide differences in health outcomes which appear little related to the level of resources channelled into health care. Some countries probably are getting more "value for money" from their health spending than others. In theory, spending money more wisely rather than seeking to spend more overall would be the appropriate policy response for those countries with low-performing health systems. But it is extremely hard to identify in just what ways a country is spending inefficiently. Health systems are complex, there are multiple objectives, and often information is inadequate.

If reallocating resources from low-performing sectors of the health system is hard, then to meet new demands for health care will require new resources. But how should policy makers decide whether such spending is justified? Judging how much public resources should be spent on health care at a given point in time can depend on two different measures of "sustainability" (Thomson et al., 2009):

- On the one hand, so long as the value produced by health care exceeds its opportunity cost, that is the value that would have been gained by spending on other areas, then growth in health spending can be said to be *economically sustainable*. Once this cost becomes too high, and better gains would be achieved by spending elsewhere (either in the private sector or for other components of public spending), then health spending becomes economically unsustainable.

- *Financial sustainability*, on the other hand, becomes a problem when governments are unable to finance the existing level of resources because of an inability or unwillingness to generate sufficient revenues to pay for them, and when they cannot – or will not – allow any further "crowding out" of other forms of government spending.

It follows that it is possible for health spending growth to be economically sustainable, and yet not financially sustainable. However, it is necessary to acknowledge that in some countries, achieving "value for money" is not enough to ensure the sustainability of the system. When fiscal constraints are binding, health systems either have to find new sources of finance – most of which have their own drawbacks – or else health spending which produces benefits greater than their costs will have to be deferred. Some of the problems currently facing countries are not because the health system is not spending money wisely, but rather that they simply cannot raise enough money because of the economic conditions. Many OECD countries may now find themselves in this situation.

This report does *not* attempt to cover all the issues that might be relevant in achieving a high-performing health system. It does not consider the different forms of financing health, or the appropriate role of competition in health system delivery, for example, in detail. Rather, it looks at the most promising policy initiatives that countries are taking in order to increase "value for money".

This introductory chapter starts with a look at recent trends – focusing on the last decade and a half – in health spending and its components. This discussion looks behind the OECD average to try and tease out some common characteristics among groups of countries. The main drivers behind health expenditure growth are then discussed and, on the basis of this, possible future spending pressure. The chapter then presents a brief assessment of the current macroeconomic situation facing OECD countries, drawing on the latest projections of countries' fiscal positions and concludes with a discussion of recent evidence on the degree of system inefficiency, suggesting that there is scope for addressing sustainability, financial or economic, by improving the efficiency of resource use to that of the best performers.

Chapter 2 looks at the range of policy options and policy instruments which might affect health care costs, health care benefits and/or the relationship between the two, including both those designed to have short run effects and those that aim to change the longer run path of spending through changes in the way health care systems are organised and governed.

The remainder of the report looks in detail at which initiatives can deliver the same care with reduced costs, or else produce more access to high quality health care services at a reasonable cost, including:

- The role of systematic, rational decision making in deciding the benefit package, paying for new technologies and applying evidence-based medicine (Chapter 3).

- The role of "pay for performance", to reward providers who increase value for money by providing better quality care and analyses (Chapter 4).

- Efforts to increase value for money in health spending by reducing the demand for care through better co-ordination by health providers (Chapter 5).

- Policies that can be used to draw all the benefits from pharmaceutical spending (Chapter 6).

- Evidence on whether greater investment in health ICTs could increase access, reduce costs and increase quality of health care (Chapter 7).

2. Health care spending: developments over recent decades

The growth of total health care spending

As noted in the preceding section, health spending has seen a near relentless rise over recent decades and had reached 9% of GDP by 2008 (Figure 1.1). Looking over the preceding 15 years, real per capita health spending grew at an annual growth rate of 3.9% for the OECD average (Figure 1.2). This compares with annual growth in GDP of around 2.6%. While the average rate of economic growth remained relatively stable throughout the period, growth in health spending has been more variable (Figure 1.3). During the mid-1990s, governments in some OECD countries applied cost-containment measures in response to the acceleration in the rate of growth of health spending experienced at the beginning of the decade. This resulted in health spending growth that was broadly comparable to average GDP growth (Huber and Orosz, 2003). However this slowing proved only temporary. Health spending began to rise rapidly again towards the end of the decade, reflecting deliberate policies in a number of OECD countries to relieve the pressures arising from the previous restrictive measures (e.g. in Canada, the United Kingdom and Ireland). The tighter budgetary controls adopted in these countries had constrained both the capacity for care and the level of activity. In the United States, a backlash against some of the more restrictive forms of managed care in the 1990s led to some easing and a rapid increase in costs at the same time (Colombo and Morgan, 2006).

Considerable country diversity

OECD countries vary enormously in how much they spend on health and the rate at which health spending grows. Developments in the share of health care spending in GDP depend on the growth rate of GDP as well as the growth rate of health care spending itself (Figure 1.4). The combined effect indicates that there has been a degree of convergence among OECD countries in the ratio of health care expenditure to GDP. Some clustering of OECD countries based on their economic and several health spending growth patterns over the period may be observed:

- A number of high income countries such as Canada and some Scandinavian countries saw stable economic growth above 2% per year, but the growth in the predominantly

Figure 1.1. **Average health spending as a share of gross domestic product (GDP) across OECD countries**

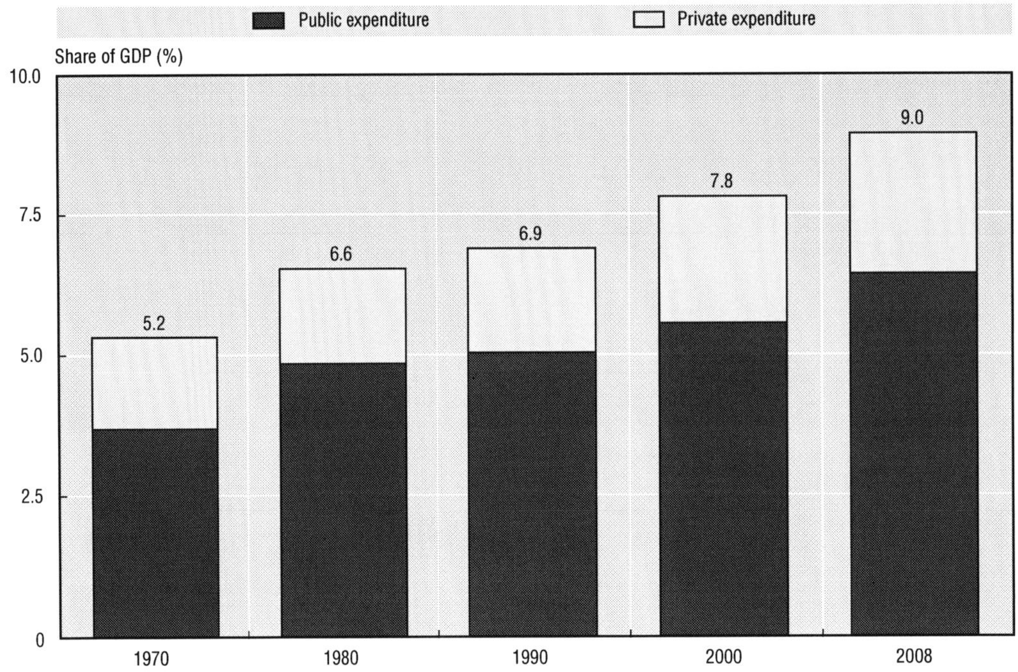

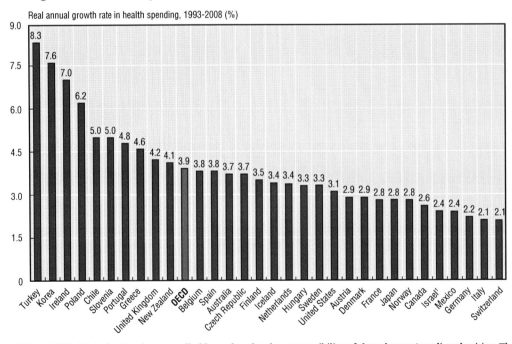

Source: OECD (2010a).

StatLink ⧉ *http://dx.doi.org/10.1787/888932319098*

Figure 1.2. **Annual growth in per capita health expenditure, 1993 to 2008**

1. The statistical data for Israel are supplied by and under the responsibility of the relevant Israeli authorities. The use of such data by the OECD is without prejudice to the status of the Golan Heights, East Jerusalem and Israeli settlements in the West Bank under the terms of international law.

Source: OECD (2010a).

StatLink ⧉ *http://dx.doi.org/10.1787/888932319117*

Figure 1.3. **Growth in total health expenditure and GDP in OECD coutries, 1993 to 2008**

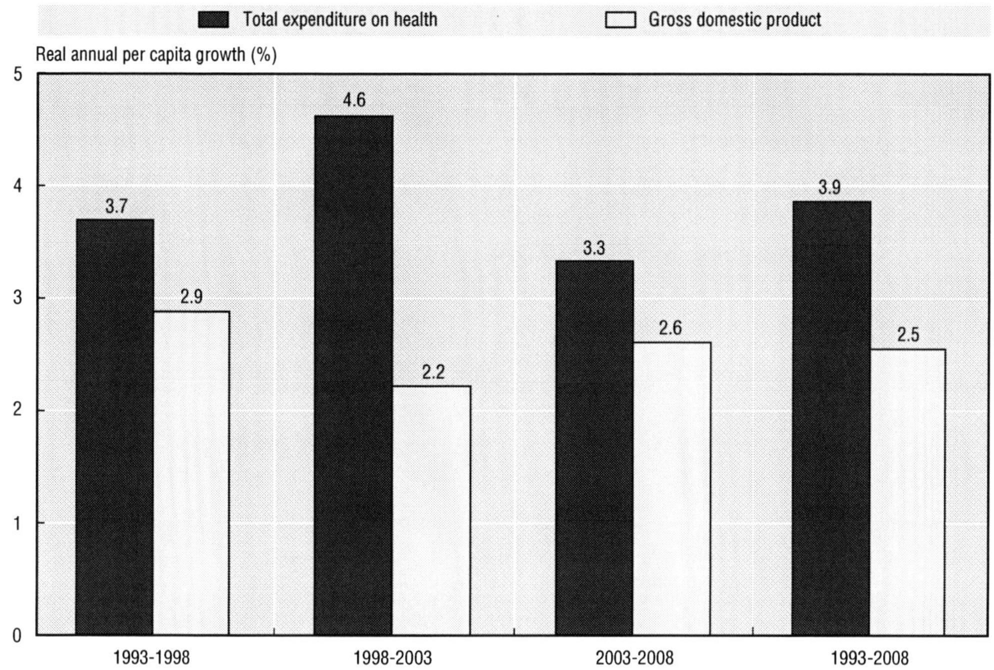

■ Total expenditure on health   □ Gross domestic product

Real annual per capita growth (%)

	1993-1998	1998-2003	2003-2008	1993-2008
Total expenditure on health	3.7	4.6	3.3	3.9
Gross domestic product	2.9	2.2	2.6	2.5

Source: OECD (2010a).

StatLink 📊 *http://dx.doi.org/10.1787/888932319136*

Figure 1.4. **Annual growth in total health spending and GDP, 1993 to 2008**

Real annual growth in per capita health spending, 1993-2008 (%)

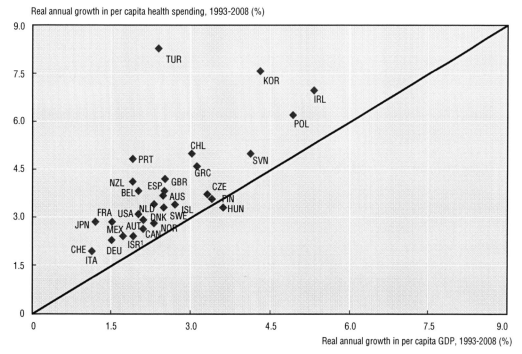

Real annual growth in per capita GDP, 1993-2008 (%)

1. The statistical data for Israel are supplied by and under the responsibility of the relevant Israeli authorities. The use of such data by the OECD is without prejudice to the status of the Golan Heights, East Jerusalem and Israeli settlements in the West Bank under the terms of international law.

Source: OECD (2010a).

StatLink 📊 *http://dx.doi.org/10.1787/888932319155*

public-funded health systems was kept in check. In the case of Canada and Finland, spending constraints by provincial and municipal governments respectively were linked to the recessions of the early 1990s to address the growing public deficits. However, since the late 1990s, spending on health has been well above that of GDP in both of these countries.

- The United Kingdom and Australia – both with moderate to strong economic growth over the period – saw health spending growth generally outpacing that of the economy. The pressure for cost containment may have been less severe and in the case of the United Kingdom, additional public resources allocated to health became a deliberate policy towards the end of the 1990s.

- Low economic growth in Germany and Italy may have contributed to the constraining of health spending and therefore limited any significant increases in the health spending to GDP ratio. Per capita health spending increased, in real terms, by 2% per year on average in both countries. On the other hand, other countries experiencing low economic growth, such as Japan, France and Belgium still saw overall health spending growth greatly exceed that of GDP resulting in an increasing health to GDP ratio.

- Among some of the lower income countries of the OECD, relatively strong long-term economic growth was more than matched by considerable increases in spending on health. This was the case in Ireland, Korea, Poland and Turkey. Other countries such as the Czech Republic and Slovenia also experienced relatively high economic growth, but – contrary to the above – health spending growth, although high, did not significantly outpace that of the overall economy resulting in only moderate increases in the health to GDP ratio. In the case of Hungary, there was in fact a fall in the health spending to GDP ratio over the period.

- Finally, countries such as Portugal (and to a lesser extent Mexico) experienced relatively high growth in health spending, although economic development remained low. While their relative economic position (in terms of GDP per capita compared with the rest of the OECD) did not improve or indeed weakened, the resources devoted to the health care system improved considerably.

Spending over time and catch-up

Focussing on growth of per capita health care spending, the very different patterns between OECD countries described above have come as a result of various economic and policy developments. Several mainly lower-income OECD countries made deliberate policy choices to finance expansions and improvements in health systems to bring their health systems up to OECD standards of care and access. Korea and Turkey, for example, saw significant reforms to increase the health care coverage of the population. There were also rapid increases in health spending in some of the eastern European countries.

Other, mostly higher-income, countries have aimed to – and been successful in – controlling costs. Real annual growth in per capita health spending varied from around 2% in Italy, Germany and Switzerland compared with well above 6% per year in Ireland, Korea and Turkey (Figure 1.5). This had led to some "catching up" or convergence across countries in the amount now spent on health.

Figure 1.5. **Per capita total spending on health in 1993 and annual growth in spending, 1993 to 2008**

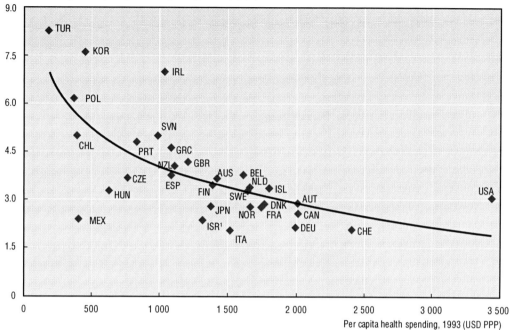

1. The statistical data for Israel are supplied by and under the responsibility of the relevant Israeli authorities. The use of such data by the OECD is without prejudice to the status of the Golan Heights, East Jerusalem and Israeli settlements in the West Bank under the terms of international law.

Source: OECD (2010a).

StatLink ᴍᴤᴸ *http://dx.doi.org/10.1787/888932319174*

Figure 1.6. **Ratio of private to public health spending growth, 1993 to 2008**

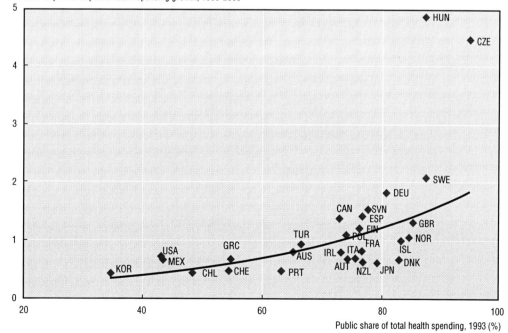

Source: OECD (2010a).

StatLink ᴍᴤᴸ *http://dx.doi.org/10.1787/888932319193*

The public share of total health spending has remained relatively stable on average across OECD countries since the early 1990s. Nonetheless, there has also been a degree of narrowing between countries in the relative importance of public and private financing of health care (Figure 1.6). That is, those countries that had a relatively high public share of health expenditure, and often more limited private insurance markets or cost-sharing arrangements (such as in the Czech Republic, Poland and Hungary) at the beginning of the 1990s, saw more rapid growth in private expenditure subsequently. In contrast, countries with a relatively low share of public health expenditure in the early 1990s tended to see public spending on health as the main driver of overall growth in health spending. This, for example, was the case in Korea, Portugal and Ireland, where, as we have seen, there were deliberate policies to widen coverage or to invest heavily in health systems.[2]

3. Spending by type of health care services

The allocation of health spending across the different types of health services and goods can be influenced by a wide range of factors, from the supply of resources and access to new or high-cost technology, to the financial and institutional arrangements for health care delivery, as well as clinical guidelines and the disease burden within a country. OECD data are able to break down spending into components of individual health care (in-patient, out-patient, pharmaceuticals, etc.) as well as those services benefiting the all or parts of the community, such as public health and administration of health care.

In-patient care (i.e. predominantly provided in hospitals) and ambulatory care together account for around 60% of health spending.[3] With in-patient care highly labour intensive and, therefore, expensive, high income countries with developed health systems have sought to reduce the share of spending in hospitals by shifting to more day surgery, out-patient or home-based care. Such services are an important innovation in health care delivery, often being preferred, when possible, by patients to staying overnight in a hospital. In the United States, elective interventions on a same day basis accounted for a quarter of the growth in US health spending between 2003 and 2006, compared with just 4% of the growth in Canadian spending.[4] Estimates of spending on same-day surgery performed by independent physicians for 2003 and 2006 suggest that this has been the fastest growing area of health care over this period (McKinsey Global Institute, 2008). In France, spending on day care now accounts for around 11% of curative care spending. By contrast, Germany, where day surgery in public hospitals was prohibited until the late 1990s (Castoro et al., 2007), reported only 2% of curative care expenditure as services of day care.[5] More generally, lower income countries seeking to invest in and expand their health systems have generally seen the growth in hospital in-patient care outpace other areas of spending such that it has been the main contributor to overall health expenditure growth (Figure 1.7).

Spending on long-term care has increased significantly across OECD countries, as the demand for care from ageing societies rises. Expenditure on long-term care, either in institutions or in a home-based setting now accounts for more than 12% of total health spending on average, and considerably more in countries where there is already a sizeable elderly population. Both Germany and Japan, with more than 20% of the population over 65 by 2008, extended their range of social insurance schemes to cover the costs of long-term care, in 1995/96 and 2000 respectively.

Figure 1.7. **Contribution to health spending growth by main functions of health care, 2003 to 2008**

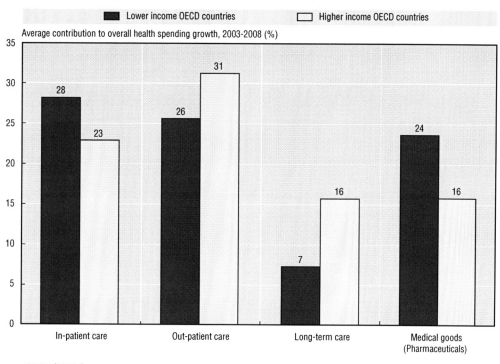

Source: OECD (2010a).

StatLink ⊞⊒⊑ http://dx.doi.org/10.1787/888932319212

In conclusion, OECD policy makers continue to be faced with unrelenting upward pressures in health care spending; population ageing, income growth and technological change will contribute to a continuation over coming decades. Nonetheless, large public sector deficits and rapidly rising public debt burdens suggest that governments may be less willing in the future to finance further increases in the supply of health care services. Health care may face cuts in financing in the same way as other areas of government responsibility. Looking beyond the economic cycle, recent OECD research suggests that there remain significant productivity reserves that many countries can draw on to mitigate future pressures. This raises the broader question of policies to slow the growth of health care spending, issues that are addressed in Chapter 2.

Spending on medical goods, being primarily pharmaceuticals, has also been rising rapidly across most OECD countries, consuming an increasing share of overall health expenditure. Since 1993, growth in pharmaceutical spending has averaged close to 4.5%, compared with the 3.9% annual rise in total health spending. By 2008, pharmaceuticals accounted for around 17% of total health spending or 1.5% of GDP. Since medical goods consume, on average, a smaller share of health spending, compared with in-patient and ambulatory care, their contribution to overall growth in health care spending has been smaller, typically accounting for about one fifth of overall health spending growth.

Again, there is much variation across countries. Although the growth in pharmaceutical spending tends to be relatively high in the lower income countries, the growth tends to be below that of in-patient and ambulatory care and therefore the share of pharmaceuticals in overall health spending has declined. In some high spending countries such as Canada, for example, medical goods have been the main driver of increasing health expenditure, contributing almost one-third of overall growth. The United States, Austria and France have also seen relatively high growth in pharmaceutical spending. This contrasts to Japan and Germany, where tighter price regulation or moves to promote more generic prescribing took greater effect.

4. The drivers of health care spending

A number of studies have attempted to identify the drivers of health spending growth and quantify their respective impact (Newhouse, 1992; OECD, 2006; Dormont et al., 2006; Smith et al., 2009).[6] Among these determinants, ageing of the population, rising national income, relative medical prices and technological progress have been given particular attention. The roles of medical supply and "defensive medicine" were also considered, especially in the United States, but found to be negligible. Most studies have used a growth accounting framework (see Denison, 1962). Within this broad framework, Newhouse (1992) estimates the contribution of known factors to health spending growth (1940-90) and assumes that most of the unexplained residual is attributable to changes in health technology. A more recent review of the earlier estimates using more recent data by Newhouse and colleagues (Smith et al., 2009) indicates that between one quarter and one half of the increase in health care spending could be attributed to technology.

According to the literature, the contribution of ageing to past health spending growth appears modest. It ranges from 6.5% to 9% of the increase in total health care spending over the period 1960 to 1990 but the results depend on estimation strategy, type of data, country and period considered (OECD, 2006; Dormont et al., 2006; Smith et al., 2009).[7] Income changes are credited with having a higher contribution to health spending growth in all studies, ranging from 28% to 58%, depending on data and hypotheses on income elasticity of health expenditures (generally assessed as being between 0.6 and 1.0[8]).

Medical price inflation is not always included in models because of measurement problems. But Smith et al. (2009) estimate a contribution of medical prices to spending growth to range between 5-18% on the basis of two alternative assumptions about productivity gains in medical care. The contribution of technological progress is often measured as the residual when respective contributions of other factors have been estimated. Initial estimates by Newhouse (1992) attributed 50 to 75% of health expenditure growth to changes in technology. More recent estimates on US data over 1960-2007 range from 27.4 to 48.3% according to alternative working hypotheses (Smith et al., 2009). Dormont et al. (2006), working on microdata, showed that "changes in medical practice" – for a given level of morbidity – explained about a quarter of health spending growth in France between 1992 and 2000.

Changing epidemiological patterns has also been put forward as a possible contributor to rising health spending. Prevention of infectious diseases together with the possibilities of long-term treatment of previously untreatable or badly treatable conditions has meant that chronic illnesses account for an increasing share of health spending. However, when controlling for the demographic effects and the quantity of services brought about through technology and treatment practice, the effect overall is thought to be minimal. Indeed, projections of health care spending in Australia between 2003 and 2033 showed that expected age standardised disease rate change actually had a favourable effect in disease areas such as cardiovascular disease and cancer, offset by dramatic increases in diabetes (AIHW, 2008).

5. Will financial sustainability be a problem in the future?

Public spending on health and long-term care amounted to, on average, some 7% of GDP in 2007. As described above, it is not always enough to show that health spending gives good value for money by delivering greater benefits than costs. If the fiscal situation is such that it simply is not possible to raise sufficient funds to cover the spending, socially desirable expenditures will have to be reduced. This section considers the long-term projections in public spending, with the subsequent section considering the extent to which current fiscal circumstances are putting more countries in this unfortunate position.

Most recent OECD projections provide some indication of likely trends for health and long-term care. Projections are made for both of these components apart since the factors driving the two components are somewhat different. The results suggest that public expenditure on health and long-term care could rise to almost double current levels – from close to 7% of GDP in 2005 to some 13% by 2050 – assuming that growth in the *residual*, which are often referred to as technological change,[9] remains unchanged throughout the period (Figure 1.8). Alternatively, if governments were successful in reducing the size of the "residual" by half over the projection period, public health and long-term care spending would still increase by 3.5 percentage points of GDP to reach around 10% of GDP.

As discussed above, these increases come from several sources. As regards the changing age structure of the population, a rising share of older age groups in the population will put upward pressure on costs because health costs rise with age. However, the average cost per individual in older age groups should fall over time for two reasons. First, the projections assume lengthening of lifetimes, thereby putting off the high costs in

Figure 1.8. **Projections of public health and long-term care spending, 2005-50**

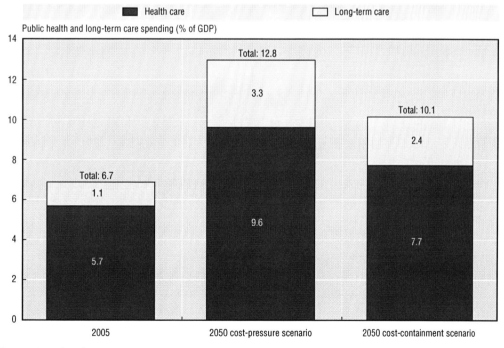

Source: OECD (2006).

StatLink ᔎᔍᔏ *http://dx.doi.org/10.1787/888932319231*

the period just prior to death into the future; and second, the effect of population ageing is also reduced because it is assumed that the longer life spans will be healthy ones.

Ageing-related effects are stronger for long-term care. Dependency on long-term care will tend to rise as the share of old people in the population increase. This effect is mitigated somewhat by the likelihood that the share of dependents per older age group will fall as longevity increases due to the assumption of "healthy ageing". Additional effects coming from non-demographic factors: expenditures are likely to be pushed up by a possible "cost disease" effect, i.e. the relative price of long-term care increasing in line with average productivity growth in the economy because the scope for productivity gains in long-term care is more limited.

These average results hide striking differences across countries. In the cost-containment scenario, a group of countries stands out with increases of health and long-term care spending at or above 4 percentage points of GDP, over the period 2005-50. It includes rapidly ageing countries (Italy, Japan, Spain), countries that will experience a dramatic change in their population structure (Korea, Mexico, Slovak Republic), and countries with currently low labour participation, which may face a substantial increase in the demand for *formal* long-term care (Italy, Ireland, Spain). In contrast, Sweden which is in a mature phase of its ageing process and already spends a relatively high share of GDP on health and long-term care, is in the lowest range with an increase below 2 percentage points of GDP.

Despite uncertainties, sensitivity analysis suggests the results are fairly robust in some key respects. For example, under the assumption of "healthy ageing", changes in longevity will have only a modest effect on spending. However, the projections for spending on long-term care are sensitive to the future development of labour market participation for the working-age population as higher participation reduces the capacity for "informal" care. An alternative scenario, where participation rates in countries where they are currently low converge towards levels in high-participation countries, has spending on long-term care rising by an additional 1-2% of GDP on average, but much more in some countries.

It is of interest to compare and contrast the results of this exercise with the many national long-term projections of public spending.[10] Table 1.1 provides the results from recent national projections together with the results from the OECD study for a selection of OECD countries. As with the OECD exercise, most of the models provide various scenarios under different sets of assumptions. The projections contained in the table are principally the base scenario, although, for example, Germany provides two forecasts based on relatively favourable and unfavourable conditions with regard to sustainability. It should also be noted that the aggregates of health and long-term care may differ from the OECD study in their definition and starting point, and thus may not be directly comparable. The national projections of spending can take into account differing assumptions of demographic, labour force and productivity changes as well as different health and policy scenarios.

The national results emphasise the range of long-term projections with increases in the health to GDP share of 2 percentage points or less in countries such as Germany, Italy, Korea, Switzerland and the United Kingdom compared to significantly higher increases in projections by France and the Netherlands. For the majority of countries, the projections appear not too dissimilar to the projection range from the OECD study.

Table 1.1. **OECD and selected national projections of public health and long-term care spending, 2005 to 2050**

		National projections						2006 OECD Study		
	Source	Sector	Share of GDP in reference year	Reference year	Projection year	Share of GDP in projection year		Sector	Share of GDP in 2005	Projected share of GDP in 2050[1]
Australia	Treasurer of Common-wealth of Australia	Public health	4.0%	2009-10	2049-50	7.1%		Public health	5.6%	7.9% / 9.7%
		Public all aged care	0.8%			1.8%		Public LTC	0.9%	2.0% / 2.9%
Belgium	Conseil Supérieur des Finances – CEV	Public health	6.1%	2008	2050	8.6%		Public health	5.7%	7.2% / 9.0%
		Public LTC	1.2%			2.5%		Public LTC	1.5%	2.6% / 3.4%
Canada	Parliamentary Budget Officer	Public health	6.8%	2007	2050-51	10.9%		Public health	7.0%	8.4% / 10.2%
								Public LTC	1.2%	2.4% / 3.2%
France	Le Sénat	Total health	9.3%	2000	2050	17.4% / 19.4%		Public health	7.0%	8.7% / 10.6%
	DREES	Total health	10.4%	2004		14.9% / 22.3%		Public LTC	1.1%	2.0% / 2.8%
Germany	Federal Ministry of Finance	Statutory health ins.	6.3%	2006	2050	7.8% / 8.5%		Public health	7.8%	9.6% / 11.4%
		LTC insurance	0.8%			1.7% / 2.3%		Public LTC	1.0%	2.2% / 2.9%
Italy	Ministero dell'Economia e Delle Finanze	Public health	~7.0%	2008	2050	9.0%		Public health	6.5%	7.9% / 9.7%
								Public LTC	0.6%	2.8% / 3.5%
Japan	MHLW	Public health	7.1%	2004	2025	11.2%		Public health	6.0%	8.5% / 10.3%
		Public LTC	1.4%			3.6%		Public LTC	0.9%	2.4% / 3.1%
Korea	Yonsei Uni./Gachon Uni.	Public health	3.1%	2005	2050	4.9%		Public health	3.0%	6.0% / 7.8%
								Public LTC	0.3%	3.1% / 4.1%
Netherlands	Ministry of Health, Welfare and Sport	Public health & LTC	9.7%	2009	2050	26.1%		Public health	5.1%	7.0% / 8.9%
								Public LTC	1.7%	2.9% / 3.7%
Switzerland	Federal Finance Administration FFA	Public health	4.4%	2005	2050	5.8%		Public health	6.2%	7.8% / 9.6%
		Public LTC	0.5%			1.4%		Public LTC	1.2%	1.9% / 2.6%
United Kingdom	HM Treasury	Public health	~8.1%	2009-10	2049-2050	~10.2%		Public health	6.1%	7.9% / 9.7%
		Public LTC	~1.3%			~2.1%		Public LTC	1.1%	2.1% / 3.0%
United States	CBO	Medicare & Medicaid	5.0%	2009	2035 (2080)	10% (17%)		Public health	6.3	7.9% / 9.7%
								Public LTC	0.9%	1.8% / 2.7%

1. Projected share of GDP under the two scenarios: "Cost-pressure" and "Cost-containment".

Source: Australia: "Intergenerational Report. Australia to 2050: Future Challenges", Treasurer of the Commonwealth of Australia. January 2010; Belgium: Rapport Annuel, Comité d'Étude sur le Vieillissement, Conseil Supérieur des Finances, June 2009; Canada: "Fiscal Sustainability Report", Office of the Parliamentary Budget Officer, February 2010; France: "Les déterminants macroéconomiques des dépenses de santé : comparaison entre quelques pays", annexe au rapport Vasselle : Rapport du Sénat sur l'assurance maladie, 2004; Germany: "Second Report on the Sustainability of Public Finances", Federal Ministry of Finance, June 2008; Italy: "Le tendenze di medio-lungo periodo del sistema pensionistico e socio-sanitario – aggiornamento 2008", Ministero dell'Economia e Delle Finanze – Ragioneria Generale dello Stato, 2008; Korea: "Forecasting Future Public Health Expenditures in Consideration of Population Ageing", 2009; Japan: "Future Prospect of Social Security Expenditure and Contributions", MHLW, May 2004; Netherlands: Ministry of Health, Welfare and Sport / Youth and Families, 2010; Switzerland: "Long-term Sustainability of Public Finances in Switzerland", Federal Finance Administration, April 2008; United Kingdom: "Long-term Public Finance Report: An Analysis of Fiscal Sustainability", HM Treasury, December 2009; United States: "The Long-term Budget Outlook", Congressional Budget Office, June 2009, OECD: "Projecting OECD Health and Long-term Care Expenditures: What Are the Main Drivers?", OECD Economics Department Working Paper No. 477, February 2006.

6. Is fiscal sustainability a problem now?

In determining how future government policy will likely affect public spending on health, it is important to recall the growing share of health in total government spending. In the years leading up to the current downturn, government spending as a share of GDP broadly declined, dropping from around 46% in 1995 to 41% in 2007 (see Joumard et al., 2010 for further details). This can be put down to total GDP rising faster than government spending over the period rather than any contraction in total public expenditures (OECD, 2009b). In only two countries, Portugal and Korea, was there an increase in government spending as a share of GDP. Over the same period, the proportion of public spending allocated to health rose from around 12% to 16% of total government spending on average – only in Hungary did the share remain unchanged.

Within this broad context, the current economic slowdown that started in 2008 differs in nature from other recent recessions in that it has been global in both scale and timing. Almost all OECD countries have been affected. The most recent *OECD Economic Outlook* (No. 87, June 2010) recorded a decline of –3.3% in OECD GDP in 2009, with only sluggish growth forecast for most countries through 2010.

Much of the recovery from recession through 2010 has been driven by the unprecedented policy stimulus packages put in place by many OECD governments to support the fragile economies rather than any renewed underlying induced consumer demand. The result of such huge government measures together with the automatic effects of a recession – largely on revenues – has meant that the fiscal position of most OECD countries has deteriorated significantly with steep rises in government deficits in 2009. These deficits are estimated to remain close to 8% of GDP across the OECD in 2010, with only modest improvement foreseen in 2011. The ratio of gross government debt to GDP is expected to rise to 100% in 2011 for the OECD as a whole, up from just over 70% in 2007 prior to the financial crisis.

Such levels of government debt raise concerns about the budgetary environment and financial sustainability, meaning that governments will need to carefully review alternative strategies to start reducing the levels of government debt whilst not undermining the stimulus driven recovery. Therefore, in the medium term, there are likely to be increased pressures on public spending either through a mix of pushing through long-planned reforms, increased efficiency measures or indeed spending cuts.

Lessons from past recessions suggest that a prolonged period of "belt tightening" throughout the economy is likely with debt consolidation lasting some years after the onset of recession, and continuing as the economy starts to grow again (McKinsey Global Institute, 2010). Thus, the high government debt ratios of the current downturn could delay the start of deleveraging leading to a rapid rise in the share of health in GDP in the first couple of years, followed by a longer period of debt reduction.

Where will pressures for restraint in health care spending likely be the strongest?

Two sets of criteria can help identify where pressures for restraint of public health care spending are likely to be the strongest:

● First, countries with high levels of debt and/or large overall public sector deficits are likely to be more concerned about public spending and fiscal sustainability than countries with low deficits and debt-to-GDP ratios.

- Second, countries where spending on health care makes up a large portion of total government spending and/or where general government spending makes up a large share of GDP.

Recent events suggest that the first criteria set is probably of more immediate importance as it concerns, as mentioned, problems of fiscal sustainability. Countries with high levels of debt and large deficits (the top right hand quadrant) will face the greatest difficulty in financing increased spending (Figure 1.10).

The second set is critical in judging the scope for further increases in public health care spending on the basis of the economic sustainability criteria. Taking into account both the overall level of public spending in the economy and the share allocated to health care (on the assumption that it is harder to raise revenues in countries which already spend a lot and that health is more likely to be affected by public expenditure constraints, the greater the proportion of public expenditure which goes on health), a first approximation may be to say that countries falling in the top right part of Figure 1.10 are going to be more concerned about health expenditures than countries in the bottom left quadrant. This assertion can be modified by many other factors, including attitudes towards taxation and public spending, and the political priority that health has in public policy.

Countries with particularly weak fiscal conditions (i.e. above the OECD average) (see Figure 1.9) are the United Kingdom, Ireland, the United States, Greece, France and Japan, and to a lesser degree Portugal, Italy and Spain. Countries where public health care spending makes up a large share of GDP (that is, above average public spending as a share of GDP and above average health spending as a share of total public spending) may face higher pressures (Austria, Denmark, France, Germany and the Netherlands). Additionally, those countries

Figure 1.9. **Forecast debt-to-GDP and general government financial balances, 2011**

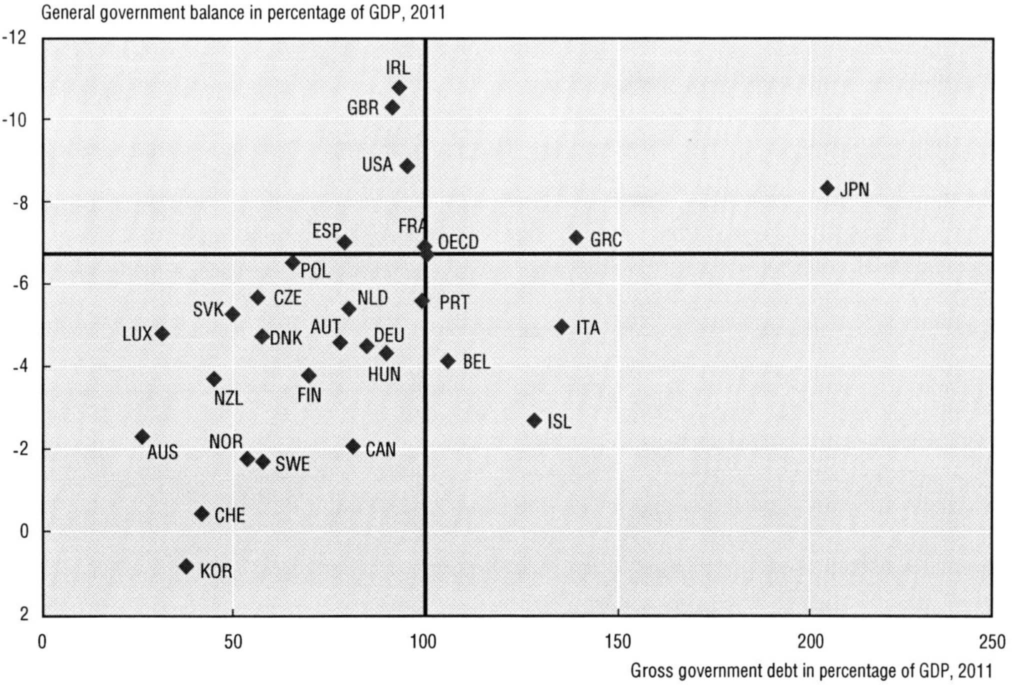

General government balance in percentage of GDP, 2011

Gross government debt in percentage of GDP, 2011

Source: OECD (2010b).

StatLink 🔗 http://dx.doi.org/10.1787/888932319250

Figure 1.10. **Public spending on health as a share
of total government spending, 2008**

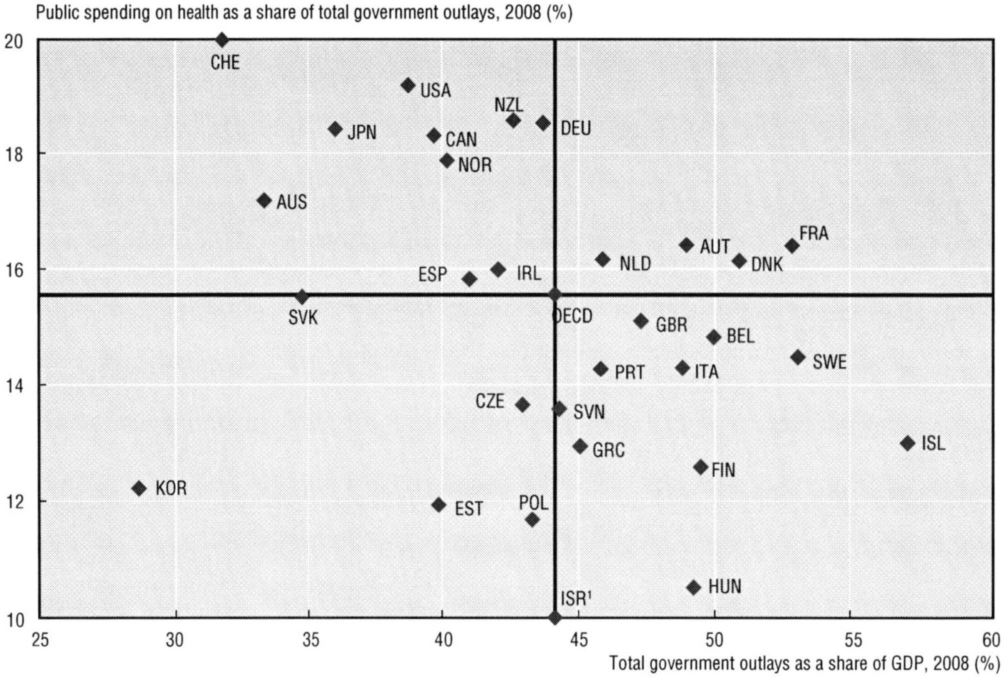

Public spending on health as a share of total government outlays, 2008 (%)

Total government outlays as a share of GDP, 2008 (%)

1. The statistical data for Israel are supplied by and under the responsibility of the relevant Israeli authorities. The use of such data by the OECD is without prejudice to the status of the Golan Heights, East Jerusalem and Israeli settlements in the West Bank under the terms of international law.

Source: OECD (2010a).

StatLink http://dx.doi.org/10.1787/888932319269

where health spending already accounts for a sizeable share of total public spending may face a different set of challenges in order to further increase the overall provision for health care.

7. How can we ensure economic sustainability of health systems?

As noted in the introductory paragraphs, the system sustainability and efficiency objectives are closely linked: making health system more efficient and effective is likely to be one of the few ways of reconciling rising demand for health care and the public financing constraints just mentioned. Recent OECD research (Joumard et al., 2008 and 2010) has examined the degree of inefficiency in OECD health systems and the scope for productivity gains. Estimates of the degree of health care spending efficiency are based on health care outcomes defined as those gains in health status that can be attributed to health care spending. A country is judged to be more efficient than another if it achieves higher life expectancy for a given level of health care spending, once confounding variables have been allowed for.

The results suggest that there is considerable scope for efficiency gains across OECD health systems. Indeed, life expectancy at birth could be raised by more than two years on average if countries were to become as efficient as the best performers. By way of comparison, a further increase in health care spending of 10% would increase life expectancy by only three to four months, holding the degree of measured inefficiency unchanged. Despite the limitations inherent in macro-level approaches, results are robust to changes in specification and estimation methods.

Correlations between overall system (outcome-based) efficiency estimates and (output-based) efficiency indicators often used for hospitals (*e.g.* average length of stays and occupancy rates for hospital acute care beds) are very low. This suggests that medical outputs can be produced very efficiently in one sub-sector but still have only a limited impact on the health status of the population. Alternatively such results may imply that high performance in the in-patient care sector is offset by inefficiencies in other sub-sectors of the health care system; and/or that co-ordination problems exist across sub-sectors.

Further tests suggest that overall system efficiency for individual countries are better correlated with quality of care indicators (such as avoidable admission rates in the in-patient care sector). Those countries with high levels of productive efficiency tend to be those with high quality of care, even though the quality of care indicators still does not have wide country coverage.

Finally, the study examined whether higher measured levels of efficiency were related to selected institutional arrangements. In this facet of the study, recent work by the OECD Secretariat (Joumard *et al.*, 2010) has served to identify institutional characteristics attributable to individual countries and to identify groups of countries with similar institutional arrangements and market or regulatory incentives (Paris *et al.*, 2009).

The results suggest that no sub-group appears to have consistently better efficiency outcomes. Indeed, within group differences appeared to be larger than across group differences in a number of cases. It would thus appear that no single type of health care system performs systematically better than another in improving the health status of the population in a cost-effective manner. In practice, OECD countries rely on quite different mixes of market and non-market regulation and need a range of policies to correct for the market failures that plague all health care systems. Put another way, the key message for policy makers is that it may be less the type of system that counts but rather how it is managed.

8. Conclusions

Health systems are economically sustainable when the benefits of health spending exceed their costs. But this is not necessarily enough to ensure the overall sustainability of the system, as sometimes fiscal constraints can be binding. This chapter has shown that health spending has gone up rapidly in many (but not all) OECD countries in recent years. Does this mean that they have become economically unsustainable? Although the chapter makes no attempt to assess the question in any systematic way, "probably not", is the most likely answer. Health systems are delivering real improvements in health, in many of the main dimensions in which we judge health spending – access, quality, responsiveness, and so on. As long as they continue to deliver such improvements, it will be economically desirable to meet the future demand for more spending. But in the short term, the sharp deterioration in the public finances means that fiscal sustainability is a problem in some countries. Chapter 2 assesses the policy options available to countries to achieve value for money in health systems in the future, but also what options are open to those countries that need to control spending for fiscal reasons in the short term.

Notes

1. Several alternative frameworks have been developed to assess the performance of health systems, either by defining the level of achievement of a defined set of goals (effectiveness), or by measuring the link between resources invested in health systems and the attainment of goals (efficiency) (WHO, 2000; Roberts *et al.*, 2004). These frameworks propose different sets of goals or objectives, for the health system itself, or for health policies but the all broadly reflect the same range of policy concerns.

2. In practice, public and private spending are closely linked. For example, in countries with cost-sharing arrangements, an increase in public spending on health care will lead, *pari passu* to a rise in private spending as well. To properly understand health spending trends over time and patterns between countries, it may be necessary to consider private and public components of expenditure together. In other words, it can be misleading to treat "private" expenditure as somehow fundamentally different from public expenditure for purposes of broad cross country analysis.

3. It is worth noting that the average shares of spending going to ambulatory and in-patient hospital care respectively have remained broadly unchanged over the past decade, despite the abovementioned rise in ambulatory spending in some countries and the need to improve ambulatory care for the growing numbers of the chronically ill (Hofmarcher *et al.*, 2007).

4. However, this shift appears to reflect regulatory issues. Public spending in the United States is largely Medicare related and prices are tightly controlled. Thus it is in the interests of hospitals to shift patients to ambulatory care where there are no controls of the price of interventions and increases in prices for private insurers appear to explain a significant part of this increase.

5. The relations between growth in health care costs and the structure of spending can be complex. While the shift from in-patient care to out-patient is expected to reduce average costs of treatment there is no clear relationship between the change in the share of health care spending on hospital care in total spending across countries between 1992 and 2007 and the real per capita growth in total (and public) health care spending over the same period.

6. Data used are for the United States (Newhouse, 1992; and Smith *et al.*, 2009) and for France (Dormont *et al.*, 2006). The time period of the data underlying the estimates are: 1960-90 for Newhouse (1992); 1960 to 2007 for Smith *et al.* (2009); and 1992 and 2000 for Dormont *et al.* (2006). Over these periods there was relatively little population ageing.

7. For the studies focusing on the United States, this may reflect the fact that over much of the earlier period under study, the baby-boom generation led to a fall in the average age of the US population.

8. Smith *et al.* (2009) explain that the raw or unadjusted elasticity between real per capita health spending and real per capita GDP is higher at between 1.4 and 1.7. However, this "expenditure elasticity" reflects not only a pure income effect but also other factors affecting health spending which are correlated with real per capita GDP such as technology, insurance and medical prices. A model used to derive an estimate of pure income effect leads to a remaining (partial) expenditure elasticity of 1.0 for 1960-2007. Taking into account medical price inflation (supposed to be higher in rich countries) further lowers the income elasticity to the range of 0.6-0.9 depending on the assumption on medical price inflation.

9. See preceding section on drivers of health care spending. The two main scenarios are referred to as the cost pressure scenario and the cost-containment scenario.

10. The *2009 Ageing Report: Economic and Budgetary Projections for the EU-27 Member States (2008-2060)* considered the demand-side effects of demographic change, health status and national income in projecting public health expenditures. The consideration of technological change based on assumptions used in the OECD projections has a significant effect on the pure demographic scenario to produce projections not dissimilar from the OECD results.

Bibliography

AIHW (2008), "Australia's Health 2008", Australian Institute of Health and Welfare.

Castoro, C., L. Bertinato, U. Baccaglini, C.A. Drace and M. McKee (2007), "Policy Brief – Day Surgery: Making it Happen", World Health Organisation on behalf of the European Observatory on Health Systems and Policies, Copenhagen.

Colombo, F. and D. Morgan (2006), "Evolution of Health Expenditure in OECD Countries", *Revue française des affaires sociales*, April-September.

Congressional Budget Office (2009), *The Long-term Budget Outlook*, United States.

Conseil Supérieur des Finances (2009), "Comité d'Étude sur le Vieillissement", Rapport Annuel, Belgium.

Denison, E.F. (1962), "The Sources of Economic Growth in the United States and the Alternatives Before Us", Committee for Economic Development, New York.

Dormont B., Grignon M. and H. Huber (2006), "Health Expenditure Growth: Reassessing the Threat of Ageing", *Health Economics*, Vol. 15, pp. 947-963.

European Commission (2009), "2009 Ageing Report: Economic and Budgetary Projections for the EU-27 Member States (2008-2060)", Joint Report prepared by the European Commission (DG ECFIN) and the Economic Policy Committee (AWG).

Federal Finance Administration (2008), "Long-term Sustainability of Public Finances in Switzerland", Switzerland.

Federal Ministry of Finance (2008), "Second Report on the Sustainability of Public Finances", Germany.

HM Treasury (2009), "Long-term Public Finance Report: An Analysis of Fiscal Sustainability", United Kingdom.

Hofmarcher, M.M., H. Oxley *et al.* (2007), "Improved Health System Performance Through Better Care Coordination", OECD Health Working Paper, No. 30, OECD Publishing, Paris.

Huber, M. and E. Orosz (2003), "Health Expenditure Trends in OECD Countries, 1990-2001", *Health Care Financing Review*, Vol. 25, pp. 1-22.

Joumard, I., C. André, C. Nicq and O. Chatal (2008), "Health Status Determinants: Lifestyle, Environment, Health Care Resources and Efficiency", OECD Economics Department Working Paper, No. 627, OECD Publishing, Paris.

Joumard, I., C. André, C. Nicq and O. Chatal (2010), "Health Care Systems: Efficiency and Institutions", OECD Economics Department Working Paper, No. 769, OECD Publishing, Paris.

McKinsey Global Institute (2008), "Accounting for the Cost of U.S. Health Care: A New Look at Why Americans Spend More", MGI report.

McKinsey Global Institute (2010), "Debt and Deleveraging: The Global Credit Bubble and its Economic Consequences".

MHLW (2004), "Future Prospect of Social Security Expenditure and Contributions", Japan.

Ministero dell'Economia e Delle Finanze (2008), "Le tendenze di medio-lungo periodo del sistema pensionistico e socio-sanitario – aggiornamento 2008", Ragioneria Generale dello Stato, Italy.

Ministry of Health (2010), "Welfare and Sport/Youth and Families", the Netherlands.

Newhouse, J.P. (1992), "Medical Care Costs: How Much Welfare Loss?", *Journal of Economic Perspectives*, Vol. 6, pp. 3-21.

OECD (2006), "Projecting OECD Health and Long-term Care Expenditures: What Are the Main Drivers?", OECD Economics Department Working Paper, No. 477, OECD Publishing, Paris.

OECD (2009a), *Health at Glance – OECD Indicators*, OECD Publishing, Paris.

OECD (2009b), *Government at a Glance 2009*, OECD Publishing, Paris.

OECD (2010a), *OECD Health Data 2010 – Statistics and Indicators for 30 Countries*, OECD Publishing, Paris.

OECD (2010b), *OECD Economic Outlook*, No. 87, OECD Publishing, Paris, June.

Office of the Parliamentary Budget Officer (2010), "Fiscal Sustainability Report", Canada.

Paris, V., M. Devaux and L. Wei (2009), "Health Systems Institutional Characteristics: A Survey of 29 OECD Countries", OECD Health Working Paper, No. 50, OECD Publishing, Paris.

Rapport du Sénat sur l'assurance maladie (2004), "Les déterminants macroéconomiques des dépenses de santé : comparaison entre quelques pays", annexe au rapport Vasselle, France.

Roberts, M. *et al.* (2004), *Getting Health Reform Right: A Guide to Improving Performance and Equity*, Oxford University Press, New York.

Seong, M.K. (2009), "Forecasting Future Public Health Expenditures in Consideration of Population Ageing", *Korean Journal of Health Economics and Policy*, Vol. 15 No. 2, pp. 1-20.

Smith, S., J. Newhouse and M. Freeland (2009), "Income, Insurance and Technology: Why Does Health Spending Outpace Economic Growth?", *Health Affairs*, pp. 1276-1284.

Thomson, S. *et al.* (2009), "Addressing Financial Sustainability in Health Systems", Policy summary for the Czech European Union Presidency Ministerial Conference on the Financial Sustainability of Health Systems in Europe, Copenhagen, WHO Regional Office for Europe on behalf of the European Observatory on Health Systems and Policies.

Treasurer of the Commonwealth of Australia (2010), "Intergenerational Report, Australia to 2050: Future Challenges".

WHO (2000), *The World Health Report 2000 – Health Systems: Improving Performance*, World Health Organisation, Geneva.

Chapter 2

Policies for Health Care Systems when Money is Tight

This chapter reviews policies that have been used in OECD countries both to control health care spending and their impact on health systems objectives. On the supply side, macroeconomic policies controlling inputs or prices of health services have been widely used. Provider incentives aimed to improve efficiency are increasingly being used. On the demand side, policies have first focused on shifting costs to the private sector; they now seek to reduce the need for health care through prevention and information, and to encourage better co-ordination of care. It explores the risks and trade-offs of quick cost-cutting fixes versus longer-term gains in efficiency.

1. Introduction

The results presented in Chapter 1 indicate strong and unrelenting pressure on the cost of health care systems. But Chapter 1 also provides evidence of significant productivity reserves that can be drawn on: wide differences in health care spending across countries are not matched by equivalent results in terms of health outcomes. Thus, this chapter examines, in greater detail, selected policies that have been used to constrain health care spending on the one hand and to ease capacity constraints (by more efficient use of these resources) on the other. This review comes in the context of one of the deepest recessions on record. Fiscal positions have deteriorated in many countries. OECD governments are now focusing more attention on sustainability issues: i.e. how to prepare for possible cuts in health care spending and how to enhance the efficiency and effectiveness of health care systems to ensure that goals of access to, and quality of, health care continue to be met (Chapter 1, Box 1.1).

As background for this discussion of instruments for fiscal restraint and improved efficiency and effectiveness, the OECD Secretariat has sketched out three possible paths for spending subsequent to reforms (Figure 2.1). These show the level of health care spending over time depending on the type of policies introduced and their success. The dotted line refers to the scenario baseline, after the introduction of reforms, while the solid line refers to actual spending under each of the three scenarios (baseline).

- In the *first scenario*, it is assumed that countries introduce policies to reduce spending of a largely temporary nature (for example, through wage and price freezes or delays in investment). These are presumed to unwind over a relatively short period such that spending returns to the same underlying path.

- In the *second scenario*, using the same example, the authorities are able to maintain, for example, aggregate wages and prices at a lower level, but they continue to increase at the same trend growth rate prior to the change in policies.

- The *third scenario* postulates that governments investing in new policies – aimed, for example, at reducing longer-term spending growth through the introduction of new cost-saving policies – may lead to an initial rise in spending. But this may be followed by a subsequent decline in the underlying *growth* of health care spending to the degree that health system efficiency and effectiveness is enhanced.

The first two scenarios affect the level of health care spending, the degree depending on their sustainability. It is probably the case that these types of policies have been the most common and this may partly explain why spending has been so difficult to control. In the current conjuncture, countries should aim at the third scenario – sometimes referred to as bending the cost curve. Such policies are clearly the most attractive goal for health policy makers as they project a slower growth of health care spending over time (Schoen, 2007; Shortell, 2009). However such a scenario is also the most difficult to achieve for at least four reasons:

Figure 2.1. **Expenditure scenarios for health: the potential impact of reforms**

Scenario 1: Short-run cost containment

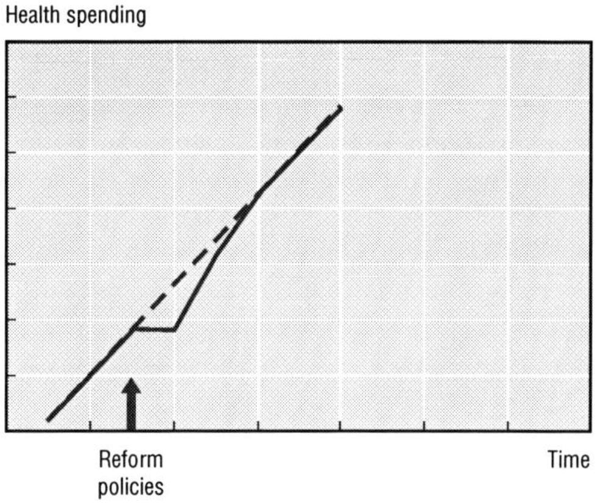

Health spending

Reform policies   Time

Scenario 2: Longer-run cost containment

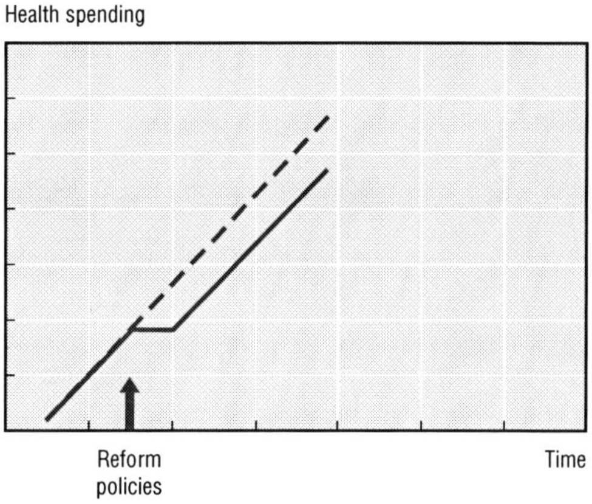

Health spending

Reform policies   Time

Scenario 3: Bending the cost curve

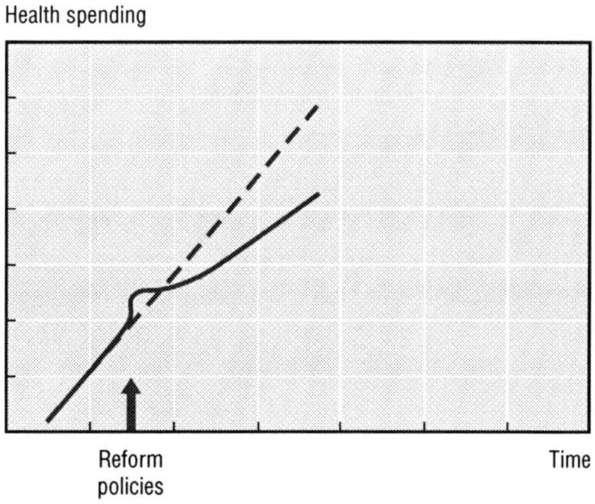

Health spending

Reform policies   Time

Source: OECD Secretariat.

StatLink ⬛ᴍˢᴮ *http://dx.doi.org/10.1787/888932319668*

- As discussed in Chapter 1, ageing populations and rising expectations will place upward pressure on health care costs.

- Rising health care costs are, to a large degree, the result of technological change. Moving onto a slower growth path may mean limiting the introduction and/or use of new medical technology or (and better) ensuring that those who develop cost-reducing technologies are rewarded adequately.[1]

- As long as the bulk of health care services received by patients is largely subsidised (if not free at point of use), governments have to find the right incentives to avoid excessive demand and over-supply of health care services.

- Governments will need to achieve continuing increases in productive efficiency in the health care sector.

The remainder of this chapter examines a selected number of key policies that could help OECD health authorities address these difficulties. There is no simple way to group or classify these policies. Past reviews of health care policies have identified four broad sequences of reform over the last several decades (Mossialos and Le Grand, 1999; Docteur and Oxley, 2004).

In addressing the need for a more efficient health care sector, authorities initially focused on policies aimed at limiting the price and volume of inputs allocated to health care systems. They then moved on to measures limiting the financial resources available to health care providers by, for example, capping the budgets of providers. Finally, they increased the share of health care spending paid by the patient (e.g. through increased cost sharing or narrowing the services covered in the basic public insurance package). These policies, while often subject to debate, have been technically easy to introduce and have been widespread.

Subsequently, countries have turned towards micro-efficiency in provision, aiming to make existing resources go further through improved incentives for purchasers, providers and patients. However, these policies have often required more in-depth reforms to health care systems that have elicited extensive debate and experimentation before being fully introduced.

The policies below are discussed in the broad order in which they have been introduced. However, they have also been broken down into those that, in the OECD Secretariat's judgement, *mainly* affect the supply as opposed to the demand side of the markets for health care services. A discussion based on this distinction will, however, need to take into account the following:

- Some policies discussed in this chapter can simultaneously affect both the demand and supply sides of the market in different ways.

- The impact of any specific policy in individual countries will depend on the regulatory and institutional environment.[2]

- Finally, there are often complementarities across policies. Some policies may be reinforced by others, and the overall impact of several policies may be stronger than that of selected policies taken separately.[3]

2. Overview of policy options

A summary of policies and their impact on spending and some of the trade-offs with respect to other health care objectives are presented in Table 2.1. This table is a very rough-and-ready guide based on the available literature and recent OECD Secretariat research and judgements. Individual policies can be assessed from a number of vantage points:

- The likely direction and size of the policy impact ("Strength" in Table 2.1);

- The speed at which policies can be introduced: policy and implementation lags can vary and there may be unforeseen negative effects as markets reassert themselves ("Impact

Table 2.1. Policies for limiting spending in a period of budget restraint

Characteristics, impacts and tradeoffs	Impact on expenditure		Objectives and trade-offs			
	Strength	Impact lag	Financial protection and access to care	Quality of care	Responsiveness	Cost efficiency
A. Macroeconomic policies aimed at expenditure restraint						
A.1. Wage and price controls (labour)	HIGH	SHORT	NONE	NONE/NEGATIVE	NEGATIVE	POSITIVE
A.2. Wage and price controls (medical materials)	HIGH	SHORT	NONE	NEGATIVE	NEGATIVE	POSITIVE
A.3. Controls on volume of inputs	HIGH	MODERATE	NONE/NEGATIVE	NEGATIVE	NEGATIVE	POSITIVE
(labour)						
(capital investment)	HIGH	SHORT	NONE/NEGATIVE	NEGATIVE	NEGATIVE	POSITIVE
A.4. Controls on volume of other inputs (high tech/drugs)	MODERATE	SHORT	NEGATIVE	NEGATIVE	NEGATIVE	POSITIVE/NEGATIVE
A.5. Budget caps (sector and global)	HIGH	SHORT	NEGATIVE	NEGATIVE	NEGATIVE	POSITIVE/NEGATIVE
A.6. Shifting costs to private sector (increased financing of cost by users)	MODERATE	MODERATE	NEGATIVE	POSITIVE/NEGATIVE	POSITIVE/NEGATIVE	POSITIVE
B. Microeconomic policies aimed at increasing efficiency						
B.1. Demand side						
B.1. Disease prevention and health promotion	LOW/MOD	LONG	POSITIVE	POSITIVE	NONE	POSITIVE
B.2. Gate-keeping/triaging	LOW	LONG	POSITIVE	POSITIVE	POSITIVE/NEGATIVE	POSITIVE
B.3. Care co-ordination integrated care/self-care	MODERATE	LONG	POSITIVE	POSITIVE	POSITIVE/NEGATIVE	POSITIVE/NEGATIVE
B.4. Better patient/doctor contact	LOW	MODERATE	NONE/POSITIVE	POSITIVE	NONE/POSITIVE	POSITIVE/NEGATIVE
B.5. Access to a PC doctor out-of-office hours (to take the pressure off hospital emergency services)	MODERATE	LONG	POSITIVE	POSITIVE	POSITIVE	POSITIVE
B.2. Supply side						
B.6. Further shift from hospital to ambulatory care	MODERATE HIGH	LONG	NEGATIVE	POSITIVE/NEGATIVE	NEGATIVE	POSITIVE
B.7. Enhancing the role of health-care purchasers	MODERATE	LONG	POSITIVE/NEGATIVE	POSITIVE	POSITIVE/NEGATIVE	POSITIVE
B.8. Improving hospital contracting/purchasing/payment systems	MODERATE	LONG	NONE	POSITIVE/NEGATIVE	POSITIVE/NEGATIVE	POSITIVE
B.9. Increasing managerial independence	LOW	LONG	UNKNOWN	POSITIVE	POSITIVE/NEGATIVE	POSITIVE
B.10. Improving payment methods/incentives for hospitals	MODERATE	LONG	POSITIVE	POSITIVE	POSITIVE/NEGATIVE	POSITIVE
B.11. Overseeing technological change and the pricing of medical goods	MOD/LOW	LONG	POSITIVE/NEGATIVE	POSITIVE/NEGATIVE	POSITIVE/NEGATIVE	POSITIVE
B.12. Increased use of ICT for information transmission	MOD/LOW	LONG	POSITIVE/NEGATIVE	POSITIVE	POSITIVE/NEGATIVE	POSITIVE/NEGATIVE

Note: Based on previous policy assessment by the OECD Secretariat and the literature. The first column refers to the type of reform policy. The following two columns refer to their potential impact on expenditure taking into account the potential size of the impact and the importance of implementation lags. The last four columns highlight some of the impacts of these policies on health care objectives, suggesting areas where trade-offs among policies may arise. A positive effect indicates a likely better achievement of the indicated policy objective while positive/ negative means that the policy could have positive or negative effects depending on the underlying institutional environment and/or the way policies have been introduced.

lag" in Table 2.1). One important issue in this context is the temptation for policy makers to choose short-term expedients which may have negative effects on health system performance if they are sustained over too long a period;

● Any possible spillover effects on other health care goals: *i.e.* access, quality of care, efficiency and effectiveness ("Objectives and trade-offs" in Table 2.1).

There is a wide range of individual policies shown in Table 2.1, and it is not possible to discuss them all in sufficient detail. More detailed reviews have been made in selected areas which appear particularly promising (see subsequent chapters in this volume).

While the OECD maintains a comprehensive database on health care outcomes (*e.g.* health status and quality of care), health care inputs (spending, health professionals and equipment) and processes (number of consultations, average length of stay, etc.), data on health policies and institutions have largely been lacking. This report draws on recent OECD Secretariat work which – to a significant degree – has helped fill this gap. Improved information on health policies, institutions and regulation – which has been presented in a number of summary tables – will now permit a better assessment of the likely impact of individual policies in different countries[4] (Paris *et al.*, 2010).

This chapter looks, first, at various supply-side policies. It then examines demand-side policies which, in the past, have often been limited to the effects of various forms of user charges on the demand for care. However, greater interest is now being paid to areas where the informed patient can become a more important actor and where a better channelling of health care demands may provide scope for increased efficiency.

3. Supply-side policies intended to restrain expenditure and increase cost efficiency

As noted, policies to restrain spending growth have first attempted to restrain the volume and price of labour and capital inputs going into health care provision; this was followed by systems of budget envelopes or caps on the health care sector as a whole or on specific sub-sectors such as hospitals.

The 1960s and 1970s saw rapid growth in supply in both ambulatory and in-patient care. With technological change and shifts in the burden of disease, the need for in-patient care has fallen while the demand – and possible scope – for treatment in ambulatory environments has increased. New drugs have played an important role in this shift: spending on medicines has taken up an increasing share of health care spending. But the net impact of this change on overall health sector efficiency seems likely to have been positive as patients have been able to shift to less costly health care settings.

While physician and nurse density has increased across the OECD over the last 30 years, this growth has slowed over the last few decades (Tables 2.2 and 2.3). This slowdown partly reflected a view by policy makers and analysts that rising numbers of doctors could induce higher demand for care and higher levels of health care spending, particularly where doctors were paid on a fee-for-service basis. Despite this general upward trend, cross-country differences in density remain large (Figure 2.2). A similar picture appears for nurses over the same period.

As regards hospital supply, there was initially some policy lag between the shift in morbidity toward chronic disease and the potential for treatment in an ambulatory environment.[5] However, over the past two decades, governments have attempted to reduce the number of high-cost acute-care beds per capita. There has also been a move to

Table 2.2. **Trends in doctor numbers per 1 000 population, 1980-2008**

	Practising physicians density per 1 000 population				Average annual growth rate (%)		
	1980[3]	1990[4]	2000[5]	2008[6]	1980-1990	1990-2000	2000-2008
Australia	1.9	2.2	2.5	3.0	1.6	1.3	2.7
Austria	2.2	3.0	3.9	4.6	3.1	2.5	2.2
Belgium	2.3	3.3	3.9	3.0	3.5	1.7	-3.2
Canada[1]	1.8	2.1	2.1	2.3	1.6	0.0	1.0
Chile							
Czech Republic	2.3	2.7	3.4	3.6	1.8	2.2	0.8
Denmark	1.8	2.5	2.9	3.4	3.5	1.6	2.3
Estonia	3.6	3.5	3.3	3.4	-0.3	-0.7	0.3
Finland			2.5	2.7			1.1
France[1]		3.1	3.3	3.3		0.7	0.2
Germany		2.8	3.3	3.6		1.9	1.1
Greece[1]	2.4	3.4	4.3	6.0	3.4	2.5	4.2
Hungary	2.3	2.9	2.7	3.1	2.5	-0.9	1.8
Iceland	2.1	2.9	3.4	3.7	2.9	1.9	1.0
Ireland[2]		1.6	2.2	3.2		3.7	4.8
Israel[*]			3.5	3.6			0.2
Italy[2]	2.6	4.7	6.1	6.2	6.0	2.6	0.3
Japan	1.3	1.7	1.9	2.2	2.7	1.6	1.4
Korea	0.5	0.8	1.3	1.9	5.8	4.6	4.6
Luxembourg	1.7	2.0	2.2	2.8	1.6	0.7	4.1
Mexico		1.0	1.6	2.0		5.3	2.6
Netherlands[2]	1.9	2.5	3.1	3.7	2.8	2.1	2.7
New Zealand			2.2	2.5			1.2
Norway	2.0	2.6	2.8	4.0	2.4	1.0	4.1
Poland	1.8	2.2	2.2	2.2	1.8	0.3	-0.3
Portugal[2]	2.0	2.8	3.2	3.7	3.6	1.2	1.8
Slovak Republic			3.2	3.0			-1.0
Slovenia			2.2	2.4			1.4
Spain			3.3	3.6			1.1
Sweden	2.2	2.6	3.1	3.6	1.6	1.7	3.1
Switzerland				3.8			
Turkey[1]	0.6	0.9	1.0	1.5	4.0	1.5	4.8
United Kingdom	1.3	1.6	2.0	2.6	2.1	1.9	3.6
United States			2.3	2.4			0.7

[*] The statistical data for Israel are supplied by and under the responsibility of the relevant Israeli authorities. The use of such data by the OECD is without prejudice to the status of the Golan Heights, East Jerusalem and Israeli settlements in the West Bank under the terms of international law.
1. Professionally active physicians data.
2. Licensed practising physicians data.
3. Data refer to 1981 for Korea.
4. Data refer to 1991 for Germany and Norway.
5. Data refer to 1999 for Norway.
6. Data refer to 2007 for Australia, Denmark, Luxembourg, the Netherlands, and the Slovak Republic and to 2005 for Sweden.

Source: OECD (2010a).

StatLink ᕦᕤ http://dx.doi.org/10.1787/888932319706

concentrate acute care in larger hospital units so as to achieve economies of scale and scope. This policy has probably limited the risk of public expenditure overruns overall, as there are fewer beds to fill. At the same time, governments have imposed tighter constraints on capital spending on new hospitals, often making them conditional on further restructuring of existing supply. Despite these shifts, some countries still find themselves with seeming imbalances in in-patient care.[6]

Table 2.3. **Trends in nurse numbers per 1 000 population, 1980-2008**

	Practising nurses density per 1 000 population				Average annual growth rate (%)		
	1980[3]	1990[4]	2000[5]	2008[6]	1980-1990	1990-2000	2000-2008
Australia	10.3	11.6	10.0	10.1	1.2	−1.5	0.1
Austria			7.2	7.5			0.6
Belgium							
Canada	9.6	11.1	10.1	9.2	1.5	−0.9	−1.2
Chile							
Czech Republic	5.9	7.2	7.6	8.1	2.0	0.5	0.8
Denmark			12.4	14.3			2.1
Estonia	7.3	7.5	6.0	6.4	0.2	−2.2	0.9
Finland			13.8	15.5			1.6
France[1]			6.7	7.9			2.2
Germany			9.6	10.7			1.4
Greece	1.9		2.9	3.4			2.1
Hungary		5.2	5.3	6.2		0.2	1.9
Iceland	8.9	12.5	13.3	14.8	3.5	0.6	1.4
Ireland[1]			14.0	16.2			1.8
Israel[*]			5.4	5.1			−0.6
Italy[2]			5.6	6.3			1.5
Japan			8.4	9.5			2.2
Korea			3.0	4.4			4.9
Luxembourg			7.4	10.9			6.8
Mexico		1.8	2.2	2.4		2.5	0.8
Netherlands			9.6	10.5			1.3
New Zealand				9.7			
Norway			12.1	14.0			2.4
Poland	4.4	5.5	5.0	5.2	2.2	−1.0	0.6
Portugal[1]			3.7	5.3			4.8
Slovak Republic[1]			7.4	6.3			−2.1
Slovenia			6.9	7.9			1.8
Spain			3.6	4.8			3.7
Sweden	6.9	8.7	9.9	10.8	1,9	1,4	1.5
Switzerland			12.9	14.9			1.9
Turkey[1]				1.3			
United Kingdom			8.7	9.5			1.2
United States[1]			10.2	10.8			0.7

[*] The statistical data for Israel are supplied by and under the responsibility of the relevant Israeli authorities. The use of such data by the OECD is without prejudice to the status of the Golan Heights, East Jerusalem and Israeli settlements in the West Bank under the terms of international law.
1. Professionally active nurses data.
2. Licensed practising nurses data.
3. Data refer to 1979 for Greece and Sweden.
4. Data refer to 1991 for Sweden.
5. Data refer to 2002 for Japan and Norway.
6. Data refer to 2006 for Luxembourg and Sweden and to 2007 for Australia, Denmark, Finland and the Netherlands.
Source: OECD (2010a).

StatLink ᴍᴙᴾ *http://dx.doi.org/10.1787/888932319725*

Cross-country differences and the scope for efficiency gains

Despite these developments, considerable diversity still exists across countries in the number of doctors, in other health care professionals and in the number of beds per capita. For example, countries such as Greece and Italy may rely too heavily on doctors while there appears to be over-supply of nurses in Ireland (Figure 2.2). The high level of acute-care beds

Figure 2.2. **Health professionals per 1 000 population, 2008**

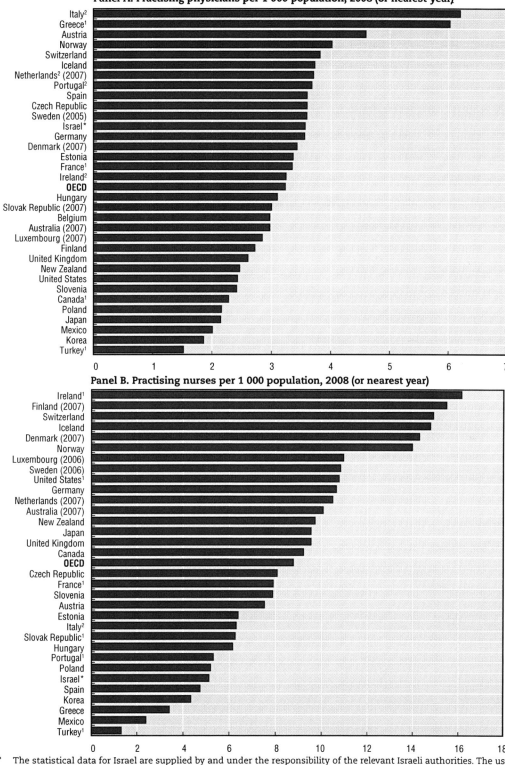

Panel A. Practising physicians per 1 000 population, 2008 (or nearest year)

Panel B. Practising nurses per 1 000 population, 2008 (or nearest year)

* The statistical data for Israel are supplied by and under the responsibility of the relevant Israeli authorities. The use of such data by the OECD is without prejudice to the status of the Golan Heights, East Jerusalem and Israeli settlements in the West Bank under the terms of international law.
1. Professionnally active physicians/nurses data.
2. Licensed practising physicians/nurses data.
Source: OECD (2010a).

StatLink ᴴᴴᴴᴴ *http://dx.doi.org/10.1787/888932319307*

per capita in a few countries suggests some scope for further adjustment (such as in Austria, Germany, Hungary, Japan and the Czech and Slovak Republics) although, in some cases, these differences in bed numbers reflect difficulties in distinguishing between acute and long-term beds (Figure 2.3) (Joumard *et al.*, 2008). Considerable diversity is also present in the ratio of nurses to doctors (from over 6 in Ireland to 0.6 in Greece) (Figure 2.4).

Figure 2.3. **Acute care hospital beds per 1 000 population, 1995 and 2008**

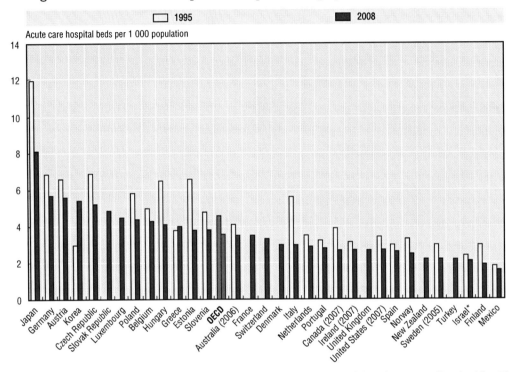

* The statistical data for Israel are supplied by and under the responsibility of the relevant Israeli authorities. The use of such data by the OECD is without prejudice to the status of the Golan Heights, East Jerusalem and Israeli settlements in the West Bank under the terms of international law.

Source: OECD (2010a).

StatLink ⇒ *http://dx.doi.org/10.1787/888932319326*

This diversity suggests that there is scope for organising health care in different ways that may encourage greater health system efficiency through a reduction in overall supply of providers in those countries with seeming over-supply or a better alignment of the skills of different types of medical professionals (*e.g.* using more nurses where doctors are in short supply). Scope for efficiency gains are supported by evidence showing that health outcomes per health practitioner vary significantly across OECD countries even after controlling for other determinants of health status, and by the fact that the productivity of health professionals appear to be higher in countries where supply has been constrained (Joumard *et al.*, 2008).

Adjusting the supply of inputs into health care

Complete reliance on markets to achieve the appropriate level, distribution and mix of medical skills is unlikely to be possible given the degree of market failure in the health sector (Smith, 2009). As a consequence, governments have considerable control over the supply of inputs of workforce, equipment/capital stock and spending on drugs. For the medical workforce, quotas for medical students are the most common method of

Figure 2.4. **Ratio of nurses to physicians, 1995 and 2008**

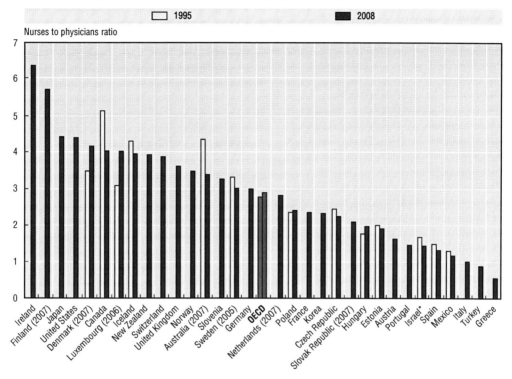

*   The statistical data for Israel are supplied by and under the responsibility of the relevant Israeli authorities. The
use of such data by the OECD is without prejudice to the status of the Golan Heights, East Jerusalem and Israeli
settlements in the West Bank under the terms of international law.

Source: OECD (2010a).

StatLink ⎚⎘⎙ *http://dx.doi.org/10.1787/888932319345*

controlling the overall number of doctors, and these constraints exist in all but three
countries (Luxembourg, the Czech Republic and Japan) (Table 2.4). Despite this, the level of
the medical workforce and the number of acute care beds, on a per capita basis, varies
considerably across countries. The degree of control and the administrative level at which
the decisions are made appears to vary considerably across countries.

There are longer-term supply problems that need to be taken into consideration when
judging the potential contribution from reduced numbers of medical staff to budgetary
restraint. First, governments in countries where the density of health care providers is low

Table 2.4. **Regulation of physician workforce**

Quotas for medical students or for students by speciality	Policy for regulation of practice location, or policy to address perceived shortages or maldistribution	
No	No	Luxembourg
No	Yes	Czech Republic, Japan
Yes	Yes	Australia, Austria, Belgium, Canada, Denmark, Finland, France, Germany, Greece, Hungary, Iceland, Ireland, Italy, Korea, Mexico, Netherlands, New Zealand, Norway, Poland, Portugal, Slovak Republic, Spain, Sweden, Switzerland, Turkey, United Kingdom

Source: Paris *et al.* (2010).

would probably be ill-advised to reduce these further, and any possible efficiency gains from reduction seem most likely to come in countries where input levels are already generous.

Second, specialisation has increased, and there are now two specialists for every generalist on average across the OECD area (OECD, 2009). This has been associated with a growing penury of primary care doctors in some countries, probably reflecting the fact that the remuneration of primary care doctors in all countries is lower than that of specialists, sometimes significantly so.[7] This problem is even more marked for rural and socially deprived areas. This appears to be leading some countries to begin treating general medicine as a specialty to attract new practitioners (Ireland) often within a context of moves towards more appropriate primary care arrangements (see below). This, in turn, may require a subsequent realignment of remuneration with those of traditional specialists. Nurses are also in short supply in some countries (Figure 2.2 and Table 2.3).

Finally the demand for health care professionals seems likely to intensify. Medical personnel may work fewer hours on average in the future, thereby reducing aggregate supply of services.[8] In addition to the general ageing of populations and the workforce, most countries are becoming concerned about the impact of the expected exit of a significant share of health care professionals as the post-war baby-boom generations move into retirement. Supply appears likely to fall just as age-related needs begin to increase (e.g. France).

A key problem in adjusting medical manpower is the long lags between the perceived increase in needs and the change in supply of trained medical staff, particularly for doctors where education can be as long as ten or more years (particularly in the case of specialists). Quotas for medical students seem to remain the most widespread regulatory tool for controlling the overall supply of medical personnel. While the number of new entrants into medical schools has recently been increased in many countries, this has not yet fed through into any marked increase in supply. Shorter-run shortages in the supply of doctors and nurses are often being partly made up by medical migration (OECD, 2008a). However, this is not a sustainable long-term policy for most countries, not least because this can mean shifting the problem to non-OECD countries where the deficiency of health care supply is even greater.

Thus, better human resource planning policies that focus on maintaining adequate supplies of qualified health care professionals over the long haul are necessary if problems of supply of health professionals are to be avoided (OECD, 2008a). Such problems have been a significant barrier to policy change. For example, Canada and the United Kingdom increased health care budgets in the 1990s following long periods of restraint but, like Denmark, they had difficulty in increasing the supply of health care because of the limited number of doctors and nurses. The reduced supply of health professionals was accompanied by upward pressure on their wages. Thus, the easing in the macro-financing constraint contributed to higher wages of health care professionals rather than the hoped-for increase in health care supply (see below) (Rapoport et al., 2009).

Increased training and migration are not the only policy measures that can be put in place. Supply blockages may be eased by: i) improving retention (particularly through better workforce organisation and management policies (particular for doctors providing in remote rural areas); ii) enhancing integration into the health workforce (e.g. by attracting former nurses or doctors back into the health workforce and by improving the procedures for recognising and, as necessary, supplementing foreign qualifications of immigrant health professionals); iii) adopting a more efficient skill mix (e.g. by developing the role of advanced practice nurses and physicians' assistants); and iv) improving productivity (e.g., through linking payment to performance).

The impact of any macro-measures will also depend on the regulatory environment (Tables 2.4 and 2.5). There are wide differences across countries in the degree to which control over the number of hospital staff is handled by individual institutions or whether limits are set at a higher administrative level. This is also the case for hospitals, the number of beds and the supply and use of high-cost equipment. Controls on hospitals and high-tech equipment are found in all countries except Finland, Greece, Iceland, Korea and Poland (Table 2.5). Note, however, that those countries with greater autonomy in hiring and remuneration at the local level can also face constraints through budgetary caps (Table 2.8).

Table 2.5. **Regulation of hospital and high-tech equipment and activities**

Open new hospitals or other institutions	Increase/decrease supply of hospital beds	Provision of specific types of hospital services	Supply of high cost medical equipment	
No regulation	No regulation	No regulation	No regulation	Finland, Greece, Iceland, Korea, Poland
No regulation	No regulation	No regulation	Regulated	Czech Republic
No regulation	No regulation	Regulated	No regulation	Slovak Republic
No regulation	Regulated	No regulation	No regulation	
Regulated	No regulation	No regulation	No regulation	New Zealand, United Kingdom
Regulated	No regulation	Regulated	Regulated	Norway, Sweden
Regulated	Regulated	No regulation	No regulation	Japan, Netherlands
Regulated	Regulated	Regulated	No regulation	Switzerland
Regulated	Regulated	Regulated	Regulated	Australia, Austria, Belgium, Canada, Denmark, France, Germany, Hungary, Ireland, Italy, Luxembourg, Mexico, Portugal, Spain, Turkey

Source: Paris et al. (2010) updated with information available in July 2010.

Controlling prices and wages

Part of the difference in spending across countries can be attributed to variation in the relative prices for health care services. Figure 2.5 shows the cost in individual countries of a similar bundle of goods and services using health-related PPPs (purchasing power parities).[9] These data show wide differences in the cost of the similar bundles of health goods and services: ranging from USD PPPs 33 in the Slovak Republic to USD PPPs 143 in Iceland. Hence, some portion of the observed differences in spending on health comes from differences in the relative prices and not volumes of services. As to country groupings, relative PPPs for health are particularly low in OECD Asian and eastern European countries.

Unfortunately, time series data showing the changes in the PPPs over time or the contribution of such changes to variation in health care spending are not yet available.[10] Nonetheless, there may be greater scope for reducing spending by reducing prices of health care services in countries with high relative prices than in those where relative prices are low. For countries with very low relative PPPs, preventing too rapid a rise in wages and prices towards the cross country average will remain a difficult policy challenge.

It is more difficult to get behind this data to judge the causes of such differences. The relative wages of health care providers is one vantage point, given the importance of wages and salaries in total health care costs and the wide range of relative wages received by health care professionals across countries. General practitioners remuneration ranges from 1.4 times the average wage of all workers in Hungary to 4.2 times for the United Kingdom. The relative

Figure 2.5. **Purchasing power parities (PPPs) for health goods and services, 2005**

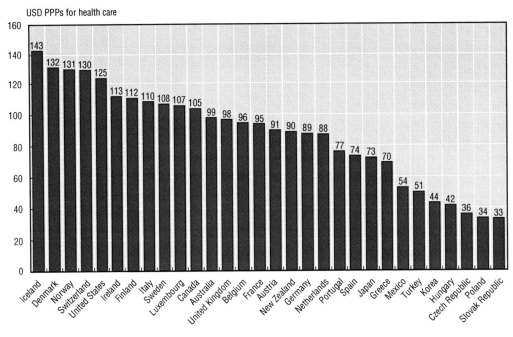

Source: OECD.Stat 2009.

StatLink ⟐ᵢ⟐ http://dx.doi.org/10.1787/888932319364

wages of specialists ranges from 1.5 times the national average wage for salaried specialists in Hungary to 7.6 times for self-employed specialists in the Netherlands (OECD, 2009). Wages for nurses (relative to the average wage) can range from 0.7 to 0.8 in some former eastern European countries to around 2.2 in Mexico (Fujisawa and Lafortune, 2008; OECD, 2009).

These cross-country differences may have reflected the capacity of countries to regulate prices. Tables 2.6 and 2.7 indicate a wide range of models for negotiating and setting of prices and the degree and nature of such arrangements varies considerably across countries. But they provide little information in themselves as to the direct role of governments. While governments often have the ultimate power to regulate, responsibility is sometimes delegated to health insurers and professionals, which may weaken governments' capacity to control spending in practice. Furthermore, the role of government in setting prices has changed over time. Caution is therefore needed when evaluating the implications of the information in these two tables for overall cost control.

In the past, wage controls have been, by their nature, particularly prevalent in systems with public-integrated models in both the hospital and ambulatory sectors if health care personnel are paid on a salary basis – Denmark (hospitals), Finland, Ireland (hospitals), Spain, Sweden, the United Kingdom (hospitals) – although this has often occurred in the context of broader public-sector pay restraint and is thus not specific to the health care sector. In some cases in the past (*e.g.* Australia, Belgium, Canada, France, Japan, Luxembourg, and Switzerland) governments have on occasion stepped in when the payers and providers could not reach an agreement on fees and prices (Docteur and Oxley, 2004). Cost control in Japan has relied heavily on price setting in both ambulatory and hospital care (Imai and Oxley, 2004).

In others, prices automatically adjust as a function of the volume of care so as not to exceed a fixed budget ceiling. In Germany, a resource-based relative value scale (RBRVS)

Table 2.6. **Regulation of prices/fees of physicians' services**

Fees/prices billed by providers (to private health insurance or to patients)

	Primary care services			Specialist services		
	Must be equal to prices/fees paid by third-party payers + "statutory co-payments" if any	Can exceed prices/fees paid by third-party payers and statutory co-payments only in some circumstances	Can always exceed prices/fees paid by third-party payers and statutory co-payments	Must be equal to prices/fees paid by third-party payers + "statutory co-payments"	Can exceed prices/fees paid by third-party payers and statutory co-payments in some circumstances	Can always exceed prices/fees paid by third-party payers and statutory co-payments
Fees/prices[1] set unilaterally by third-party payers at central level			Australia	Poland[2]		Australia
Fees/prices negotiated at central level between third-party payers and/or government and providers	Czech Republic, Japan, Korea, Luxembourg, Netherlands, Norway	Austria, Belgium, France, Denmark		Czech Republic, Iceland, Japan, Korea, Luxembourg, Netherlands, Norway	Austria, Belgium, France, Greece[4]	
RBRVS established at central level and local negotiation on point value	Switzerland,[2] Germany			Switzerland, Germany		
Fees/prices negotiated at local level	Canada		New Zealand	Canada	New Zealand	
Fees/prices are negotiated with each insurer						
Capitation or salary unilaterally set by third-party payer or government at central level	Poland,[2] Slovak Republic[2]	Hungary[4]		Slovak Republic[2, 6]	Hungary[4]	
Capitation or salary negotiated by interested parties at central level	Iceland, Italy, Portugal, Spain, United Kingdom, Turkey	Finland, Greece,[4] Ireland,[5] Mexico[3]		Denmark, Italy, Portugal, Spain, Turkey	Finland,[3] Ireland,[3] Mexico,[3] United Kingdom[3]	
Capitation or salary negotiated by interested parties at local level	Sweden			Sweden		

1. Fees/prices can include or not "statutory co-payments".
2. Physicians can charge any price if they do not participate to the national or health insurance systems or provide not-covered services, but those circumstances are considered to be of marginal importance.
3. For private services paid on a fee-for-service basis, physicians are most often free to charge any price they will.
4. Physicians are not allowed to charge extra-fee fees in principle, but informal payments are common practice.
5. For two-thirds of the population, GPs set their prices freely.
6. An RBRVS is set at central level, health insurers negotiate volume caps and point values.

Source: Paris et al. (2010).

Table 2.7. **Regulation of hospital prices for covered services**

Price paid by third-party payers (basic primary health coverage)	Prices billed by providers		
	Must be equal to prices/fees paid by third-party payers + "statuory copayments" if any	Patients may pay supplements for superior accomodation	Patients may pay supplements for superior accomodation AND supplemental fees charges by physicians
Determined by central government	Norway		Ireland, United Kingdom (private practice)
Negotiated by interested parties at central leval	Australia (public patients in public hospitals[1]) France ("public" hospitals[2]) Greece, Hungary, Japan	Austria, Korea	Australia (private patients in public or private hospitals), Belgium, France (private hospitals, or private practice in public hospitals), Turkey
DRG weights defined at central level with negotiation of rates at local level or with insurers	Denmark, Italy, Poland		Germany
Negotiated by interested parties at local level	Finland, Spain, Sweden	Canada, Switzerland	
Negotiated at central level with possible further negotiations between individual providers and insurers	Czech Republic,[3] Netherlands, Slovak Republic[3]		
Negotiated between individual third-party payers and providers			Mexico (private hospitals)
Payment by global budget	Iceland, Luxembourg, Mexico (public hospitals), New Zealand, Portugal		

1. Public patients are not charged for treatment.
2. Include most not-for-profit private hospitals.
3. Informal payments are common.

Source: Paris *et al.* (2010).

has been introduced with the value of the points earned by individual practitioners declining as the overall number of points (for all practitioners) increases so as to ensure that the budget envelope is not exceeded. Similar arrangements are used for specialists in the Slovak Republic (Table 2.7).

Tighter control over both volumes of inputs and, particularly prices and wages, should permit governments to engineer a strong short-term negative effect on spending, if desired, in a period of retrenchment, and the impact could be even stronger in the presence of high rates of inflation. Nonetheless, the impact will depend on a number of factors:

● Existing contractual relations between payers and providers – for example, whether labour contracts are pluri-annual and whether remuneration is formally indexed to the rate of inflation.

● Whether the authorities can fix the number of providers supplying care.

● The degree to which cost reductions can be eroded by supplier responses. On the one hand, lower prices may trigger a substitution effect for providers and lower volumes of health services because treating patients becomes less lucrative. On the other hand, an income effect may result in higher volumes of care as physicians attempt to compensate for the loss of remuneration by increasing supply.[11, 12]

In attempting to reduce relative wages of health care providers, policies will need to take into account the possible negative effects in countries where wages are particularly low. Low wages may lead to medical personnel having more than one job to make ends meet and, as a consequence, they may face greater difficulties in maintaining their knowledge and skills, or may shorten their working hours, thereby reducing supply. In some countries (Greece, Hungary, the Czech and Slovak Republics and Poland), informal payments have become widespread.[13] In Japan and Korea, low fees can lead to induced demand, higher volumes of care than necessary, and patient dissatisfaction. Most importantly for the long-term sustainability of the health system, low wages may lead to out-migration of medical professionals.

Setting pharmaceutical prices

Setting prices in the pharmaceutical sector requires special attention because of the specific characteristics of that market (Docteur and Paris, 2009). Although pharmaceutical drugs account for a small share of total health care costs (17% of total health care spending for the OECD area on average), spending has been rising faster than for other main components of health care in the past. The level of drug prices is much higher for a few countries (mainly the eastern European countries, Mexico and Greece). The key problem for policy makers in this market is to find the appropriate balance between obtaining good value for money for patients and payers now while ensuring that the incentives for continued innovation remain strong enough to encourage further innovation – i.e. adequate to ensure the development of better drugs in the future. Finally, it also means finding ways of limiting demand in a market where patients rarely face the full cost of the drugs that are prescribed and ensures that the distribution system for drugs – which represents as much as one-third of the total cost – is operating efficiently.

A wide range of techniques is available for pricing, coverage and for influencing the demand for and the mix of pharmaceuticals (see Docteur and Paris, 2009 and Chapter 6 of this publication). These include: external benchmarking using prices in other countries as a guide, internal reference pricing, pricing using pharmaco-economic assessment and risk-sharing schemes. Possible reforms in this area include:

- Changes to reimbursement and pricing so as to better steer consumers towards lower-cost products (e.g. encouraging generic substitution), and providing incentives for more efficient distribution mechanisms;

- Increasing the role of pharmaco-economic assessment in determining value;

- Price-volume agreements where prices are adjusted when drug spending increases beyond agreed ceilings.

Price controls can be an effective tool for cost-cutting policies – for example, research-based drug manufacturers in Ireland have recently agreed to cut prices by 40% for nearly 300 widely prescribed medicines.

Budgetary caps and constraints

With public health care spending continuing to rise, budgetary caps or envelopes progressively became a more widely used instrument for controlling health spending. Such tools can take the form of an overall limit on public spending or it can be sector specific (e.g. hospitals). Table 2.8 shows that all countries – with the exception of Austria, Japan, Korea, and Switzerland, together with the United States – have set some form of budget caps or spending constraint. The remaining countries have constraints either at a national, regional level or for individual hospitals or use other techniques to limit spending (e.g. Japan through price setting).

Table 2.8. **Stringency of the budget constraint**

Nature of budget constraint	
No budget constraint	Austria, Japan, Korea, Switzerland
Expenditure target without further allocation	Luxembourg
Expenditure target with silo *or* regional allocation	Australia, Belgium, Czech Republic, Denmark, Finland, France, Germany, Greece, Iceland, Netherlands, Slovak Republic, Spain,[1] Turkey
Expenditure target with silo *and* regional allocation	Canada, Mexico
Strict health budget without further allocation	
Strict health budget with silo *or* regional allocation	Hungary, Ireland,[2] Italy[2]
Strict health budget with silo *and* regional allocation	New Zealand, Norway, Poland, Portugal, Sweden, United Kingdom

1. Sub-targets by region/sector in Spain whereas sub-targets for different health services (silo approach) for other countries.
2. Sub-targets by region/sector/area in Italy and Ireland whereas sub-targets for different health services (silo approach) for Hungary.

Source: Paris *et al.* (2010).

Initially directed at the hospital sector (the most costly element of the system), they have been often complemented by global and supplementary spending caps on ambulatory care and pharmaceuticals, reflecting the difficulty for controlling overall spending by focusing on only one care component. In general, policies to control and reshape supply and to cap spending in the hospital sector appear to have been more successful than for ambulatory care or pharmaceutical drugs, although institutional differences lead to considerable variation across countries.[14] Spending control through budgetary caps also appears to have been most successful in countries such as Denmark, Ireland, New Zealand and the United Kingdom where integrated models of health care financing and supply are or were the rule and in mainly single-payer countries, such as Canada, where health care budgets are generally explicitly set through the budget process (Mossialos and Le Grand, 1999).

A few countries with social-insurance systems have established indicative budgets or targets (Belgium, France, Luxembourg and the Netherlands), but these limits have often not been respected, partly because of their less-than-compulsory nature and, sometimes, because there was no means to claw back over-spending in subsequent years.[15, 16] Others have imposed spending limits indirectly: the Czech government set budget caps on individual providers in 1994 (after a sharp increase in spending in 1992-93), but operated the policy via the main insurer; and, in countries where supply is organised at lower levels of government, the central authorities limited the amount of intergovernmental transfers (Canada, Finland) or set limits on tax increases at lower levels of government (Denmark and Sweden).

New budget controls have also involved a move from retrospective payments – i.e. paying the provider *ex post* on the basis of costs – to prospective or forward-looking budgets. At the simplest level, this has meant that providers have been given a hard-budget constraint while being expected to continue to adjust supply to meet the increasing demand for care.

However, top-down spending constraints in the form of budget caps can have undesirable incentive effects depending on the governing regulations. They do not encourage (and may actively discourage) providers to increase output or to enhance productivity. For example, where the budget is allocated independently of output, there is no financial cost to the provider if output falls or compensation for higher costs where output is increased. Where budgets have been set on the basis of historical cost, this may favour inefficient providers and penalise efficient ones and hinder the geographical re-distribution of scarce resources on the basis of need.

Furthermore, where savings are clawed back by payers, fixed budget ceilings encourage suppliers to spend up to the ceiling. And since budget caps and controls on inputs are often associated with cuts to staff and increasing workloads, staff morale may suffer while restrictions on wage rates and on hiring can interfere with personnel policies and the capacity to attract labour. In any case, most governments have found themselves obliged to finance the cost over-runs when faced with bankruptcy of hospitals, particularly where these are unique regional providers (*e.g.* Italy, Greece, New Zealand and Portugal). As a consequence, governments have been moving increasingly to combine budget setting with measures that take more account of levels of efficiency and output across hospitals and differences in needs across geographical areas.

Cost control in a decentralised environment

A number of countries combine significant control over overall health care spending at the central level with decentralisation of responsibility for health care provision to lower levels of government. Some of these have been particularly successful in limiting the growth of the aggregate health care costs (Canada and Finland over certain periods at least). In these cases, a reduction in financial resources to lower levels of government (*e.g.* equalisation grants) has forced the latter to a reduce spending and/or introduce measures to improve the efficiency of provision. Where supply is affected, lower levels of government face the brunt of criticism from patients and providers, while the central authorities benefit politically from reduced public spending overall and smaller public sector deficits.[17] But even under these circumstances, countries cannot sustain spending control indefinitely. Progressively increasing political pressure – often related to public dissatisfaction with supply and lengthening waiting times – almost inevitably force governments to reverse policies and increase spending, sometimes substantially.

Supply-side restraint and the impact on other health care objectives (see Table 2.1)

Policies for controlling public health care expenditure may affect other health care system objectives although the magnitude will depend on the time frame over which the policies are considered: in general, the longer the policies are sustained, the greater the potential for unwanted side effects. On the positive side, there may be positive effects on system efficiency – for example, where the health care system is supply constrained and hospitals are called on to do more with fewer resources. Nonetheless, even in such cases, issues of access to health care and the quality of that care may arise. Reduced resources may lead providers to supply less care or limit the introduction of new technologies, a problem that may be particularly pertinent where there are cutbacks on investment.

Using incentives to improve supply-side performance

As mentioned in OECD (2005) and Docteur and Oxley (2004) more attention is being paid to reforms that focus on improving incentives both on the demand and the supply dimensions of health care systems. This sub-section selectively reviews supply-side reforms introduced to this end and the impact where information is available. It is probably fair to say that most attention has been focused on measures to enhance the functioning of the supply side of health care systems. But subsequent paragraphs pay somewhat more attention to demand-side issues than in the past.

The purchaser-provider split and increased purchasing and contracting

The purchaser-provider split permits a better mapping of responsibilities and governance of health care systems. In theory, the purchasers, acting as agents of patients and/or government administrations identify health care needs and contract with providers to fulfil them. They also can monitor whether the objectives of health systems are being achieved – and propose remedial action where they are not. There has been widespread scope for purchasing and contracting in (social) insurance systems. But such models have become increasingly prevalent in countries with integrated systems (*e.g.* Italy, New Zealand, selected Nordic countries, Spain and the United Kingdom).

The purchaser-provider split is an appealing model for furthering health system goals. Nonetheless, such an approach has also proved difficult to introduce in an effective manner (Figueras *et al.*, 2005). First, purchasers require informations on health needs to inform the purchasing agent: such information is, most often, either unavailable or prohibitively costly to obtain. Purchasing may also be poorly linked to overall objectives of the health system as the responsibility of the purchaser may not include all the health care needs of the population – for example in some countries, purchasing institutions may only cover spending for treatment and spending on prevention may be too low.[18] The process of contracting can also be long and costly and monitoring of contract compliance requires a large amount of timely information and technical expertise which may be costly.

Despite these difficulties, the basic model does form an important building block for a more policy-oriented approach to health care arrangements. Health care objectives and targets can be set, resource needs assessed and system performance evaluated. But national administrations will need to examine carefully how best to introduce purchasing and build the data systems that are necessary, especially for monitoring performance.

More efficient deployment of resources in ambulatory care

The growing role of the ambulatory sector is raising issues as to how this sector should best be organised and, more specifically, how the personnel should be remunerated. While there is no hard and fast rule, independent contractors operating in solo practices and paid on the basis of fee-for-service are the form of organisation that is, probably, least conducive to the treatment of the growing numbers of patients with chronic diseases in a cost-effective manner. In the United States for example, the concept of a "medical home" where the doctor follows the patient through time and co-ordinates needs is gaining ground and, as noted, the recent moves towards partial gate keeping in Germany and France have included scope for the introduction of managed care systems. More innovation is needed in this area, although developments in individual countries will be guided by the existing strengths of each national approach (see Chapter 5).

In this context, there is considerable diversity in the way in which ambulatory care is organised. This may partly reflect the difficulty in designing payment systems that, at once, limit the incentive to oversupply (as in fee-for-service) while preventing low levels of consumer satisfaction through, for example, waiting lists for specialist visits and elective surgery, something that appears more frequently in systems where providers are paid by capitation or on the basis of wages and salaries. But whatever the system, there has been little change in recent years in the capacity of the system to channel patients and co-ordinate care and virtually all OECD countries see this as a major area in need of improvement (Hofmarcher et al., 2007).[19]

As regards payment arrangements, some countries have been moving towards mixed payment systems that combine fee-for-service, capitation and wage and salaries which are thought to perform better than using a single payment method.[20] For example, group practices in England have taken on a limited purchasing role, and a significant part of their remuneration package is based on achieving public health and quality goals/targets. However, mixed systems also pose challenges and require oversight by the authorities to ensure that the overall goals of the health care system are being met, in particular as regards patient responsiveness and access to specialist or hospital care when needed.

Improving cost efficiency in the hospital sector

While the hospital and acute care sector continues to contract in most OECD countries, it remains the largest single component of health care expenditure (Figures 2.6 and 2.7).[21] It is also an area where the scope for efficiency gains is likely to be particularly

Figure 2.6. **Percentage of in-patient care in total health expenditure, 1980, 1990, 2000 and 2008**

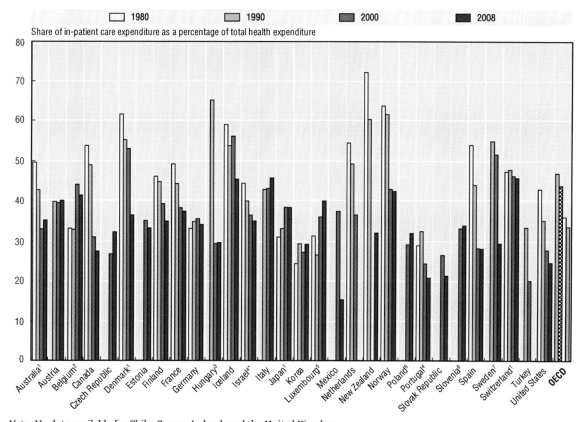

Note: No data available for Chile, Greece, Ireland, and the United Kingdom.
1. Data refer to 2007 instead of 2008; 2. 2003 instead of 2000; 3. 1991 instead of 1990; 4. 2006 instead of 2008; 5. 2005 instead of 2008; 6. 2002 instead of 2000; 7. 1993 instead of 1990.
* The statistical data for Israel are supplied by and under the responsibility of the relevant Israeli authorities. The use of such data by the OECD is without prejudice to the status of the Golan Heights, East Jerusalem and Israeli settlements in the West Bank under the terms of international law.
Source: OECD (2010a).

StatLink ⟨⟨⟨ http://dx.doi.org/10.1787/888932319383

Figure 2.7. **Health care spending by component, 2008 (or most recent year)**

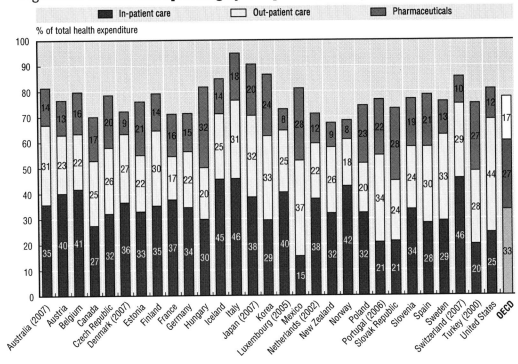

Note: No data available for Chile, Greece, Ireland, Israel, and the United Kingdom.

Source: OECD (2010a).

StatLink ━━━ http://dx.doi.org/10.1787/888932319402

important, reflecting, among other things, the growing use of day surgery and reduced lengths of hospital stay. There has been a series of important reforms undertaken in this sector. Hospital systems, particularly those run by national health systems, have most often faced tight budget limits with little management freedom for some time now. More recently, management capacity has been enhanced and the cost accountability and independence of hospital management has been increased (Italy, Spain, the United Kingdom and the Netherlands) (although to varying degrees). Budget periods have also been lengthened and there is greater flexibility in the use of any surpluses – i.e. they can be used by the hospital rather than being taken back by the budget authorities. Greater autonomy of hospital management has led to more contracting out of non-essential services. Although the costs of ensuring that the quality goals are met can be non-negligible, there is widespread agreement that this can lead to lower costs as long as there is sufficient competition in the market for these services (OECD, 2006).

The method of financing hospital services is of paramount importance in assessing whether there is scope for efficiency improvements. The arrangements formerly used to pay hospitals in many countries have not encouraged efficiency and may have had the opposite effect – for example, where costs were reimbursed *ex post*, or where the prices used were out of line with the underlying cost of supply because of technological change and falling prices of equipment. As noted, budget caps have often been set on an historical basis, thus locking in the poor performance of inefficient providers while failing to reward the efficiency of the efficient ones.

A growing number of countries have moved to prospective case-related payment schemes such as those using diagnosis-related groups (DRGs) to set, in advance of service provision, payments based on the estimated cost of hospital care for a particular episode. These encourage hospitals to increase the volume of treatments and they also have the advantage of encouraging providers to reduce the cost of each episode of care. However, where there is excess supply, they may lead to budget over-runs if providers are able to induce additional demand or there is pent-up demand. As a consequence, many countries now monitor supply and provide feedback in relation to the existing budget ceilings. Similar arguments and policies apply to other sectors of the health system, including physicians' services (Table 2.9).

Table 2.9. **Policies to control volumes of care**

	Existence of policies to control volume		
	Is there any regulation/control on health provider activity?	Is direct-to-consumer advertising of pharmaceuticals permitted?	Physicians' payment linked to volume targets?
Australia	No	Yes for some medicines	Yes, reduction in physicians' fees[1]
Austria	Yes, activity volume monitored, feedback, prescription targets/budgets	Yes for some medicines	Yes, reduction in physicians' fees
Belgium	Yes, activity volume monitored, feedback, prescription targets/budgets	Yes for some medicines	No
Canada	Yes, activity volume monitored	Yes for some medicines	Yes, reduction in physicians' fees
Czech Republic	Yes, activity volume monitored, feedback, prescription targets/budgets	Yes for some medicines	Yes, refund to health insurance funds
Denmark	Yes, activity volume monitored	Yes for some medicines	Yes, reduction in physicians' fees
Finland	Yes, feedback	Yes for some medicines	Yes, refund to health insurance funds
France	Yes, feedback	Yes for some medicines	No
Germany	No	Ys for some medicines	No
Greece	No	Yes for some medicines	No
Hungary	Yes, activity volume monitored, feedback	Yes for some medicines	No
Iceland	Yes, activity volume monitored	Yes for some medicines	No
Ireland	No	Yes for some medicines	No
Italy	Yes, activity volume monitored, feedback	Yes for some medicines	Yes, refund to health insurance funds
Japan	No	Yes for some medicines	No
Korea	Yes, activity volume monitored, feedback	Yes for some medicines	Yes, reduction in physicians' fees
Luxembourg	Yes, feedback	Yes for some medicines	No
Mexico	No	Yes for some medicines	No
Netherlands	No	Yes for some medicines	No
New Zealand	No	Yes for all medicines	No
Norway	Yes, activity volume monitored	Yes for some medicines	No
Poland	Yes, activity volume monitored	Yes for some medicines	No
Portugal	Yes, prescription targets/budgets	No	No
Slovak Republic	Yes, activity volume monitored	Yes for some medicines	No
Spain	Yes, activity volume monitored, feedback, prescription targets/budgets	Yes for some medicines	No
Sweden	Yes, feedback, prescription targets/budgets	Yes for some medicines	No
Switzerland	Yes, activity volume monitored, feedback	Yes for some medicines	Yes, reduction in physicians' fees
Turkey	Yes, activity volume monitored, prescription targets/budgets	No	No
United Kingdom	Yes, activity volume monitored, feedback	Yes for some medicines	Yes, reduction in physicians' fees

1. In some jurisdictions (*e.g.* Victoria).

Source: Paris *et al.* (2010).

For hospitals, decentralisation of decision making and more management independence is desirable where it is accompanied by enhanced managerial capacity, more independence in decision making and greater cost accountability. Increased managerial independence may help create more efficient deployment of human resources, for example, in the context of changing scope-of-practice rules for health professionals.

Competition in insurance and provider markets

In the search for greater efficiency, a number of countries have introduced market or market-type mechanisms either at the level of insurers or providers (Germany, the Netherlands and Switzerland). At the levels of insurance markets, the aim is to encourage insurers to become more administratively efficient, provide better services to their clients and to eventually search for better and more efficient providers. However, the degree to which this competitive pressure spills over into provider markets varies considerably across countries, reflecting, among other things, differences in the regulatory environment.

In general, insurers compete for clients on the basis of a universal mandatory premium for a basic care package, often with options for coverage of elements not included in the basic health care package. Insurers must take all comers on the basis of a community-rated premium. Due to the fact that the pattern of risks differs across insurers, risk adjustment mechanisms have been put in place to create a level-playing field for competition in this market. However, as risk adjustment can never be complete, insurers have an interest to "cream skim", to attract the best risks and avoid the worst, with potential negative effects on access (Smith, 2009).

In order to secure the major benefits of competitive insurance, insurers must be able to contract selectively with providers, thereby creating the potential to extract cost efficiencies and quality improvements in the provision of care. This was successful to some degree in the United States for managed care arrangements. However, in other countries which are attempting to introduce greater competition in social insurance markets (such as Switzerland and the Netherlands), this is only partly the case and, in a number of health care systems, prices are set after bilateral negotiation between insurers and providers or set directly by the authorities. With the scope of services open to negotiation becoming progressively wider in the Netherlands, time will tell whether such approaches lead to increased cost containment.[22].

Even without introducing competitive insurance markets, collectively purchased health services – where a purchaser seeks to place contracts for specified health services for a defined population group – can permit purchasers to place pressure on health care providers. Purchasers can take on many forms, such as employer-based insurers in the United States, social insurers (such as those just considered), local governments or national or regional health services. But competitive pressure can arise only where there is some flexibility in where the contracts are placed and there is some control over where the patients can obtain the care that they need.

The potential for gains, however, will depend on the regulatory framework, the market conditions, and the capacity of the purchaser to write and monitor contracts. In practice, competition may be limited by the presence of a single provider, the complexity of the contracting process and the lack of information to assess whether contracts are being met, particularly as regards responsiveness to patient needs and clinical quality. These difficulties may require recourse to other forms of competition, *e.g.* through benchmarking and yardstick competition.

Improving data systems and information transfer to promote quality of care

Studies in a number of countries, most notably the United States (Institute of Medicine, 2001) have noted widespread problems of health care quality; such dysfunctions have been recorded in many other countries as well. There appears to be general agreement that quality problems are likely to have a significant impact on health and health care budgets because of the cost of rectifying the ensuing errors – for example, hospitalisation because of incorrect medication. Lack of co-ordination and communication among providers and between providers and patients is a major cause of the observed quality deficits. Improving the quality of care would reduce such waste and could lead directly to significant improvements in population health and well-being.

Meeting this challenge seems difficult in the absence of better statistical information to delineate the dimensions of the problem. In this context, more widespread use of ICT in order to permit rapid transmission of the information to agencies providing oversight is needed (see Klazinga and Ronchi, 2009; OECD, 2010b; and Chapter 7 of this publication). Achieving improved quality of care also requires systems which reward good performance and new methods of paying providers that take the quality of the care into account. Pay for performance (P4P) represents one such response (see Chapter 4). Improvements in medical information and its transfer – from patients to providers, among providers and from provider to payer – also have the potential to improve care co-ordination, reduce the delivery of duplicative services, reduce administrative costs, give feedback to providers and provide the basis for better planning of system enhancements.

But while the potential for reduced costs and better population health are there, the introduction and maintenance of the associated ICT systems are proving to be more costly than anticipated: information technology is capital-intensive, and the costs must be balanced against any purported gains. As with a number of other programmes, more information on the cost effectiveness of such programmes is needed.

There is a widespread consensus that increases in health care spending have been driven to a large degree by technological change and that some part of this has had only marginal benefit in terms of health outcomes. There remain wide cross-country differences in the supply of high-tech equipment (such as imaging) without much difference in health outcomes (OECD, 2009). Thus, there is certainly a need for reviewing whether all the new medical materials or procedures meet certain cost-effectiveness criteria as defined by each country. In this context, there is widespread interest in health technology assessment (HTA) as a means of sorting out which techniques, drugs and equipment have the highest benefits relative to the cost. While institutes such as the British National Institute for Health and Clinical Excellence can make judgements of the costs and potential benefits, governments must make the final choices in light of its capacity and willingness to pay (see Chapter 3).

4. Demand-side issues and policies

Evidence of weak efficiency can be found on the demand as well as the supply dimensions of health care systems, although distinguishing between what is demand-related and supply-related is often difficult.[23] As regards the demand for care, OECD (2004) for example, notes wide variation in the rates of ischemic health disease across OECD countries which do not appear to correlate with the levels of specific treatments (*e.g.*

coronary revascularisation). Similar problems occur for other diseases. Thus, there is too much practice variation both within and across countries (Mulley, 2009). Greater adherence to widely accepted care protocols might improve care quality as well as reducing overall treatment costs. Such practice variation is reflected, as well, in the marked differences in pharmaceutical drug consumption across countries ranging from USD PPPs 350-420 in Denmark, New Zealand and Switzerland to USD PPPs 888 in France (Figure 1.11 from OECD, 2008b).[24]

At the same time, there are wide differences in the use of health care services by patients, as measured by doctor consultations and discharges from in-patient care. The number of annual doctor contacts ranges from around four or fewer to over ten (for the clusters of OECD Asian and eastern European countries) while there is a three-fold difference in the number of hospital discharges across OECD countries. Little correlation is apparent between: i) consultations and the number of doctors; and, ii) the number of discharges and the supply of beds (Figures 2.8 and 2.9).[25]

Neither of these differences can be easily attributed to either supply or demand factors alone and, in practice, it would appear that institutional norms, incentives (payment arrangements) and patterns of patient behaviour all contribute to this variation.[26] Nonetheless, policy makers need to assess the reasons for such large differences in system use and whether narrowing them may provide scope for greater cost efficiency without loss in terms of health outcomes or quality of care.

Figure 2.8. **Doctors consultations and density of physicians, 2008**

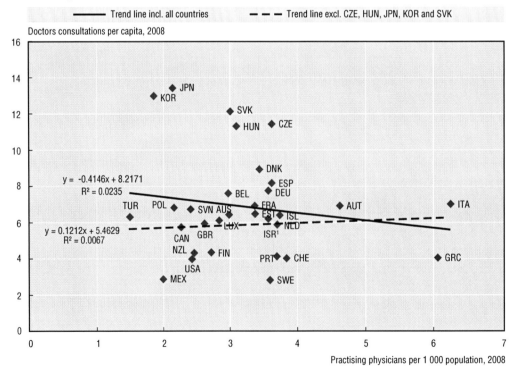

1. The statistical data for Israel are supplied by and under the responsibility of the relevant Israeli authorities. The use of such data by the OECD is without prejudice to the status of the Golan Heights, East Jerusalem and Israeli settlements in the West Bank under the terms of international law.

Source: OECD (2010a).

StatLink http://dx.doi.org/10.1787/888932319421

Figure 2.9. **Discharges per capita and number of beds, 2008**

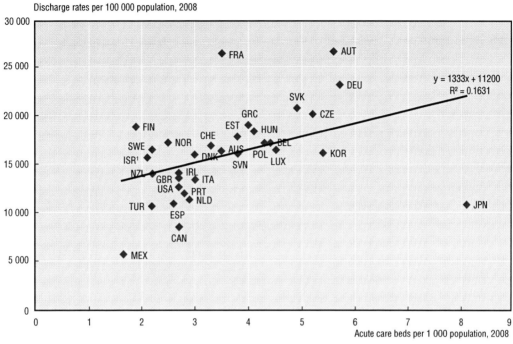

1. The statistical data for Israel are supplied by and under the responsibility of the relevant Israeli authorities. The use of such data by the OECD is without prejudice to the status of the Golan Heights, East Jerusalem and Israeli settlements in the West Bank under the terms of international law.

Source: OECD (2010a).

StatLink ⏩ *http://dx.doi.org/10.1787/888932319440*

Increasing the share of total health care spending paid for by private households

The level of *public* health care spending can be reduced by placing a larger share of the responsibility for health risks onto private households. This can take on various forms:

● *Government reduction in the scope of the "benefit basket"*: for example, most public systems do not cover certain surgery or may not cover treatments or drugs that have no or only limited therapeutic value (France, Spain).

● *Shift costs of health care for selected risks (e.g. dental treatment)* from public insurance to private complementary or supplementary insurance.

● *Require patients to pay for a larger share of the health care that they receive.* Such cost sharing takes on a variety of forms, ranging from flat rate payments per doctor visit or hospital stay to co-payments for drugs.

Most OECD countries provide full or near-to-full population coverage for a core set of health care services. However, this measure, when used in isolation, is a poor indicator of coverage. For example, where services such as dental treatment or pharmaceutical drugs are excluded from the basic package or are covered in a very limited way (Canada and France), the degree of cost sharing may be more important than it seems. In such cases, patients can face significant out-of-pocket spending, unless they are covered by some form of private or mutual insurance. In contrast, there can be wide exemptions from co-payments for certain vulnerable groups which increase, sometimes substantially, the share of health care costs paid for by public health systems (Table 2.10).[27] Such measures can also increase the administrative costs of cost-sharing systems substantially.

Table 2.10. **Exemptions from co-payments**

	Are there exemptions from co-payments?	If exemptions exist:							
		for those with certain medical conditions or disabilities	for those whose income are under designated thresholds	for beneficiaries of social benefits	for seniors	for children	for pregnant women	for those who have reached an upper limit for out-of-pocket payments	other
Australia	Yes								X[1]
Austria	Yes	X	X					X	
Belgium	Yes	X	X	X	X			X	X[2]
Canada	Yes	X	X	X	X				
Czech Republic	Yes	X	X	X	X	X		X	X
Denmark	Yes	X			X	X		X	
Finland	Yes							X	
France	Yes	X	X	X			X		X[3]
Germany	Yes	X	X	X		X			
Greece	Yes	X	X	X			X		
Hungary	Yes	X							
Iceland	Yes	X		X	X	X	X	X	
Ireland	Yes	X	X	X		X	X	X	
Italy	Yes	X	X		X	X	X		
Japan	Yes	X			X	X	X	X	X[4]
Korea	Yes	X	X	X	X	X		X	
Luxembourg	Yes	X					X	X	
Mexico	-								
Netherlands	Yes	X				X		X	X[5]
New Zealand	Yes	X	X	X		X	X	X	
Norway	Yes					X	X	X	
Poland	Yes	X				X			X[6]
Portugal	Yes	X	X	X	X	X	X		
Slovak Republic	Yes	X	X	X	X	X	X		
Spain	Yes	X			X				
Sweden	Yes	X				X		X	
Switzerland	Yes	X	X	X	X	X	X	X	
Turkey	No	–	–	–	–	–	–	–	–
United Kingdom	Yes	X	X	X	X	X	X	X	

"–": not applicable.
1. In Australia, while no universal exemptions apply, full or partial exemptions and safety nets apply in various parts of the health system.
2. Chronic patients.
3. Accidents at work.
4. Public assistance beneficiaries.
5. GP visits.
6. E.g. war invalids and disabled veterans, drafted soldiers

Source: Paris *et al.* (2010).

Although it is difficult to establish clear patterns, there appears to have been some limited increase in the share of out-of-pocket spending in total health care spending, on average, during the 1990s with increases in the share of out-of-pocket spending in total spending increasing in 13 out of 22 countries for which data were available (Figure 2.10).[28] This increase, however, appears to have been marginally reversed in the current decade with declines in 24 out of 32 countries for which data were available.[29, 30] Greater increases in cost sharing has mainly concerned pharmaceutical drugs, while increased private payments for in-patient care and doctor visits have been less widespread (France,

Figure 2.10. **Out-of-pocket payments as a percentage
of total health expenditure, 1990, 2000 and 2008**

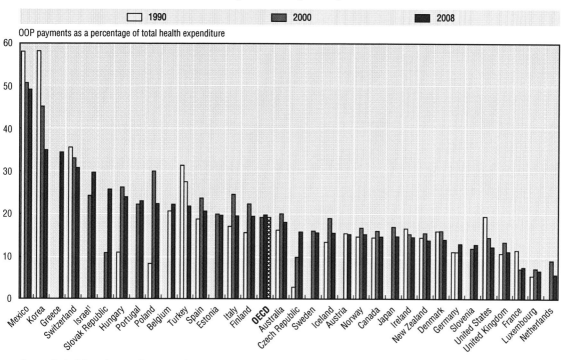

1. The statistical data for Israel are supplied by and under the responsibility of the relevant Israeli authorities. The use of such data by the OECD is without prejudice to the status of the Golan Heights, East Jerusalem and Israeli settlements in the West Bank under the terms of international law.
Note: Authors' estimate for Greece. Data for Chile are not available.
Source: OECD (2010a).

StatLink ᵃˢᵖ *http://dx.doi.org/10.1787/888932319459*

Germany, Italy, Sweden). The number of drugs not reimbursed has risen, very often for "comfort" drugs or those without proven therapeutic value. In a number of cases, flat-rate payments per prescription have been introduced (the Czech Republic, France, Germany, the United Kingdom). Elsewhere, pharmaceutical reference price systems have been introduced (Germany, Canada, France). These arrangements increase cost sharing for individuals using branded or higher cost products while assuring access to drugs of a generic nature.

The limited increase of cost sharing possibly reflects concern by the authorities over ensuring widespread access to care. But whatever the motivation, the very limited changes in cost sharing over recent decades for most countries (as measured in Figure 2.10), and the widespread exemption for vulnerable groups[31] (Table 2.10), any effects on the demand for care seem likely to have been limited. In any case the wide difference in cost sharing across countries is not correlated with cross-country differences in health status. While increased cost sharing can limit the demand for care, the size of the change necessary to ensure a significant impact on the demand for health care services would certainly have a negative effect on access (Smith, 2009). But larger increases than those experienced up to now could form one element of a wider package to reduce the pressure on public finances, if balanced by protection for vulnerable groups.

Reducing the need for health care through disease prevention and health promotion

Government programmes for health promotion and disease prevention represent roughly 5% of health care spending in the OECD area. A superficially persuasive idea is that increased investment in prevention policies would have a high payoff in terms of reduced health care costs at some time in the future. In this context, there is ample evidence that a number of standard prevention programmes – such as vaccination against communicable diseases – are highly cost effective. However, OECD governments have implemented a wide range of interventions in this area, particularly during the past five years, but without a strong body of evidence of the effectiveness of interventions and virtually no evidence on their efficiency and distributional impacts (OECD, 2010b).

Given the long and uncertain lags between spending and outcomes and the need to address large population groups, there is no assurance that prevention will be less expensive than subsequent cure. For example, before the beginning of the recent OECD work on prevention of obesity, the state of the evidence was very poor, especially concerning the efficiency and distributional implications of such interventions. However, new evidence produced by the OECD through micro-simulation analysis, does show favourable cost effectiveness and distributional profile for the interventions evaluated in the analysis (OECD, 2010b).

Better communication between patients and care providers may help

Better two-way communication between doctors and their patients regarding the (human) cost and potential benefits of treatment might be beneficial and in line with the growing trend towards more active consumerism in health care. There is some evidence (Mulley, 2009) that patients may be less willing than their doctors to choose highly invasive and intensive forms of treatment if they are better aware of the chances of success and/or serious longer-term side effects. Improved decision aids may help both patients and providers reduce unwarranted variation in provision. Second opinions may also help in this regard, as can a stronger role of primary care doctors in helping patients come to a reasoned position.

With an increasingly educated population and rising chronic disease, there should be greater scope for self-care and prevention than in the past. A better understanding by patients as to when they should make contact with the health system – e.g. through better health education and widespread dissemination of information on early warning signs – is desirable. Such policies, however, would need to be structured within the context of broader efforts aimed at disease prevention and health education and promotion. For minor treatment problems, telephone hotlines may help, as can well-screened information provided through the Internet.[32]

Improved care co-ordination and gate keeping may reduce the need for high-cost care

With a very large share of the health care services being consumed by a relatively small share of the population, the demands for care could be reduced by ensuring that these individuals are kept out of high-cost institutional environments as much as possible (see Chapter 5 and Hofmarcher et al., 2007).[33] Issues of reduced need for high-cost care have gained greater prominence as the prevalence of chronic diseases (and often multiple chronic diseases) increases as populations age. Barriers to improved co-ordination appeared to arise from a range of institutional impediments:

- fragmented financing of health care (most notably between medical care on the one hand and social services and long-term care on the other);

- the growing complexity (*e.g.* growing specialisation) within health care systems, while information flows between levels of care are often inadequate to meet the challenge of the new care needs; and,

- possibly most important, co-ordination activities do not formally exist in some systems: health professionals charged with co-ordination are not explicitly recognised and co-ordination activities are rarely remunerated. At the same time, scope-of-practice rules can sometimes prevent nurses and other health professionals from taking on a stronger role in this area (Hofmarcher *et al.*, 2007).

Improving care co-ordination will require policies aimed at improved information transfer between different providers and provider levels, reconfiguration of provider systems (particularly at the primary care level) with appropriate and explicit incentives for care co-ordination. Particular attention needs to be given to transitions between care levels (*e.g.* between acute hospital care and long-term care).

Despite the perceived importance of improved care co-ordination, available evidence suggests that, while improved co-ordination will enhance care quality, there is no clear evidence that specific forms of care co-ordination – such as disease management – will lead to overall cost savings (IGAS, 2006). Indeed, the introduction of improved information systems (ICT) may entail large up-front costs. A similar conclusion arises concerning cost efficiency for programmes of healthy ageing – *i.e.* programmes aimed at keeping individuals fit and in good health as they age, rarely appear to be cost effective, or lead to overall reductions in health care costs (Oxley, 2009).

But whatever the degree of cost efficiency, such measures are probably best served within the context of primary care gate-keeping systems which regulate access to specialist and hospital care and more generally act as the patient's agent within the health care system for a fixed period of time.[34] Primary care gatekeepers can help guide the patient through the health system, thereby improving care co-ordination. Table 2.11 shows the intensity of gate keeping across countries.

Table 2.11. **Gate keeping**

		Primary care physicians referral to access secondary care is:		
		Compulsory	Encouraged by financial incentives	Not compulsory, not financially encouraged
Registration with a primary care physician is:	**Compulsory**	Denmark, Italy, Netherlands, Norway, Portugal, Slovak Republic, Spain		
	Encouraged by financial incentives	Hungary, New Zealand, United Kingdom	Belgium, France, Germany, Switzerland	
	Not compulsory, not financially encouraged	Canada, Finland, Mexico, Poland	Australia, Ireland	Austria, Czech Republic, Greece, Iceland, Japan, Korea, Luxembourg, Sweden, Turkey

Source: Paris *et al.* (2010).

5. Conclusions

Improving health system performance remains an overarching goal

Health care spending has continued to climb throughout the OECD area over recent decades, reaching around 9% of GDP on average in 2008. Health spending is taking up a growing share of total public expenditure. On average, public health spending has risen from 12% of total general government spending in 1992 to 16% in 2008. There is nothing inherently wrong in growing health spending as long as the additional benefits from the additional spending are, at the margin, greater than benefits from the alternative use of these resources. But, with three-quarters of health spending funded from public budgets, concerns about the allocation of resources and the efficiency of spending come to the forefront, especially so when money is tight and governments face difficulties in financing public sector deficits. In such circumstances, issues of system sustainability and increased value for money in the provision of health care become more important. This chapter has described a range of policy measures that may help policy makers address this issue.

Countries can reduce spending quickly by rationing inputs, and limiting input costs and prices

Within this context, this chapter points to two main sets of cost-reducing responses to economic crises in the health sector: i) controls over inputs into the health care, their price and/or budgetary caps; and ii) enhanced productive efficiency and effectiveness through better supply and demand incentives. These two policy sets are closely linked. Greater productive efficiency will help ease overall financing constraints.

Past country experience and the size of the current fiscal challenge suggests that the first set of policies will probably be needed in the early stages of retrenchment. Wage and price controls are likely to have the strongest short-term effects, particularly when supplemented by tight budgetary caps.

In most OECD countries, governments can exercise considerable control over the supply of inputs and their prices. As a consequence, they can achieve strong reductions in spending over shorter periods and they have been widely used, albeit with different degrees of intensity and success over time and across countries.

But such policies cannot be sustained for long periods

There are risks and trade-offs in relying solely on quick cost-cutting fixes. When reductions in the supply of health professionals are prolonged or pushed too far, they can lead, subsequently, to upward pressures on wages and difficulties in scaling up supply when budget restraints are eased. It is even possible that measures taken to restrict spending in the short run can increase spending over the longer run – for example, if necessary investments are delayed and desirable prevention policies are not implemented.

Thus, governments may need to consider exit strategies before the underlying pressures build up and force governments to make sub-optimal health care policy decisions. One element of such an approach might be to link any subsequent wage increases with micro-reforms aimed at increasing the efficiency of provision – *i.e.* using remuneration increases to buy change. However, for this to be credible, wages and salaries would need to follow the introduction of reforms, something which will be difficult to achieve.

Changing the incentives that people face will offer better payoff in the longer term

There are significant productivity reserves in health systems and there are a wide range of policies that might lead to greater efficiency. But getting value for money requires continuous efforts to close the evidence gap on what measures could produce meaningful value for money over coming decades. In assessing possible avenues for reform, much attention has been focused on the supply side of the health care system as the scope for efficiency gains are arguable the largest. However, promising demand-side interventions that go beyond the traditional issue of cost sharing should also be considered.

The change in disease patterns need to be matched by new methods of organising and providing care

Supply-side strategies are complex undertakings and require a close review of the facing providers to provide cost-effective care with the important caveat that any reform needs to take into account the existing institutional environment in the country in question. As shown, there are very wide differences across countries in the level and pattern of resource use that may provide avenues for future exploration. Supply-side policies evoked in the main text include:

- The separation of purchaser and provider functions needs to be strengthened to monitor better system performance. The separation of the purchaser and provider functions provides scope for a clearer identification of responsibilities within health care systems and potentially to better governance. It can help identify needs and monitor whether health system goals of access and quality are being met. However, such arrangements – which can take on different forms – require large amounts of information to provide adequate oversight.

- Most OECD countries have probably not fully adjusted to the shift in morbidity towards chronic disease and the potential for treatment in an ambulatory environment. Thus, countries need to explore models of primary or ambulatory care that are better adapted to the emerging epidemiological landscape. More efficient deployment of resources in the ambulatory sector is needed and, underlying this, new payment arrangements – for example various "pay for performance" schemes – will need to be identified;

- There is considerable scope for efficiency gains through better organisation and use of health care resources in the hospital sector. Despite the widespread reduction in the number of beds over the past two decades, the hospital sector remains the largest single component of health care spending. Moves to introduce prospective payment systems seem likely to positively affect efficiency if accompanied by tight control over activity. Designing better payment arrangements is one function that could be delegated to health care purchasers.

- Alternatively, a greater role in setting incentives in both the ambulatory and hospital sectors could come from the increased play of markets. Such arrangements have become increasingly popular in a number of countries (Germany, the Netherlands, Switzerland and the United States.) However, introducing a competitive model in an environment fraught with market failures makes it difficult to say whether such measures will lead to increased efficiency and lower costs.

- The adoption of information technology and computerisation of providers' practice may bring value to health systems by improving the scope for care co-ordination, minimising duplication of medical tests, reducing the administrative cost of processing claims and potentially increasing the quality of care where this is monitored.

More attention needs to be given to demand-side issues

Wide differences also exist across countries in user charges suggesting that there is probably scope for shifting a greater part of the cost of health care on to users, at the very least in countries where out-of-pocket payments make up a very small share of total health care costs and where vulnerable groups are adequately protected. High-cost health care may also be reduced by cost-effective prevention.

The main text also describes the inexplicably large differences in the demand/use of health care systems across countries. One possibility is that some countries are better at prevention than others. Cost-effective prevention may be one way of reducing the need for curative care. But there is potentially scope for additional savings by arrangements such as primary gate keeping or care co-ordination so as to channel patients towards the most appropriate care settings and to prevent high-cost hospitalisations.

Bending the cost curve requires addressing technological change

A sustained reduction in the growth of public health care spending (the third scenario in Figure 2.1) will, however, require addressing technological change, which is one of the key drivers of health care spending. Up to now, most countries have been able to ensure that most mainstream interventions are included in their basic package of publicly subsidised health care services. If technological change accelerates as some authors suggest (Aaron, 2003), the authorities may need to become more selective in what is introduced into the basic package.

Notes

1. Newhouse (1992) estimated that up to half of the increase of expenditure in the United States is linked to technology. Research by the CBO (2008) confirms this broad picture. However, most recent estimates for the United States suggest that technology might explain from one quarter to one half of the total increase in health care spending (Smith et al., 2009).

2. For example, policies to control directly the supply of inputs of health sector personnel may be more difficult if regulatory control is decentralised to providers.

3. For example, the introduction of more market competition in provider markets will be reinforced if there are policies for increased information on prices and quality and the potential for selective contracting.

4. This is referred to in the text as Paris et al. (2010). Details of the construction of the policy and institutional indicators are provided in that document.

5. Political economy factors underlay some of the increases in hospital supply. In many countries, there were strong political pressures for increases in hospitals in municipalities and cities to ensure local access and jobs. These hospitals were also important employers. In addition, there were strong financial incentives because the investment in increased capacity was often paid for at other levels of government or institutions.

6. Paris et al. (2010) finds that 16 countries reported shortages of non-acute beds and, in five countries, patients frequently experienced extended acute care hospital stays awaiting appropriate follow-up care.

7. For example, earnings of GPs are less than half that of specialists in Australia, Belgium and the Netherlands.

8. The growing feminisation of the medical workforce is a factor as women doctors tend to work shorter hours than male doctors. Regulatory changes have also contributed – such as the European Working Time Directive which limits the number of working hours in hospitals in the European Union.

9. These data need to be treated with caution as individual components of health care spending can be input- rather than output-based. Data are for 2005.

10. While such work is in progress at the OECD, changes in these data over time are not yet available. However, recent research (Farrell *et al.*, 2008) argues that the increase in spending in the United States over the period 2004 to 2007 was largely driven by price increases in the ambulatory sector. This, in turn, reflects a further shift from in-patient care – where prices tend to be tightly controlled in the Medicare system – to ambulatory care where price controls have been less strict.

11. Only limited information is available on which impact will be more important. Recent changes in primary care in Norway, for example, have shown little income effect on service production (Grytten *et al.*, 2008), while in Japan, strict regulation of physician fees has been accompanied by very short and repeated physician consultations (OECD, 2009) (see below).

12. This can occur, for example, by increasing volumes to compensate for limitations on price (or wage) increases (*e.g.* ambulatory care in Australia, France and Japan and the hospital sector in Sweden), providing higher cost services (*e.g.* more on-site diagnostic tests) (France, Germany and the United States), up-rating of patients into higher cost classifications (*e.g.* Medicare in the United States) or shifting services into areas where there are no price controls (the United States). Doctors operating in both the public and private sectors (the United Kingdom, Finland, Greece and Ireland) can also attempt to shift care into the private sector where government controls are less strict.

13. In Greece for example, doctors in the public sector have also tended to shift patients into their private practices (Economou and Giorno, 2009).

14. Nonetheless, such outcomes are not a foregone conclusion and may depend on the period under review. Budget caps have been, generally, less well met or not met at all in Greece, Italy, Portugal and Spain even though they have similar institutional arrangements. Alternatively, countries with integrated models have also deliberately increased resources to the health care sector over certain periods – for example, Canada, New Zealand and the United Kingdom in the most recent period – or have experienced rebounds in spending after periods of tight budget restraint (Ireland).

15. The outcome may depend on the amount of excess supply in the system. For example, spending limits have traditionally been kept tight in the UK National Health Service. With pressure to improve efficiency, and reduce waiting lists, considerable productivity gains were achieved in the 1980s and 1990s (Light, 2001).

16. France, however, has strengthened its system of spending control in 2004 with certain positive results.

17. The issue here is one of political economy rather than one relating to specific tools for restraining health care expenditure.

18. The French *Agences régionales d'hospitalisation* when they were initially set up in France in the late 1990s covered only hospital care. More recently their mandate has expanded to cover ambulatory care and they were renamed *Agences régionales de santé*.

19. The "Survey on health system characteristics" (Paris *et al.*, 2010) reports that 14 countries have disease management systems and that ten have case management arrangements for patients with complex conditions. However, the extent of these programmes is unknown. The implementation of purchasing requires a health-needs assessment which is not necessarily available in all countries.

20. Currently, considerable use of fee-for-service is made in North America and in Austria, France Germany and Switzerland.

21. Excluding Korea, Mexico, Turkey, Spain, the Slovak Republic, Sweden and the United States.

22. In the Netherlands, selective contracting covers 34% of health care supply.

23. Demand-side policies consider attempts to channel the demand (or need) for health care so as to minimise cost and or maximise the effect on health outcomes (an example is the use of GP gate keeping for triaging patients). Supply-side effects concern incentives and regulatory measures facing providers that lead to greater cost efficiency and effectiveness in supply. An example, here, is the introduction of market forces (out-sourcing of laundry or meals) where market conditions permit competition.

24. Differences in prices across countries can reflect differences in prices and in the mix of drugs (see OECD, 2008b).

25. However, variation in the share of the elderly in the population may partly explain some of these differences in discharges (OECD, 2009).

26. For example, some of these differences reflect poor measurement: the low number of doctor consultations in Sweden and Finland may reflect the fact that the first contact with the health care

system is very often with nurses (Bourgueil *et al.*, 2006). Data for the Netherlands exclude contacts for maternal and child care. As regards regulation, many doctor contacts in Japan are for the renewal of prescriptions which may be unnecessary in the case of long-term conditions. (Note, however, that this regulation may have been changed recently.) Alternatively, some countries require doctor check-ups before undertaking sport activities and this is often still paid for by the insurer (France). Doctors that are paid on a fee-for-service basis also tend to have higher consultation rates than those paid a salary. Some of the countries with low levels of contacts may be supply constrained (*e.g.* Mexico).

27. See Paris *et al.* (2010) for additional information on the breadth, depth and height of coverage.

28. This appears to be sensitive to the presentation. Out-of-pocket spending appears to have risen in both the 1990-99 and 2000-07 periods when taken as a share of total household consumption.

29. Note that the negative changes were generally small.

30. Increases were most marked in the following countries: Greece, the Slovak Republic, Hungary, Sweden, Austria and Japan.

31. For example, over half of the countries in the survey have ceilings for individuals or households that have reached an upper limit for out-of-pocket payments (see Table 2.10, penultimate column).

32. See NHS direct website in the United Kingdom as an example – *www.nhsdirect.nhs.uk*. However, given the diversity and unclear origin of much of the medical information found on the internet, such information needs to be carefully screened by health ministries.

33. For example, the top 25% of US Medicare beneficiaries in terms of their care costs accounted for 85% of annual expenditures in 2001 and for 68% of five-year cumulative expenditures from 1997 to 2001 (CBO, 2005).

34. Gate keeping aims at encouraging appropriate use of health services. The concept of the primary care doctor acting as a chief agent and co-ordinator has been one response to rationally allocate scarce resources of specialists and hospitals in the face of the increasing complexity of medical knowledge and specialisation. Gate keeping is supposed to reduce consumers' search costs to steer demand for specialised services in a way to ensure appropriate use of different levels of care. Whether these arrangements are successful depends on whether the primary care doctors are skilled enough to judge the quality of care of other providers, and in certain circumstances its cost (Paris *et al.*, 2010).

Bibliography

Aaron, H. (2003), "Should Public Policy Seek to Control the Growth of Health-care Spending?", *Health Affairs*, January.

Bourgueil, Y. *et al.* (2006), "Vers une coopération entre médecins et infirmières – L'apport des expériences européennes et canadiennes", DREES, Série Études, No. 57, Paris.

Congressional Budget Office (CBO) (2005), *High-Cost Medicare Beneficiaries*, Washington DC, available at *www.cbo.gov/showdoc.cfm?index=6332&sequence=0*.

Congressional Budget Office (CBO) (2008), *Technological Change and the Growth of Health Care Spending*, Washington DC.

Docteur, E. and H. Oxley (2004), "Health System Reform: Lessons from Experience", *Towards High Performing Health Systems: Policy Studies*, OECD Publishing, Paris.

Docteur, E. and V. Paris (2009), "Ensuring Efficiency in pharmaceutical pricing", *Achieving Better Value for Money in Health Care*, OECD Publishing, Paris.

Economou, C. and C. Giorno (2009), "Improving the Performance of the Public Health Care System in Greece", OECD Economics Department Working Paper, No. 722, OECD Publishing, Paris.

Farrell, D. *et al.* (Mckinsey Global Institute) (2008), "Accounting for the Cost of U.S. Health Care: A New Look at Why Americans Spend More", available at *www.mckinsey.com/mgi/publications/US_healthcare/index.asp*.

Figueras, J., R. Robinson and E. Jakubowski (eds.) (2005), *Purchasing to Improve Health System Performance*, Open University Press and European Observatory on Health Systems and Policies.

Fujisawa R. and G. Lafortune (2008), "The Remuneration of General Practitioners and Specialists in 14 OECD Countries: What Are the Factors Explaining Variations Across Countries?", OECD Health Working Paper, No. 41, OECD Publishing, Paris.

Grytten, J., F. Carlsen and I. Skau (2008), "Primary Physicians' Response to Change in Fees", *European Journal of Health Economics*, HEPAC, Health Economics in Prevention and Care, Vol. 9, No. 2, pp. 177-125.

Hofmarcher, M.M. *et al.* (2007), "Improved Health System Performance Through Better Care Coordination", OECD Health Working Paper, No. 30, OECD Publishing, Paris.

IGAS (2006), "Améliorer la prise en charge des malades chroniques : les enseignements des expériences étrangères de 'disease management'", Rapport présenté par Pierre Louis Bras, Gilles Duhamel et Etienne Grass, Paris.

Imai, Y. and H. Oxley (2004), "Managing Public Costs in the Japanese Health and Nursing Care Sector", *Osaka Economic Paper*, Vol. 58, No. 2, September.

Institute of Medicine Committee on Quality of Health Care in America (2001), *Crossing the Quality Chasm, A New Health System for the 21st Century*, National Academy Press, Washington.

Joumard, I. *et al.* (2008), "Health Status Determinants: Lifestyle, Environment, Health Care Resources and Efficiency", OECD Economics Department Working Paper, No. 627, OECD Publishing, Paris.

Klazinga, N. and E. Ronchi (2009), "Improving Data Systems to Promote Quality of Care", *Achieving Better Value for Money in Health Care*, OECD Publishing, Paris.

Light, D. (2001), "Managed Competition, Governmentality and Institutional Response in the United Kingdom", *Social Science and Medicine*, Vol. 52.

Mossialos, E. and J. Le Grand (eds.) (1999), *Health Care and Cost Containment in the European Union*, Aldershot, Ashgate.

Mulley, A. (2009), "The Need to Confront Variation in Practice", *British Medical Journal*, Vol. 339.

Newhouse, J.P. (1992), "Medical Care Costs: How Much Welfare Loss?", *Journal of Economic Perspectives*, Vol. 6, pp. 3-21.

OECD (2004), *Towards High Performing Health Systems*, OECD Publishing, Paris.

OECD (2005), *Towards High Performing Health Systems*, OECD Publishing, Paris.

OECD (2006), "Competition in the Provision of Hospital Services", DAF/COMP(2006)20, OECD Publishing, Paris.

OECD (2008a), *The Looming Crisis in the Health Workforce: How Can OECD Countries Respond*, Paris.

OECD (2008b), *Pharmaceutical Pricing Policies in a Global Market*, OECD Publishing, Paris.

OECD (2009), *Health at a Glance*, OECD Publishing, Paris.

OECD (2010a), *OECD Health Data*, OECD Publishing, Paris.

OECD (2010b), *Obesity and the Economics of Prevention*, OECD Publishing, Paris.

Oxley, H. (2009), "Policies for Healthy Ageing: An Overview", OECD Health Working Paper, No. 42, OECD Publishing, Paris, February.

Paris, V. *et al.* (2010), "Health System Institutional Characteristics: A Survey of 29 OECD Countries", OECD Health Working Paper, OECD Publishing, Paris, forthcoming.

Rapoport, J., P. Jacobs and E. Jonnson (2009), *Cost Containment and Efficiency and in National Health Systems: A Global Comparison*, Wiley, Weinheim.

Schoen, C. (2007), "Bending the Curve: Options for Achieving Savings and Improving Value in Health Spending", Presentation, The Commonwealth Fund, 18 December.

Shortell, S. (2009), "Bending the Cost Curve: A Critical Component of Health Care Reform", *JAMA*, Vol. 302, No. 11, pp. 1223-1224.

Smith, P. (2009), "Market Mechanisms and the Use of Health-care Resources", *Achieving Better Value for Money in Health Care*, OECD Publishing, Paris.

Smith, S. *et al.* (2009), "Income, Insurance and Technology: Why Does Health Spending Outpace Economic Growth", *Health Affairs*, Vol. 28, No. 5, pp. 1276-1284.

Chapter 3

Rational Decision Making in Resource Allocation

Patients, providers and payers have a common interest in ensuring that health care systems do not waste resources. Evidence-based medicine (EBM) and health technology assessment (HTA) can help by focusing on two simple questions: does it work, and is it worth it? This chapter explores potential efficiency gains that might be achieved by introducing more rational decision making into clinical care and looks at how clinical guidelines and health technology assessment can be used to inform these decisions. It then reviews how these functions are realised in institutions throughout the OECD.

1. Introduction

Most patients assume that doctors and other health care providers are giving them care of the highest quality possible, using the latest knowledge and most efficient technology. Health care funders would like to think they are getting the best possible value for their money. Both groups are often wrong. A number of studies over the past few decades have examined the evidence concerning the medical and cost effectiveness of treatments and techniques across a wide spectrum of health care activities. Whatever the level of analysis, and whatever the specific concern examined, the findings are similar: you do not always get what you pay for.

For one, higher spending on health at country level does not always correlate with better health outcomes for the population. Likewise, there are widespread variations in health spending by regions and even cities that appear to have no discernable impact on health outcomes.

Patients, providers and payers have a common interest in ensuring that health care systems do not waste resources. Evidence-based medicine (EBM) and health technology assessment (HTA) can help by focusing on two simple questions: does it work, and is it worth it? The first question is so simple it seems absurd, but analyses have shown that a large percentage of medical interventions – up to a third in some cases – has questionable benefits.[1] Technology assessment (in the wide sense of drugs as well as machines and other technical supports) asks not only whether a molecule or medical act works, but whether it represents a significant improvement over previous methods, and if it is the most efficient use of limited resources.

This chapter examines the potential to achieve efficiency gains by introducing more rational decision making into clinical care. It reviews the methods for doing so: clinical guidelines and health technology assessment. It then looks at how these functions are realised in institutions throughout the OECD. There are many different ways to organise these functions and countries could benefit from learning from each other's experience.

2. The potential for enhanced efficiency

Evidence from a number of studies suggests that health systems have some room to achieve efficiency gains.

Macroeconomic studies suggest potential efficiency gains in many countries

In a recent study (Joumard et al., 2008), the OECD estimated the impact of health care spending on population health status, controlling for other determinants of health (income, education, life-style factors and pollution). Taking life expectancy as the best available proxy for population health status, panel regressions suggest that health care spending does not provide the same value for money across OECD countries. If all countries were to become as efficient as the best performers, people would live two additional years on average across

OECD countries, for the same level of spending. Similar conclusions arise when using data envelopment analysis to derive relative efficiency scores (Joumard *et al.*, 2010).

These estimates should not be taken at face value, however: identifying health gains that can be unambiguously attributed to the health system is challenging and many health care services are not designed to increase length of life but instead to improve the *quality of life* of patients. However, the 2008 study suggests that health spending growth contributed by 46% to the observed increase in life expectancy of women and 39% for men in OECD countries between 1991 and 2003, which means that "health spending matters for longevity gains".

International variations in medical practice cannot entirely be explained by epidemiology and uptake of innovation

Variations in medical practice have been observed both across countries and within countries since the early 1970s (Mullan and Wennberg, 2004). Data regularly collected by the OECD provide multiple examples of such variations *across countries*. For instance, the rate of revascularisation procedures per 100 000 population ranges from 5 in Mexico to 692 in Germany (see Figure 3.1, Panel A). The consumption of anticholesterols varied from 49 defined daily doses per 1 000 people in Germany to 206 in Australia (see Figure 3.1, Panel B). The number of MRI exams ranges from 12.7 per 1 000 population in Korea to 98.1 in Greece (see Figure 3.1, Panel C).

Figure 3.1. **International variations in medical practice**
Panel A. Coronary revascularisation procedures per 100 000 population, 2008

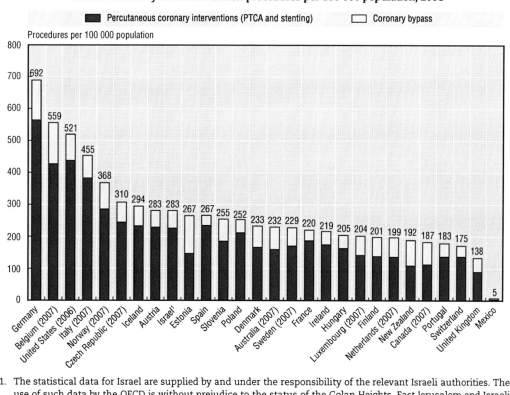

1. The statistical data for Israel are supplied by and under the responsibility of the relevant Israeli authorities. The use of such data by the OECD is without prejudice to the status of the Golan Heights, East Jerusalem and Israeli settlements in the West Bank under the terms of international law.

Note: Some of the variations across countries are due to different classification systems and recording practices.

Source: OECD (2010).

Figure 3.1. **International variations in medical practice** (*cont.*)

Panel B. Anticholesterols consumption, defined daily doses per 1 000 people per day, 2000 and 2007

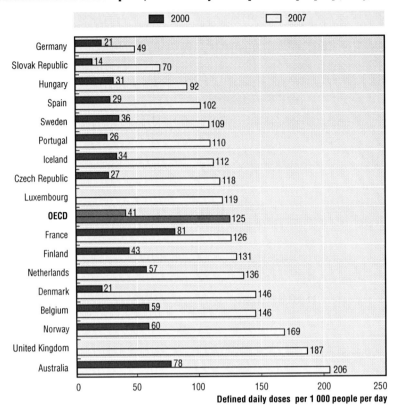

Source: OECD (2009).

Figure 3.1. **International variations in medical practice** (*cont.*)

Panel C. Number of MRI exams per 1 000 population, 2008 (or latest year available)

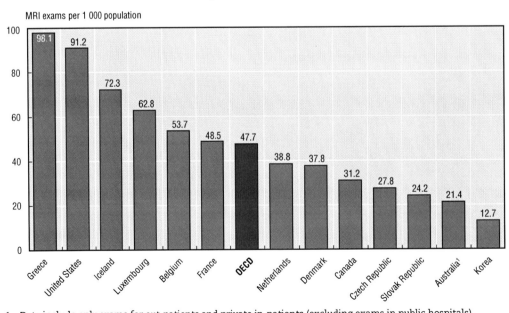

1. Data include only exams for out-patients and private in-patients (excluding exams in public hospitals).

StatLink ᴍᴘᴀ http://dx.doi.org/10.1787/888932319478

These variations cannot entirely be explained by differences in the epidemiologic context, though it certainly plays a role. Differences in the adoption of new technologies, itself influenced by ability and willingness to pay, payment methods for providers, manufacturers' strategies, professional skills and preferences, are deemed to explain most of these variations. For example, whether or not the treatment or procedure is covered by health insurance is an important factor.

Local variations in medical practice suggest a potential for increasing the effectiveness and efficiency of health care provision

Studies on medical practice variations (MPV) also suggest that savings could be achieved for the same level of health outcomes with a more efficient care process. Local variations in medical practice have been observed in several OECD countries (Denmark, the Netherlands, Norway, and Sweden) and even documented in great detail in the United States (Mullan and Wennberg, 2004; Mulley, 2009). The Dartmouth Institute has been providing information for many years about local practice variations and their explanatory factors. Working on Medicare data, researchers of this Institute have shown that some geographical areas tend to offer more care to chronically ill patients – care that yields no added benefits and sometimes even adverse outcomes (see Figure 3.2; Dartmouth Institute, 2008; Mulley, 2009).

Such variations are found elsewhere too: studying utilisation rates of stents and implantable cardioverter defibrillators (ICDs) in Spain in Italy, Capallero et al. (2009) observed variations both across and within countries. In 2006, the rate of percutaneous coronary interventions (PCIs) was 2 112 per million population in Italy and 1 276 per million in Spain. The proportion of PCIs performed with at least one stent was slightly higher in Spain than in Italy (96.1% against 92.5%) just like the number of stents implanted per procedure (1.59 against 1.45). The proportion of drug-eluting stents was similar (55% in Italy and 59% in Spain), but showed high variations across regions (from 23% to 78% in Italy and from 40% to 78% in Spain). ICD implantation rates differed both between and within countries. In 2006, Italy reported 189 implants per million population and Spain 60, with regional variations ranging from 39 to 285 in Italy and from 24 to 116 in Spain.

Most of those studies on MPV have tried to identify explanatory factors. In the United States, local variations can be partly explained by differences in coverage, organisation of care or payment methods. Researchers of the Dartmouth Institute conclude that a share of observed practice variations is "supply sensitive" – i.e. explained by differences in supply. For instance, regions served by organised systems of care (group practice or integrated hospital systems) typically provide less intensive care. In countries with uniform coverage policy, institutional features and providers' payment schemes, other factors have been identified, such as the influence of peers or industry, personal characteristics of physicians (such as age, gender, initial medical education, training and aversion to uncertainty) or of their patients (see de Jong et al., 2010; Mousques et al., 2010 for reviews).

In conclusion, if part of MPVs can be explained by socio-economic characteristics and the health needs of different populations, another part remains unexplained and potentially indicates inefficient use of resources.

Figure 3.2. **Local variations in medical practice**
Hostpital utilisation, prevalence of severe chronic illness,
and Medicare spending among 306 Dartmouth Atlas Regions

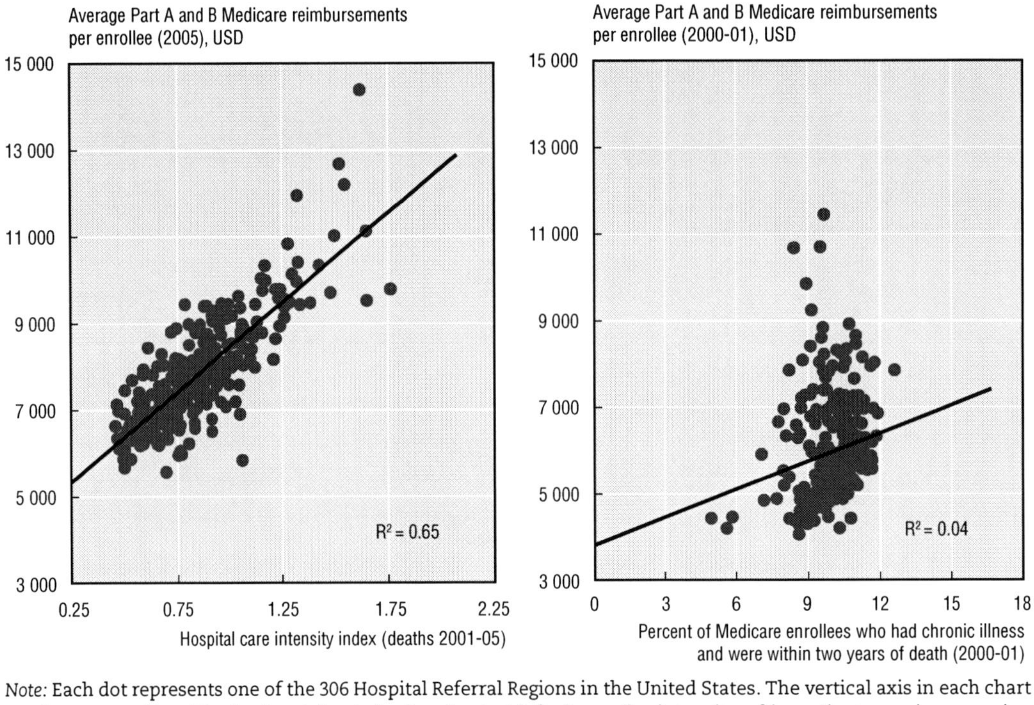

Note: Each dot represents one of the 306 Hospital Referral Regions in the United States. The vertical axis in each chart shows spending. The horizontal axis in the chart at left shows the intensity of in-patient care in managing chronic illness; about 65% of the variation in Medicare per capita spending is explained by the variation in use of inpatient care ($R^2 = 0.65$). At right, the horizontal axis shows prevalence of severe chronic illness, which is only slightly correlated with Medicare per capita spending ($R^2 = 0.04$). Prevalence of severe chronic illness accounts for about a USD 1 500 per capita difference in spending between regions where patients are the sickest compared to regions where patients are healthiest.

Source: Dartmouth Institute (2008).

Clinical practice often deviates from effective care as defined by evidence-based medicine research

The American Institute of Medicine estimates that half of all health care is currently provided in the United States without any evidence of its effectiveness (Institute of Medicine, 2009). In addition, where evidence exists, health care services are not always provided in accordance with best practice recommendations.

A study conducted by the Rand Corporation in 1998-2000 in the United States showed that patients received only 54.9% of recommended care for a set of 439 quality indicators defined for 30 acute and chronic conditions. Quality care indicators were based on recommendations pertaining to screening, diagnosis, treatment and follow-up for each condition. While more than 75% of recommended care was provided for senile cataract or breast cancer, this percentage did not exceed 50% for ten conditions. Only 22.8% of recommended care was provided for hip fracture and 10.5 for alcohol dependency. In many but not all cases, non-adherence with recommended care corresponded to an underuse of health care services (McGlynn *et al.*, 2003).

Other studies have produced more anecdotal evidence of non-adherence to recommended care in medical practice. For instance, in France, the High Authority in Health (HAS) issued a recommendation about pharmaceutical treatments for hypercholesterolemia: initial drug treatments should only be prescribed above a certain level of LDL-cholesterol and after the failure of a diet. In 2002, more than half of patients who received a first prescription of anticholesterol drugs had not undertaken any diet. For one-third of patients with new treatments, the level of LDL-cholesterol had not been tested, and for another third, drugs were prescribed in spite of a LDL-cholesterol level lower than the recommended threshold. Similarly, antibiotics were too often prescribed for viral and non-bacterial conditions in the 2000s. For some anxiolytics, prescribed dosages exceeded the maximum recommended dose in one-third to one-fourth of cases, and treatment duration exceeded the recommendation in 30 to 50% of cases. As many as 500 000 patients received a single prescription of long-term asthma treatment, which is inappropriate and does not conform to recommendations (see Polton *et al.*, 2007 for a summary).

Patients' preferences are not always taken into account

The participation of well-informed patients in clinical decision making is another promising way to improve efficiency. Sometimes, when evidence is produced about the relative benefits and harms of alternative treatments for a given condition, no solution is found to be superior to its alternative(s) in all respects. In such cases, clinicians and patients have to trade-off different types of benefits and harms, with a variable level of uncertainty for each of them. Ideally, the selection of the treatment should reflect patient preferences, which is not always the case.

The treatment of prostatic hyperplasia is an example. A study showed that when patients are informed through "decision aids" about the benefits and harms of surgical treatment, the rate of surgery falls by 40% from baseline levels. The experience showed that patients more bothered by their symptoms were more likely to choose surgery than those who were more worried about the prospect of sexual dysfunction (Mulley, 2009). The preference for less invasive treatment options has also been identified for some conditions, such as back pain and osteoarthritis of the knee or the hip (Dartmouth Institute, 2008). This suggests that the consideration of well-informed patients' preferences may not only increase patients' well-being and satisfaction but has also the potential to save money in some circumstances.

3. EBM and HTA offer opportunities to rationalise health care provision

Evidence-based medicine (EBM) and health technology assessment (HTA) have very different origins and do not serve identical purposes, though they can both influence health care provision.

Evidence-based medicine

EBM has been a gradual revolution in medical thinking. This movement began after the Second World War with the application of experimental design – randomised controlled trials (RCTs) – into medical practice. The first RCT, performed for tuberculosis by Bradford Hill and Archie Cochrane, created a new paradigm of experimental clinical epidemiology. This technique became widely used for the introduction of new drugs as part of the drug regulatory process from the 1960s. However, its diffusion into the rest of medical practice has been slower.

In the 1990s, evidence-based medicine developed into a more formal movement based on new techniques for synthesizing RCTs into meta-analysis including comprehensive bibliographic searches of all available literature. These techniques were first brought to bear on obstetrics, by Sir Ian Chalmers and a team that systematically reviewed all available literature on childbirth including positions, bed rest, use of steroids, etc. What they found was striking: many techniques long in use had no firm basis in evidence. Some things were unequivocally wrong and others had relatively firm evidence that they worked. This meant that some practices should be encouraged, some discouraged, and some studied further. This realisation spawned a whole international movement known as the Cochrane collaboration, institutions that systematically review medical literatures. There are now several groups studying most domains of health care.

To practically implement evidence-based medicine required a new generation of clinical protocols or guidelines. There have always been protocols in medicine. This is what constitutes a medical textbook: a summary of knowledge in the field. In any clinical domain, there are textbooks that lay out clinical treatments for different diseases like myocardial infarction or stroke. Societies of specialists often put out guidelines for their members on how to treat different diseases. The main change was that new guidelines were developed using comprehensive reviews of medical literature, meta-analysis, and other methods of critical appraisal.

Comparative effectiveness research (CER), recently promoted in the United States by the 2009 American Recovery and Reinvestment Act, aims to generate and synthesise evidence on comparative benefits and harms of alternative treatments. This is not a new activity, since many payers and institutes, including in the United States, have been doing such research for years. However, the additional USD 1.1 billion invested by the government to scale up CER increases the initial government budget by 73% (Docteur and Berenson, 2010). Just as EBM, CER's primary goal is to inform decision making at the patient level. Both have the potential to foster patient involvement in treatment choice, provided that results are made available to patients. It may also be used by third-party payers to inform decisions about coverage.

4. Health technology assessment

Health technology assessment goes one step further than EBM or CER. It does not only try to answer the question: "does it work?" or "what works best?" but also the question: "is it worth it?"

Health technology assessment has a different lineage through economics. It began with cost-benefit analysis which was introduced as part of the managerial revolution in government. It was widely used in many government departments such as the treasury and defence and diffused into health care in the late 1970s, as a response to the pressure of technological progress and the spread of high cost equipments. Cost-benefit analysis was closely linked to the introduction of new technologies. The first assessments, in the health field, were produced for CT scanners.

In 1993, Australia was the first country to use cost-effectiveness analysis for decision making on drug coverage. It was followed by several OECD countries. The largest and most visible example was the UK National Institute of Health and Clinical Excellence (NICE).

Any HTA process includes a systematic review of the available clinical evidence about the benefits and harms of the technology considered (i.e. EBM, and CER when available). But HTA usually considers a broader set of benefits – not limited to patients' outcomes – and often includes an economic assessment. Institutions in charge of HTA have some latitude to define HTA method and process to reflect the preferences of their targeted audience (an insurer, the government, the general public, etc.), though guidelines exist in

Box 3.1. **Evidence-based medicine, comparative effectiveness research and health technology assessment: working definition**

Evidence-based medicine (EBM) was defined by Sacket and colleagues in 1996 as "the conscientious and judicious use of current best evidence from clinical care research in the management of individual patients". As noted by Drummond *et al.* (2008), this definition was "expanded by usage to policy and group-focused evidence-based decision processes to produce evidence-based guidelines, make insurance coverage decisions, and develop drug formularies".

A definition of comparative effectiveness research (CER) is proposed by the American Institute of Medicine: CER is the generation and synthesis of evidence that compares harms and benefits of alternative methods to prevent, diagnose, treat and monitor a clinical condition or to improve the delivery of care. The purpose of CER is to assist consumers, clinicians, purchasers, and policy makers to make informed decisions that will improve health care at both the individual and population levels.

Many definitions have been proposed for health technology assessment (HTA). According to the International Network of Agencies for Health Technology Assessment (INAHTA), HTA is defined as "a multidisciplinary field of policy analysis. It studies the medical, social, ethical, and economic implications of development, diffusion, and use of health technology". However, in practice, HTA processes do not always consider the wide range of social, ethical and economic implications of the use and diffusion of new technologies and instead focus on health and organisational impacts. The main objective of HTA is to inform decisions of coverage, but it can also inform clinical guidelines.

Use of EBM and HTA

Source: Adapted from Drummond *et al.* (2008), Institute of Medicine (2009), *www.inahta.org/HTA/*, consulted on 8 March 2010.

this domain too. The main objective of HTA is to inform decision making, but it can also inform practice guidelines (see Box 3.2).

In OECD countries, there is a trend towards the institutionalisation of EBM[2] and HTA, as well a trend towards an increased used of both for the production of clinical guidelines and coverage decisions. However, countries show a high diversity in development stages. The sections below describe briefly the current use of EBM and HTA in OECD countries, as well as perspectives for the future.

5. The current use of technology assessment in OECD countries

Attempts have been made to draw a comprehensive picture of HTA settings and use at the European level (Sorenson *et al.*, 2007; Velasco-Garrido *et al.*, 2008), as well as in other countries (special issue of the *International Journal of Technology Assessment in Health Care*, 2009). A survey undertaken by the OECD in 2008-09 collected a minimum set of information on the effective use of health technology assessment in decision making (see Table 3.1). According to this survey, all but four countries (the Czech Republic, Greece, Luxembourg and Turkey), reported the existence of structures or capacities for health technology assessment. However, HTA capacities vary widely across countries.

Most countries reported that HTA is used to determine the coverage of medical procedures, medicines and high cost equipments. In some countries, such as Portugal, HTA is only used to determine coverage of pharmaceuticals. Many countries indicated that HTA results are also taken into account to establish reimbursement prices, especially for drugs. Finally, in a majority of countries, HTA is also used to produce clinical guidelines. All countries using HTA but France reported that cost effectiveness and affordability are considered in health technology assessment.

Institutions: status, mandate and range of activities

The first national HTA agency was created in Sweden in 1987[3] (see Box 3.2), followed by many countries. Today, most OECD countries have national agencies responsible for health technology assessment, with different institutional settings (independent or attached to the ministry of health or national insurance), scope (in terms of technologies to be assessed) and mandates (inform decision making, issue practice guidelines, horizon scanning, accreditation of health care institutions). However, HTA activities are not limited to national agencies. HTA efforts have preceded the creation of such agencies and, in several countries, ministries in charge of health have been funding activities for decades (*e.g.* Mexico). In several European countries, and in Canada, regional or hospital HTA agencies co-exist with national agencies (Velasco-Guarrido *et al.*, 2008). In the United States, public payers (Medicare, the Veterans Health Administration) and private insurers undertake HTA activities to inform formulary decisions. Korea and the Slovak Republic have recently created HTA agencies (Kim, 2009).

Only a few OECD countries have not established national HTA agencies, among which are the United States and Japan. In Japan, the Ministry of Health and Welfare funds HTA activities, and the production of EBM practice guidelines are commissioned to academic centres. Yet there is no formal link with decision making on reimbursement and pricing (Hisashige, 2009).

Use of HTA to inform coverage decisions

In a few cases, agencies responsible for HTA are also responsible for the "appraisal" of technology, as is the case for NICE in England and Wales or for the Swedish LFN (in charge of assessing new drugs for coverage decisions). Most often however, their role is confined

---

Box 3.2. **Health technology assessment in Sweden**

The *Swedish National Agency for Health Technology Assessment* (SBU) was created in 1987, as an independent organisation. Its mandate is defined by the government: "SBU is mandated to *make scientific assessments* of new and established technologies from a medical, economic, societal, and ethical perspective. The agency shall *present and disseminate* these assessments so that providers of health care and others may be able to use the findings of the assessments. The agency shall *assess* how the findings have been used and what results have been achieved" (Jonsson, 2009).

The SBU actively disseminates the results of its assessments. Full reports, as well as syntheses for different audiences, including the general public and the international community (English versions). The latest results are available on its website and in pharmacies. SBU organises press releases and press seminars, as well as local and national conferences and education programmes. Experts who participated in the assessment process used to be, on a voluntary basis, appointed as "ambassadors" and travelled in the country to inform colleagues and other stakeholders. This process recently changed and now, "receivers" are appointed in each county to promote the dissemination of results. Finally, assessment results are published in the Journal of the Swedish Medical Association and in other national and international journals.

The SBU regularly evaluates the use of assessment reports in medical practice and publishes the results of evaluations in its annual activity report. Studies have shown a positive impact of SBU reports. For instance, in accordance with SBU recommendations, the use of pre-operative routine tests has been reduced for young and healthy patients, as well as the prescription of sick-leave for back pain, and investments in equipment for bone density measurement. The prescription of diuretics and beta-blockers, shown to be as effective as newer and costlier drugs in the treatment of mild hypertension, increased after the publication of the SBU report. In the treatment of depression and alcohol and drug abuse, the prescription of more effective drugs increased, in accordance with SBU recommendations.

The *Pharmaceutical Benefits Board* (LFN) was created in 2002, as an independent agency in charge to determine whether a drugs will be reimbursed under the national pharmaceutical benefit scheme. For each new drug applying for reimbursement, the LFN assesses the extent to which it satisfies three criteria: cost effectiveness (from a societal perspective); human value (*i.e.* absence of discrimination); and the "need and solidarity principle" (which can justify to prioritise treatments targeting people with the greatest needs). The LFN has also undertaken the systematic review of several classes of drugs since 2003, which led to delisting in some occasions.

For example, the evidence assessed by the Swedish CBU on drug use among the elderly people is synthesised in a 28 pages document (including an English version) *www.sbu.se/ upload/Publikationer/Content1/1/Drug_Consumption_among_Elderly_summary.pdf*.

Source: Jonsson (2009); Moïse and Docteur (2007).

---

to scientific assessment while third-party payers, government or joint associations of bodies make decisions.

In the pharmaceutical sector, where the use of HTA is the most developed, HTA agencies or independent scientific institutes normally conduct the assessment while coverage decisions remain in the hand of governments or third-party payers. In France, the High Authority in Health (HAS) provides recommendations about the coverage of pharmaceuticals

Table 3.1. **Use of HTA in OECD countries**

	Structure and capacity for health technology assessment	Cost-effectiveness and affordability taken into account in HTA	New medicine			New procedure			New high-cost equipment		
			Coverage	Reimbursement or price	Guidelines	Coverage	Reimbursement or price	Guidelines	Coverage	Reimbursement or price	Guidelines
Australia	Yes	Yes	X	X	X	X	X	X	X	X	X
Austria	Yes	Yes	X	X							
Belgium	Yes	Yes	X	X	X	X		X	X		
Canada	Yes	Yes	X	X	X				X	X	X
Czech Republic	No	–									
Denmark	Yes	Yes	X	X	X	X	X	X	X	X	X
Finland	Yes	Yes	X	X	X			X			
France	Yes	No	X	X		X	X		X		X
Germany	Yes	n.a.	X	X		X					
Greece	No	–									
Hungary	Yes	Yes	X	X	X	X			X		X
Iceland	Yes	n.a.	X	X							
Ireland	Yes	Yes	X	X	X						
Italy	Yes	n.a.									
Japan	Yes	Yes	X	X	X	X	X	X	X	X	X
Korea	Yes	Yes	X	X	X	X	X	X	X	X	
Luxembourg	No	–									
Mexico[1]	Yes	Yes	X	X	X	X		X	X	X	X
Netherlands	Yes	Yes	X	X	X	X	X	X	X	X	X
New Zealand	Yes	Yes	X	X	X	X		X	X	X	
Norway	Yes	Yes	X		X	X		X	X		X
Poland	Yes	Yes	X	X		X		X	X		
Portugal	Yes	Yes	X	X	X			X			X
Slovak Republic	Yes	n.a.									
Spain	Yes	Yes	X	X		X		X	X		X
Sweden	Yes	Yes	X	X	X						
Switzerland	Yes	Yes	X			X					
Turkey	No	–									
United Kingdom	Yes	Yes	X					X			X

Note: HTA: Health technology assessment; n.a.not available; "–": not applicable.

1. In Mexico, the use of HTA is yet limited.

Source: Paris et al. (2010), updated with information available in July 2010.

but the government and health insurance funds make ultimate decisions. In Germany, the Institute for Quality and Efficiency in Health Care (IQWiG) makes recommendations to the Federal Joint Committee of Health Insurance Funds, Hospitals and Physicians (G-BA), which issues final guidance.[4] In Canada, the intergovernmental Common Drug Review, part of the Canadian Agency for Drugs and Technology in Health, issues recommendations about the coverage of new drugs but provincial and federal governments remain responsible for their inclusion in the formularies of their programmes (Paris and Docteur, 2006; OECD, 2008).

Recommendations for coverage decisions do not always result in "yes or no" options. They may suggest restricted coverage (to some indications or population sub-groups) or "coverage with evidence development". This last option, conditioning coverage to the generation of further research on effectiveness, has been used increasingly, especially when there is a high level of uncertainty about the effects of the assessed treatment.

HTA has also widely been used in OECD countries to design public health programmes for the early detection of cancer. It allowed for example to define that systematic breast cancer screening by mammograms only "worth it" after the age of 50. Under this age, direct and indirect costs exceed the benefits of such programmes.

Use of HTA to establish practice guidelines

Many HTA agencies only inform coverage decisions and do not provide clinical guidance for professionals. A few agencies, however, integrate the two functions. The extent to which clinical guidelines condition reimbursement or are binding for physicians varies across systems.

NICE guidance, for instance, defines what should be covered by the NHS and in which circumstances. NICE's clinical guidance typically restricts coverage to a target population or to second line treatment, but guidance also defines patients' rights to access treatments when appropriate. In principle, clinical guidelines are thus binding for NHS practitioners. However, there is no national programme to monitor or control professional behaviour, since the system relies on confidence in professional judgement and economic incentives received by Primary Care Trusts. Recently, NICE has been involved in the definition of quality targets used in the Quality and Outcomes Framework (QOF), which provides incentives to physicians to improve the quality of care through pay-for-performance payments.

On the contrary, the Swedish SBU and the French HAS produce guidelines that are not binding for health professionals. Efforts are made to promote professional adherence, including academic detailing by health insurance funds (in France), but there is no formal obligation to comply with guidelines. The pay-for-performance scheme recently introduced in France includes quality targets drawn from HAS guidelines, thus providing economic incentives to comply with these guidelines for the one-third of physicians who participate in this programme in 2010.

The role and methods of economic evaluation

Many countries use economic evaluation in HTA, especially for recommendations pertaining to the coverage of new drugs and technologies. Each country or agency determines the methods to be used. Most countries compute incremental cost-effectiveness ratios (ICERs), which indicate additional costs incurred by the new treatment for an additional unit of benefit or outcome. Outcomes are generally measured in quality-adjusted life years (QALYs). The German Institute IQWiG, which was asked to develop its methodology in 2007, decided to use efficiency frontiers to determine the most efficient therapy among the set of all alternatives for which costs and benefits are known. This method is original and may be adopted by France but it does not allow the comparison of costs and benefits across therapeutic areas (IQWiG, 2009).

Health economists have been debating for years about methodological aspects of economic evaluation in health (costs and outcomes to be considered, modelling and assessing uncertainty, discount rates to be used for future costs and benefits, etc.), that are not addressed here. Instead, the focus is on two subjects which are particularly relevant for policy makers: should there be a single and explicit ICER threshold beyond which technologies would not be funded? What should be the role of budget impact assessment?

Threshold or not?

In 2008, the Belgian institute KCE issued an extensive set of reflexions on the rationale and current practice of ICER thresholds (Cleemput et al., 2008). In theory, the ICER threshold should be the value of the ICER which maximises health gains under a budget constraint: if payers were able to establish a league table ranking all health systems interventions according to their (decreasing) ICER and compute budget impact for each intervention, the ICER threshold would be the ICER of the last intervention to be funded before the exhaustion of the available budget[5]. However, with the exception of the experience in the Oregon Medicaid programme, no payer or government has ever considered the construction of such a league table for several reasons, including the lack of information on costs and benefits for all interventions and the fact that all interventions cannot be considered independent. In addition, policy makers often have goals other than the maximisation of health gains. For instance, they may favour distributional aspects (e.g. favour interventions which will offer less "QALYs per unit cost" but for a high number of people over a more cost-effective intervention useful for a small number of people). A further argument against such thresholds is that it could provide incentives for manufacturers to set prices at the highest possible level to meet the threshold criteria. All these constraints suggest the adoption of a flexible threshold rather than a fixed one. This is indeed the strategy usually adopted by policy makers (for NICE, the Swedish LFN and the Canadian Common Drug Review).

Budget impact analysis

Economic evaluation may or may not include budget impact analysis (BIA), i.e. a measurement of the prospective impact of the adoption of the assessed technology on health care costs (or public budget). The role of BIA in decision making is often ambiguous and not clearly defined (Niezen et al., 2009). HTA-based recommendations may incidentally lead to cost savings, in which case BIA is always welcome. However, most often, BIA provides estimates of the additional amount of money needed for the implementation of an HTA recommendation (e.g. adoption of a new technology). Then, decision makers have to consider whether the implementation of this recommendation is affordable.

BIA is not always performed and published in a transparent manner, but it is hard to imagine that decision makers do not use it, at least for planning and budgeting purpose. Does BIA have a role to play in HTA and decision making? Niezen et al. (2009) spell out rationales for the consideration of BIA in decision making. First, any decision entailing additional spending has opportunity costs: this amount of money will have to be diverted from other health care interventions, or from other public sector investments. BIA allows the consideration of those opportunity costs. Second, if trade-offs have to be made within the health systems, the loss aversion or endowment effect – i.e. the fact that people typically value more what they do not want to lose (e.g. a reimbursed drugs that could be delisted to supply a new one) than what they could gain (e.g. the new drugs), make policy makers adverse to the delisting of current benefits. These preferences increase the opportunity costs of new decisions, especially those with high budget impact. Third, when benefits of health care interventions are assessed with a high degree of uncertainty, policy makers may be more reluctant to engage large amounts of money. Fourth, BIA can serve policies aiming to preserve "equal opportunity". The fact that budget impact is small is often mentioned to justify the reimbursement of orphan drugs which are not cost effective (by common standards). In conclusion, budget impact cannot be ignored by decision makers: more explicit consideration of BIA would make decisions more transparent, though it may not be possible to establish definitive rules for joint consideration of cost effectiveness and affordability.

Dissemination of HTA results

The publication of an HTA report is important both for transparency and for implementation (as far as guidelines are concerned). HTA complete reports typically include hundreds of pages of complex information compiled in a more or less friendly manner. Consequently, HTA agencies must make efforts to disseminate information to various stakeholders.

The minimum that HTA agencies should do is to provide a summary of the assessment and recommendations, that professionals can easily consult and use in their current practice. Most HTA agencies do so. However, more active strategies of dissemination, as adopted by the SBU in Sweden (see Box 3.2), are desirable.

Communication with patients and the general public is all the more important in a context of overwhelming information, whose quality is not always easy to assess for lay people. Some HTA agencies publish useful information for patients and their relatives. In the United States, the Agency for Healthcare Research and Quality (AHRQ) publishes guides for patients in both English and Spanish on its website, as well as audio versions.[6] Sixteen guides are currently available, for instance on treating prostate cancer, antidepressant medicines, treating high-cholesterol and osteoporosis treatments. They typically include a description of the disease or symptoms, benefits and risks associated with alternative treatments and prices for monthly supply of the main medications.

NICE publishes booklets on its website named "Understanding NICE guidance" and written for NHS users. For instance, the booklet on depression in adults[7] describes the usual symptoms of depression, alternative treatments that can be supplied by the NHS for the different degree in severity of depression, and proposes sets of questions that patients should ask to their doctors to better understand their disease and treatment. Costs of alternative therapies are not mentioned since all treatments are provided free of charge by the NHS.

Monitoring of implementation

Evidence-based practice guidelines are not always binding for health professionals, except when they determine funding by a national health system or an insurer. Third-party payers, however, should be interested to know whether recommendations produced by HTA agencies are followed.

Third-party payers should first monitor the compliance of medical prescriptions with conditional reimbursement clauses, where they exist. In a few cases, prior authorisation is required for the treatment to be reimbursed, but most often, physicians are responsible for the appropriateness of prescription. In many countries, third-party payers do not have access to patients' diagnoses and cannot assess whether the prescribed treatment is adequate. However, the analysis of reimbursement claims can sometimes shed some light about compliance with conditional reimbursement clauses. For instance, it can reveal that the initial target population has been widened to ineligible populations.

Similarly, compliance of health professional practices with HTA-based practice guidelines should be assessed, if only to measure the effectiveness of HTA. However, very few countries have institutionalised systematic review of impact of HTA reports, Sweden being one of them (see Box 3.2). In England, NICE produces and commissions reports on the uptake of implementation of guidelines.[8] More than 30 reports have been published to date mainly using administrative data on prescription claims.

6. The impact of health technology assessment

Velasco-Garrido *et al.* (2008) carried out a systematic literature review on the impact of health technology assessment, using a framework with six types of impact: awareness (knowledge of HTA reports by stakeholders), acceptance by stakeholders, impact on the policy process, impact on policy decisions, impact on clinical practice and outcomes (health gains and economic impact). The following paragraphs will concentrate on three important aspects: impact on decision making, impact on practice and impact on costs.

Impact of HTA on decision making

When HTA is conducted to inform coverage decisions, recommendations are generally not binding for the government(s), health insurance funds or other bodies who ultimately make decisions. For instance, in Canada, formulary decisions of provincial drug plans generally follow recommendations from the Common Drug Review, with varying delays, but tend to add restrictions to initial listing recommendations (McMahon *et al.*, 2006). In France, HAS positive recommendations for drug coverage are generally followed, while recommendations for delisting are not always implemented or are only implemented with a considerable delay.

Do HTA-based guidelines contribute to changes in medical practice?

In their literature review, Velasco-Garrido *et al.* (2008) identified 17 studies on the impact of HTA on clinical practice, concentrated on two countries: the United Kingdom (NICE recommendations) and Sweden. Results of these studies are mixed.

Sheldon *et al.* (2004) analysed the impact of 12 sets of NICE guidance produced between 1999 and 2001 and found mixed results. In several cases, NICE did not have a significant impact on current practice trends (*e.g.* wisdom tooth extraction, hearing aids, implantable cardioverter defibrillators, prescription of zanamivir in influenza). In other cases, the recommendation was followed by a significant change in practice (*e.g.* higher prescription of Orlistat for obesity, and of taxanes for breast cancer) and/or a reduction of practice variations (Orlistat and drugs for Alzheimer's disease). However, in the Orlistat case, a closer audit showed that the drug was prescribed in accordance with the guidance only in 12% of cases (age, BMI and weight loss). The authors concluded that professional acceptance to published guidance largely influences their compliance.

In Sweden, impact studies conclude that SBU's recommendations impacted medical practice in conformity with recommendations in most cases (see Box 3.2).

HTA does not always reduce costs

The primary objective of HTA activities is to enhance the effectiveness, quality and efficiency of health care. HTA activities can save costs when coverage of a new technology is denied or restricted, or when guidelines recommend cheaper treatment alternatives. On its website, NICE published a list of NICE guidance expected to reduce costs.[9]

However, the use of HTA does not obviously always lead to savings. In fact, empirical estimates show that NICE's recommendations for the adoption of new technologies have cost the NHS an additional GBP 1.65 billion per year (Chalkidou *et al.*, 2009).

7. The future of health technology assessment

There is no consensus among OECD countries on the use of health technology assessment, and more specifically, economic evaluation. Several arguments, regularly developed against its use are discussed below, along with key principles developed by an international expert group for the improved conduct of HTA for resource allocation decisions (see Box 3.3; and Drummond *et al.*, 2008).

Discussing three arguments against the use of HTA and economic evaluation

The first argument against the use of HTA and CEA (cost-effectiveness analysis) is that they do not encourage innovation in health care and may indeed compromise private investments in R&D. In fact, the extent to which HTA will affect technological innovation, negatively or positively, depends on methods used, especially for the valuation of outcomes.

By using HTA and economic assessment in coverage decisions, government and third-party payers send signals to manufacturers about the type of innovation they value and their willingness to pay. The selection of outcomes of interest is a first type of signal. For instance, while some HTA agencies will consider surrogate markers as reasonable measures of outcomes,[10] others will be more reluctant to do so. By making this choice explicit, policy makers provide useful information to innovators about the type of evidence they must produce for the adoption of their products. Similarly, when HTA agencies assess the degree of innovativeness of a new product to inform price decisions, as is the case in France,[11] the industry receives a transparent and explicit assessment of the value attributed to incremental (or radical) therapeutic improvements of their products. This may help the industry to direct investments towards the most valued therapeutic areas and the most valued incremental changes of existing therapies.

The impact of the use of the cost-effectiveness criteria on private R&D investments is not straightforward. Vernon *et al.* (2005) show how firms can use cost-effectiveness thresholds in their R&D investment decision-making process to determine a range of expected returns on investments, according to different levels of effectiveness, price and volume. The existence of (implicit or explicit) ICER thresholds may potentially reduce the firm's uncertainty about policy makers' decisions and willingness to pay but, on the other hand, it may discourage R&D investments with low returns on investments at the given threshold.[12, 13]

It is worth noting that HTA and economic assessment do not always result in negative recommendations and indeed have in the past promoted the use of new technologies and increased their uptake in systems otherwise under tight budget constraints (for instance in the United Kingdom).

The second argument is that the length of HTA and CEA processes delay patients' access to innovation. Typically, the production of an HTA report can take several years (*e.g.* two to three years in Sweden for reports on the treatment of a condition which compares several alternatives). However, in many countries, products and treatments can be marketed and sometimes reimbursed before being assessed through an HTA process. Access is thus not delayed in principle. This is the case in the United Kingdom, where a new drug, for instance, can be supplied to NHS patients until NICE decides it should not be.[14] In addition, countries have the possibility to create accelerated procedures for promising technologies. For instance, in Sweden, the SBU developed a specific programme (Alert) to quickly review new and innovative treatments (Jonsson, 2009). Finally, third-party payers may design special access programmes to provide immediate access to promising treatments for patients with life-threatening diseases, pending the results of the assessment and appraisal process. Several Canadian federal and provincial drug coverage plans have introduced such programmes (Paris and Docteur, 2006).

The third argument is that HTA raises ethical concerns and is not accepted by the population, especially when HTA recommendations are negative. Such decisions are often perceived as rationing by the general public or patients and receive high attention from the media (especially in the United Kingdom). However, budget constraints, strict or soft, entail trade-offs. HTA just provides an opportunity to make trade-offs more explicit, rational, consistent and equitable. This argument certainly needs to be popularised among professionals, patients and the general public. The involvement of stakeholders in the HTA process, its transparency, the publication of criteria considered to make final decisions should contribute to a wider acceptability of the process and the final decisions (Gruskin and Daniels, 2008).

Principles for good conduct and good use of HTA

Among the principles proposed for HTA good practices (Box 3.3), many have already been adopted by several OECD countries and are consensual while others have been subject to national adaptations. Some of these recommendations seem particularly relevant given the current status of HTA practices in OECD countries.

The idea that HTA should include all technologies is probably one of the most important one, with several implications. In many countries, HTA activities focus on new drugs and costly medical devices, which are assessed against existing ones. Resource limitations partly explain such a focus. However, HTA should ideally be extended to all technologies (all products, diagnostics and procedures, disease management) and to the review of existing treatments for a more rational decision-making process. Even if countries do not need to generate HTA reports for the thousands of medical procedures and products that are currently used, there is scope for improvement in this matter in a number of countries. The experience from most countries is that major savings can be achieved in existing clinical practice, not new technologies. The real savings or efficiency

---

Box 3.3. **Key principles for the improved conduct of HTA for resource allocation decisions**

- *The goal and scope of the HTA should be explicit and relevant to its use:* they should be agreed by a wide range of stakeholders; the link between HTA and decision making should be explicit.

- *HTA should be an unbiased and transparent exercise:* HTA should be conducted by bodies independent from decision-making bodies, third-party payers or professional associations; HTA process and criteria for decision making should be transparent. HTAs should be freely and publicly accessible to stakeholders.

- *HTA should include all relevant technologies, i.e.* drugs, devices, diagnostic procedures and treatment strategies, to prevent distortions in resource allocation. The current focus on drugs and new technologies is not ideal.

- *A clear system for setting priorities for HTA should exist,* to ensure cost-effective HTA activities. For instance, NICE selects technologies to be assessed on six criteria: burden of disease, resource impact, clinical and policy importance, presence of inappropriate variations in practice, potential factors influencing the timeliness of guidance, and likelihood of the guidance having an impact.

- *HTA should incorporate appropriate methods for assessing costs and benefits:* methods should be adapted to purpose and context, be transparent and consistent across assessments, and be periodically reviewed. HTAs should be conducted by trained experts.

- *HTAs should consider a wide range of evidence and outcomes:* randomised clinical trials data may need to be completed by observational studies, surrogate endpoints must be considered and extrapolated to outcomes of interest; benefits, risks and costs must be defined broadly. Outcomes should include changes in quality of life for patients, as well as benefits for patients' relative, employers and the society. Variations in costs and benefits across population sub-groups should be assessed.

- *A full societal perspective should be considered when undertaking HTA* to ensure efficient resource allocation at the level of the society.

- *HTA should explicitly characterise uncertainty surrounding estimates* and include sensitivity analyses and confidence intervals for results.

- *HTA should consider and address issues of generalisability* and transferability across patients, populations and settings of care.

- *Those conducting HTAs should actively engage all key stakeholder groups,* in the definition of objectives of HTA reports, of treatment alternatives and patient populations to be considered and modeling. They should be given opportunities to comment HTA drafts and appeal decisions.

- *Those undertaking HTA should actively seek all available data,* including confidential data, though this may contradict the transparency principle.

- *The implementation of HTA findings should be monitored.*

- *HTA should be timely:* ideally, HTA should follow marketing authorisation and be subject to review periodically, or when new information is available.

- *HTA findings need to be communicated to different decision makers, i.e.* decision makers, managers of health care institutions, health professionals, patients and the general public.

- *The link between HTA findings and decision-making processes needs to be transparent and clearly defined.* Criteria for decision makers can legitimately differ across payers or jurisdictions, ideally they should be transparent.

Source: Based on Drummond *et al.* (2008).

---

gains come from rationalising the current medical practice. This means not only discountinuing out-dated techniques that are marginally effective, but also making sure that effective procedures and technologies are properly disseminated and used by all.

The involvement of stakeholders (producers, professionals and patients) in the HTA process is certainly desirable. However, the involvement of these stakeholders should be clearly defined (consultation or participation?). It is interesting to note that stakeholders' involvement does not necessarily mean stakeholders' "endorsement" of HTA conclusions. In the case of NICE, manufacturers have appealed against 30% of decisions, half of which have been upheld, in spite of their involvement in the process (Drummond *et al.*, 2008).

Two recommendations, however, do not make consensus. First, while Drummond *et al.* (2008) recommend adopting a full societal perspective in health technology assessment, many countries only consider costs for "health care" payers. In theory, the societal perspective should be used in order to maximise social welfare. In practice, however, the policy mandate of people in charge of health policy is to maximise gains obtained from health budgets or health spending. Therefore, economic evaluation often considers costs for the public payer or for all health care payers (Johannesson *et al.*, 2009).

Second, some countries consider that confidential data cannot be taken into account in health technology assessment, because it would break the rule of transparency.

8. Conclusions

Rationalising health care provision is a promising way to achieve efficiency gains. The production and dissemination of clinical guidelines, based on evidence-based medicine (EBM), can contribute to such a rationalisation process. Health technology assessment (HTA) can complement the use of evidence-based clinical guidelines by informing coverage decisions to make sure that new technologies are worth it.

Conducting HTA requires information. The development of information systems, providing data on volumes and costs of procedures performed and treatments prescribed is a prerequisite to the development of HTA. Some countries also need to develop a skilled workforce necessary to perform assessments.

Countries should seek more actively to monitor the implementation of HTA recommendations, especially for guidelines. Currently, only a few HTA agencies or institutions undertake or commission studies to monitor the impact of recommendations.

Countries that are interested can build on an already rich international collaboration in the field of HTA. European and international networks exist and allow participants to share experiences and skills, to produce guidelines for HTA good practice, and to co-ordinate early detection of technologies needing assessment.[15] Consumers and payers would probably benefit from more standardised HTA methods. Though results of economic evaluation will inevitably differ across countries – due to differences in the organisation of care, in relative prices of various inputs, and in professional practices and epidemiological contexts – uniform standards in data requirements would be desirable.

Institutions matter. It appears promising to combine the functions of looking at new drugs and technologies with the development of evidence-based guidance. It is important to bring together medical thinking about clinical effectiveness with economic thinking about cost effectiveness and the use of economic evaluation techniques. This is leading to clinical-economic appraisal that lies at the heart of rational decision making for health care.

Notes

1. From a synthesis of several studies conducted in the United States, researchers concluded that one-third or more of all procedures performed in the United States in the 1990s were of questionable benefit (RAND, 1998).

2. However, due to a long tradition of self-regulation of the medical profession, these activities still rely on medical associations and colleges in several countries. For instance, in Switzerland, the promotion of good practices for pharmaceutical prescriptions mainly rely on quality circles gathering physicians and pharmacists (Paris and Docteur, 2007), with no intervention from the government and only logistic support (for data collection) from insurers.

3. The OTA, created in 1972, was dissolved by the US Congress a few years later.

4. The German Institute for Medical Information and Documentation (DIMDI) manages HTA programmes, commissions HTA reports to qualified experts and maintains a database with all HTA reports, including IQWiG's reports (see *www.dimdi.de/static/en/index.html*).

5. According to this definition, ICER thresholds should not exist in social security systems with no strict budget constraints or when the societal perspective is adopted.

6. *www.effectivehealthcare.ahrq.gov/index.cfm/guides-for-patients-and-consumers/*, consulted on March 8, 2010.

7. *http://guidance.nice.org.uk/CG90/PublicInfo/pdf/English*, consulted on 8 March 2010.

8. *www.nice.org.uk/usingguidance/evaluationandreviewofniceimplementationevidenceernie/ niceimplementationuptakecommissionedreports/nice_implementation_uptake__commissioned_reports.jsp*, consulted on 8 March 2010.

9. See *www.nice.org.uk/usingguidance/benefitsofimplementation/costsavingguidance.jsp*.

10. Surrogate markers are sort of "intermediary measures of outcomes". For instance, the available evidence can show that a drug effectively lowers the cholesterol level (which is known to lower mortality risks) without demonstrating yet that it effectively reduces mortality.

11. The French HAS rates on a five-level scale a "degree of innovativeness" for each new drug, by comparison with existing competitors. Though no formal economic assessment is conducted, this assessment, together with the prices of existing competitors, will inform price decisions. The most innovative products will be granted higher "price premium".

12. Hollis (2005) suggests that policy makers should publish ICER thresholds for orphan drugs (which will be typically higher than usual thresholds) to encourage firms to invest in this type of products.

13. In addition, some authors argue that ICER thresholds could encourage firms to set higher prices than they would have done without regulation, but without exceeding the threshold.

14. However, in such cases, providers may prefer to wait for NICE's decision (and NHS additional funding) to uptake the innovation.

15. See for example: EUnetHTA (European Network for Health Technology Assessment: *www.eunethta.net/*); INAHTA (International Network of Public Agencies for HTA: *www.inahta.org/ Publications/*) – INAHTA was established in 1993 and has now grown to 46 member agencies from 24 countries; Euroscan Network (*www.euroscan.org.uk*); and Inno HTA (HTA methodology for innovative healthcare technologies: *www.inno-hta.eu/*).

Bibliography

Baker L. *et al.* (2008), "Expanded Use of Imaging Technology and the Challenge of Measuring Value", *Health Affairs*, Vol. 27, No. 6, pp. 1467-1478.

Battista, R.N. and M.J. Hodge (2009), "The 'Natural History' of Health Technology Assessment", *International Journal of Technology Assessment in Health Care*, Vol. 25: Suppl. 1, pp. 281-284

Capallero, G., G. Fattore and A. Torbica (2009), "Funding Health Technologies in Decentralised Systems: A Comparison Between Italy and Spain", *Health Policy*, Vol. 92, pp. 313-321.

Chalkidou, K. *et al.* (2009), "Comparative Effectiveness Research and Evidence-based Policy: Experience from Four Countries", *The Milbank Quarterly*, Vol. 87, No. 2, pp. 339-367.

Cleemput I. *et al.* (2008), "Threshold Values for Cost-effectiveness in Health Care Health Technology Assessment", KCE Reports No. 100C, Belgian Health Care Knowledge Centre (KCE), Brussels.

Dartmouth Institute (2008), "An Agenda for Change: Improving Quality and Curbing Health Care Spending: Opportunities for the Congress and the Obama Administration", A Dartmouth Atlas White Paper, The Dartmouth Institute for health policy and clinical practice.

de Jong, J. et al. (2010), "Do Guidelines Create Uniformity in Medical Practice?", *Social Science and Medicine*, Vol. 70, pp. 209-216.

Docteur, E. and R. Berenson (2010), "How Will Comparative Effectiveness Research Affect the Quality of Health Care?", Timely Analysis of Immediate Policy Issues, Urban Institute and Robert Wood Johnson Foundation.

Drummond, M. et al. (2008), "Key Principles for the Improved Conduct of Health Technology Assessments for Resource Allocation Decisions", *International Journal of Technology Assessment in Health Care*, Vol. 24, No. 3, pp. 244-258.

Gómez-Dantés, O. and J. Frenk (2009), "Health Technology Assessment in Mexico", *International Journal of Technology Assessment in Health Care*, Vol. 25: Suppl. 1, pp. 270-275.

Gruskin S. and N. Daniels (2008), "Justice and Human Rights: Priority Setting and Fair Deliberative Process", *American Journal of Public Health*, Vol. 98, No. 9, pp. 1573-1577.

Hisashige, A. (2009), "History of Health Care Technology Assessment in Japan", *International Journal of Technology Assessment in Health Care*, Vol. 25: Suppl. 1, pp. 210-218.

Hollis, A. (2005), "An Efficient Reward System for Pharmaceutical Innovation", Research Paper, Department of Economics, University of Calgary.

Institute of Medicine (2009), *Initial National Priorities for Comparative Effectiveness Research*, Institute of Medicine of the National Academies, Washington.

IQWiG (2009), "General Methods for the Assessment of the Relation of Benefits to Costs", Version 1.0, IQWiG, Köln.

Johannesson, M. et al. (2009), "Why Should Economic Evaluations of Medical Innovations Have a Societal Perspective?", OHE Briefing, No. 51, Office of Health Economics, London.

Jonsson, E. (2009), "History of Health Technology Assessment in Sweden", *International Journal of Technology Assessment in Health Care*, Vol. 25, Suppl. 1, pp. 42-52.

Joumard, I., C. André and C. Nicq (2008), "Health Status Determinants: Lifestyle, Environment, Health Care Resources and Efficiency", OECD Economics Department Working Paper No. 627, OECD Publishing, Paris.

Joumard, I., C. André and C. Nicq (2010), "Health Care Systems: Efficiency and Institutions", OECD Economics Department Working Paper No. 769, OECD Publishing, Paris.

Kim, C.-Y. (2009), "Health Technology Assessment in South Korea", *International Journal of Technology Assessment in Health Care*, Vol. 25, Suppl. 1, pp. 219-223.

McGlynn, E.A. et al. (2003), "The Quality of Care Delivered to Adults in the United States", *New England Journal of Medicine*, Vol. 348, No. 26, pp. 2635-2645.

McMahon, M., S. Morgan and C. Mitton (2006), "Common Drug Review: A NICE Start for Canada?", *Health Policy*, Vol. 77, No. 3, pp. 339-351.

Moïse, P. and E. Docteur (2007), "Pharmaceutical Pricing and Reimbursement Policies in Sweden", OECD Health Working Paper, No. 28, OECD Publishing, Paris.

Mousques, J., T. Renaud and O. Scemama (2010), "Is the 'Practice Style' Hypothesis Relevant for General Practitioners? An Analysis of Antibiotics Prescription for Acute Rhinopharyngitis", *Social Science and Medicine*, forthcoming.

Mullan, F. and J. Wennberg (2004), "Wrestling With Variation: An Interview With Jack Wennberg", *Health Affairs*, Web Exclusive, pp. VAR73-VAR80.

Mulley, A.G. (2009), "The Need to Confront Variation in Practice", *British Medical Journal*, Vol. 339, pp. 1007-1009.

Niezen, M.G. et al. (2009), "Finding Legitimacy for the Role of Budget Impact in Drug Reimbursement Decisions", *International Journal of Technology Assessment in Health Care*, Vol. 25, No. 1, pp. 49-55.

OECD (2005), *Health Technologies and Decision Making*, OECD Publishing, Paris.

OECD (2008), *Pharmaceutical Pricing Policies in a Global Market*, OECD Publishing, Paris.

OECD (2009), *Health at a Glance – OECD Indicators*, OECD Publishing, Paris.

OECD (2010), *OECD Health Data*, OECD Publishing, Paris.

Paris, V. and E. Docteur (2006), "Pharmaceutical Pricing and Reimbursement Policies in Canada", OECD Health Working Paper, No. 24, OECD Publishing, Paris.

Paris, V. and E. Docteur (2007), "Pharmaceutical Pricing and Reimbursement Policies in Switzerland", OECD Health Working Paper, No. 27, OECD Publishing, Paris.

Paris, V., M. Devaux and L. Wei (2010), "Health Systems Institutional Characteristics: A Survey of 29 Countries", OECD Health Working Paper, No. 50, OECD Publishing, Paris.

Polton, D., P. Ricordeau and H. Allemand (2007), "Peut-on améliorer à la fois la qualité et l'efficience de la prescription médicamenteuse? ", *Revue française des affaires sociales*, Vol. 61, No. 3-4, pp. 73-86.

RAND (1998), "Assessing the Appropriateness of Care", *Rand Health Research Highlights*, Rand Corporation.

Sheldon, T.A. *et al.* (2004), "What's the Evidence that NICE Guidance Has Been Implemented? Results from a National Evaluation Using Time Series Analysis, Audit of Patients' Notes and Interviews", *British Medical Journal*, Vol. 329, p. 999.

Sorenson, C., P. Kanavos and M. Drummond (2007), *Ensuring Value for Money in Health Care: The Role of HTA in the European Union*, London School of Economics and University of York, London.

Velasco Garrido, M. *et al.* (2008), "Health Technology Assessment and Health Policy Making in Europe – Current Status, Challenges and Potential", *Observatory Studies Series*, No. 14, WHO Regional Office for Europe on behalf of the European Observatory of Health Systems and Policies, Copenhagen.

Vernon, J., W.K. Hughen and S.J. Johnson (2005), "Mathematical Modelling and Pharmaceutical Pricing: Analyses Used to Inform In-Licensing and Developmental Go/No-Go Decisions", *Health Care Management Science*, Vol. 8, pp. 167-179.

Chapter 4

Improving Value for Money in Health by Paying for Performance

Many OECD countries are experimenting with new methods of providing incentives to providers to improve the quality of health care, often known as "pay for performance" (P4P). Yet it remains unclear – in part due to a lack of good data – whether these new ways of paying providers (hospitals, primary care, integrated systems) significantly improve the quality of care and increase value for money in health. Experience to date suggests that it is possible to improve quality and efficiency by paying for it, for example in public health interventions such as cancer screening, and in getting physicians to follow evidence-based guidelines for chronic conditions like diabetes and cardiovascular disease. This chapter looks at cases where P4P appears to be producing good results and analyses the numerous factors that affect the implementation of incentive programmes, such as the challenges involved in establishing quality measures, collecting data, and monitoring it for performance – a prerequisite for designing effective P4P schemes.

1. Introduction

Many OECD countries are experimenting with new methods of paying providers and sometimes patients to improve the quality of health care, often known as pay for performance (P4P) or payment for results.[1] There are growing numbers of schemes testing new models for rewarding quality: in OECD countries like the United States, United Kingdom and New Zealand; in middle-income countries like Brazil, China, and India; and low-income countries like Rwanda. These P4P schemes are testing whether new ways of paying providers (hospitals, primary care, integrated systems) that use some type of synthetic measure of quality show improvements in the *quality* of care and also improve *value for money* in health. Although the evidence at the moment is limited, given that these schemes are new and many have limited formal evaluation, the experience to date suggests that it is possible to improve quality and efficiency by paying for it.

Today, most health care providers are not rewarded for improving quality. The traditional methods for paying physicians such as salary, fee-for-service or capitation pay for quantity not quality. For example, a fee schedule, which is common in many insurance systems, only pays for the unit of service, not the quality of the service, or whether it improves intermediate health outcomes. Capitation payments (paying per person enrolled in practice) leave quality assessment up to patients, assuming that they can change practice if quality is inadequate. In hospitals, even new payment methods like diagnostic-related groups (DRGs), which pay a fixed amount per patient based on diagnosis (to adjust for case mix), do not formally measure quality of care.

Some believe that competition between providers will drive up quality by allowing patient choice, but competition alone does not solve the perennial problem of information asymmetry between physicians and patients, and also between physicians and payers. Assessing quality requires information (such as hospitalisation rates, nosocomial infection rates, and overall effectiveness of treatments) that is beyond what patients can know at reasonable cost. In fact, determining what constitutes quality and devising appropriate measurements is a prerequisite for designing effective P4P schemes.

2. Difficulty in defining and measuring quality of care

As one can imagine, it is difficult to measure something as multidimensional as quality of care. There has been a revolution in our thinking about quality of care in the last two decades beginning with the lessons from Deming and Juran on quality in industrial processes that showed the importance of measuring quality to improve it. The issue was highlighted in two influential United States Institute of Medicine reports: *Crossing the Quality Chasm* which created a new paradigm for thinking about quality and *To Err is Human* which highlighted that medical errors killed more people than traffic accidents in the United States. IOM defined quality as "the degree to which health services for individuals and populations increase the likelihood of desired health outcomes and are consistent with current professional knowledge".

At the heart of quality is clinical effectiveness – whether a given health intervention improves health outcomes. Outcomes, however, are themselves complex and multidimensional. They include domains beyond clinical effectiveness such as quality of life and consumer satisfaction. To illustrate the complexity of measuring quality, consider the example of the quality of treatment for a woman diagnosed with breast cancer. The stage at which the cancer is diagnosed will determine how long she lives. This means that in order to understand difference in outcomes between different physician groups or hospitals, it is necessary to account for the differences in stage in order to adjust for the severity of disease – what is known in health policy jargon as case mix. The stage at which a cancer is detected will depend on the coverage and quality of cancer screening programmes, and in many countries coverage is low. Therefore, one measure of quality would be on the coverage of cancer screening and this metric is used in many primary care P4P schemes.

But what is the quality of care for the actual treatment (health service) of cancer? The first objective is to improve health outcomes. Mortality is a population measure, but for individuals the more meaningful statistic is survival from time of diagnosis. For Stage 1 breast cancer, where the cancer has not spread beyond the breast, over 90% of women live beyond five years, and most now commonly live beyond ten years. Therefore, measuring outcomes is a lengthy process and quality measures depend on more intermediate process indicators such as whether the correct cancer protocol was given. For most interventions, it is necessary to assume that intermediate outcomes like lowered blood pressure or cholesterol lead to improved health outcomes.

Beyond these issues of clinical effectiveness or technical quality, there are also other dimensions of quality, including quality of life. For example, cataract surgery improves vision, but does not prolong life. Furthermore, patients often judge the quality of health care on more human factors like whether the clinical staff were polite, treated them with respect, did not make them wait for long periods of time, and the facilities. Patients often judge the quality of health care by non-clinical factors.

Although the issues of measuring the quality of health care are difficult, it is a tractable problem. Quality has three dimensions: clinical effectiveness, patient safety, and patient experience. Over the last five years, the OECD has been gathering data on standardised outcomes measures across most clinical domains. Increasingly, quality of life is being incorporated into measures of outcomes including patient experience. The United Kingdom has been experimenting with new methods of incorporating patient satisfaction in the Patient Reported Outcomes Measurement (PROM) with promising results. Finally, P4P schemes are developing new methods for incorporating quality measures into payment systems like the Quality Outcomes Framework for primary care in the United Kingdom.

3. Pay for performance: a new paradigm

Pay-for-performance schemes are changing this by formally measuring quality of care and paying for it. There are now many new examples in OECD countries and beyond that are attempting to explore a new frontier in payment systems that incorporate quality. Though the evidence is still insufficient to draw definitive conclusions, results from P4P schemes suggest what common sense would tell you: that quality of care increases when you pay for it. Paying for preventative and public health services appears to be particularly effective and can increase coverage of cancer screening, vaccination rates, etc. Often, primary care physicians neglect preventative services such as screening for cancer, measuring blood pressure and treating it, counselling patients to stop smoking or to improve their diet. The most successful P4P programmes pay additionally for providing these services or reaching some target. These programmes generally show significant increases in the use of these important public health interventions that are likely to maximise health gain.

P4P is also useful in offering incentives for prevention and co-ordination of care of chronic diseases like diabetes. It can ensure that diabetics undertake important preventative tests and also help encourage co-ordination between specialists in diabetes, often based in hospitals, and primary care providers.

One of the critical issues that has bedevilled P4P programmes is monitoring the quality indicators. In many instances, information on quality is not routinely collected. Therefore, part of the P4P programme is to collect information, requiring potentially costly up-front investment in computers, training, and software. In addition, there is generally no culture for physician practices to report clinical indicators and they need to be cajoled into providing the information. Many programmes pay physicians incentives for providing the information, including funding to computerise their record keeping. These up-front costs are often larger than the savings generated in the short run.

Pay-for-performance systems typically cost more in the first couple of years, but may return this investment over time as the system works and people are healthier. Furthermore, the cost savings may occur in other parts of the system. For example, better preventative care in primary care will lead to decreases in hospitalisations. In unitary systems like the UK NHS, this type of cross savings is internalised by the single purchaser, the Department of Health. In multipayer systems, however, assessing the savings is more difficult, since the payer may not realise the benefits. Whether P4P actually saves money will depend on whether the long-term cost savings can be internalised by the body that introduced the P4P scheme. But the more important question is not if it saves money, but whether it improves quality commensurate to its costs, in other words, whether or not it achieves value for money.

It can be hard to know for sure whether quality of care has improved, or whether the system is merely adjusting to reporting on quality; P4P systems often require new collection of quality data that did not exist before, but it may be that physicians were providing high quality care, but not reporting on it. It is also difficult to know if P4P schemes improve efficiency because they require long-term collection of costs across the health system. Most of the P4P schemes also suffer from limited evaluation, particularly in the use of control groups, making it difficult to draw conclusions. However, the experience of P4P schemes in a number of countries is that they do appear to increase the quality of care. The experience of California primary care P4Ps suggests that it can be used to incentivise important public health interventions like screening for cancer, immunisation, smoking cessation, etc., that are highly cost effective and some of the best buys in health care. This model was replicated in Brazil and a similar model was used in Rwanda and it also demonstrated increased use of preventative and public health services.

4. Getting the design right in P4P: multiple agent problem

One of the most complex tasks in designing P4P schemes is finding the optimal reimbursement scheme for health care providers. Doctors have specialised knowledge about what patients need which is why patients go to the doctor, but patients cannot judge whether what the doctor is telling them is true, because to do so would require patients to possess that same specialised knowledge – essentially to become a doctor. This is the classic problem of information asymmetry, in this case compounded by the problem of uncertainty in medical knowledge. Even doctors do not necessarily know what will work for an individual patient. Medical knowledge is about the average patient, but no patient is average, and there will be a distribution of outcomes for any given intervention.

Information asymmetry and medical uncertainty make the "principal-agent problem" almost intractable in health care. Since the doctor knows more, a patient hires him to be his agent or to act on his behalf, to act as if they were the patient with the knowledge of the doctor: the doctor is supposed to act in the patient's interest, but often they do not since patients and physicians have different interests, objectives, and information.

The situation is further complicated by the fact that the patient often does not pay for the treatment, but instead it is paid by a third party like an insurance company or government. This means that in health care it is very difficult to align incentives to promote quality at the lowest cost because we have three parties all with different objectives and different levels of information – the multiple agent problem.

In a traditional fee-for-service model, physicians have a strong incentive to provide extra care, since they are reimbursed according to the number of services they provide. Patients, for many reasons, including a lack of information but also cultural factors generally accept the advice of physicians. In fee-for-service systems, there is a strong tendency to increase the volume of services to increase payment. An extreme example is the exponential increase in the volume of services by Chinese health providers who are now paid almost exclusively by fee-for-service. There has been an explosion in hospital admissions, since hospitals are paid by the number of admissions (Wagstaff, 2009; Herd, 2010). This increase in services is largely paid for out people's own pockets, since health insurance is very limited though increasing rapidly.

In OECD countries, most of the spending is by a third party – government or an insurance company. Since patients do not face the true costs of services, they have a tendency to overuse them. When physicians have an incentive to do more, and patients face virtually no costs in using services, there is strong pressure to increase utilisation, making it essential/necessary for third party payers to find some method for controlling ever-increasing costs.

As the example above illustrates, it may be difficult to align patient and provider incentives to get maximum value for money out of health care. One of the problems is that there is no measure of quality of care as part of the transaction. If one could make quality of care visible, by formally measuring it, this would decrease the information asymmetry between doctors, patients, and payers, and it might be possible to align physician and patient incentives by paying based on quality of care – this provides the theoretical foundation for why P4P should work.

5. Defining P4P

There is no accepted international definition of pay for performance (P4P). It is often used interchangeably with the term paying for results or *results-based financing* (RBF). RBF is used particularly in global health, as in the case of the large global fund set up by Norway, the United Kingdom and Australia at the World Bank. This fund provides grant funding for countries to introduce P4P schemes and to properly evaluate them including the use of good experimental design with randomisation into P4P interventions versus comparable control groups without the intervention.

Table 4.1 presents the definitions of pay for performance used by some of the most important stakeholders in the area. Given that the P4P movement started in the United States, the first three definitions are from a United States perspective: 1) Agency for Healthcare Research and Quality (AHRQ), 2) Centers for Medicare & Medicaid Services (CMS), and 3) RAND Corporation. These all focus on quality improvement, although they are defined somewhat differently. The RAND Corporation also includes efficiency as a measure. The latter three definitions take a broader approach and are more concerned with developing countries: 4) World Bank, 5) United States Agency for International Development, and 6) Center for Global Development. The World Bank, USAID, and Centre for Global Development definitions include both incentives on the supply side to providers and also demand-side incentives to patients like conditional cash transfers. In addition, the definitions from development agencies emphasize more productivity of health care including output-based measures such as visits, tests, vaccines, or health assessment.

This review uses the more restrictive definition of P4P focusing on supply-side interventions (*i.e.* payments to providers, not to patients) that include some measure of quality of care.

Table 4.1. **Pay-for-performance definitions**

Organisation	P4P definition
AHRQ	Paying more for good performance on *quality metrics* (*source:* AHRQ, undated)
CMS	The use of payment methods and other incentives to encourage *quality improvement* and patient-focused high value care (*source:* Centers for Medicare and Medicaid Services, 2006)
RAND	The general strategy of promoting *quality improvement* by rewarding providers (physicians, clinics or hospitals) who meet certain performance expectations with respect to health care quality or efficiency (*source:* RAND Corporation, undated)
World Bank	A range of mechanisms designed to enhance the *performance of the health system* through incentive-based payments (*source:* World Bank, 2008)
USAID	P4P introduces incentives (generally financial) to reward attainment of *positive health results* (*source:* Eichler and De, 2008)
Center for Global Development	Transfer of money or material goods conditional on taking a *measurable action or achieving a pre-determined performance target* (*source:* Oxman and Fretheim, 2008)

Note: Definition emphasis added by authors.

6. P4P programme design framework

To show how P4P programmes are designed and implemented, a general P4P programme framework is presented in Figure 4.1. The framework includes measures, the basis for the reward, and the reward. Quality and efficiency are the two major categories of measures. These are also known as supply-side P4P measures, because they are provider-based measures related to health care delivery.

The first component of a P4P scheme is the measurement of quality – the first box in Figure 4.1. The quality measures follow a well-known paradigm of structure, process, and outcomes (Donabedian, 2005). Structure refers to the health care setting, including the facility, equipment, supplies, pharmaceuticals, information technology, and human resources. When P4P programmes reward structure, it is often for investments in information technology. Process, broadly defined, are the procedures used to provide health care services, including practice guidelines, disease management protocols, and vaccination and screening rates. P4P programmes often use process measures like whether

Figure 4.1. **P4P programme framework**

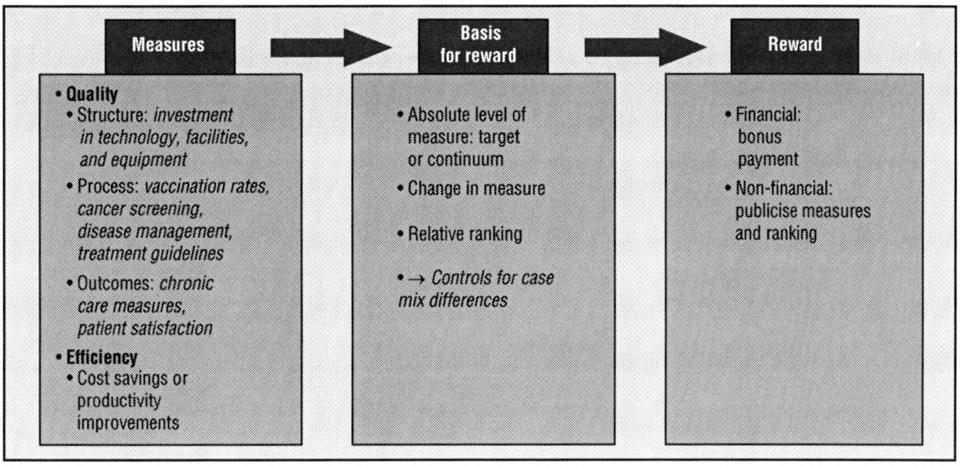

P4P: Pay for performance.

Source: Adapted from Scheffler (2008).

a child was fully vaccinated or a woman screened for breast and cervical cancer as quality measures.

Outcomes measures are the most difficult and rarely include mortality or morbidity. For example, survival for breast cancer that has not spread beyond the breast, is now commonly more than ten years and it is difficult to reward providers for outcomes that take place so far in the future. As a result, measuring quality depends more on intermediate outcomes such as blood pressure, blood sugar levels, and cholesterol levels. The efficiency measures focus on costs. For example, a physician's performance may be measured by the number of in-patient days per 1 000 enrolees, the ratio of out-patient procedures occurring at a hospital versus a lower-cost health care facility. These measures should be adjusted for case mix, since the severity of patients' illness is one of the main determinants of cost. Often, age and sex are used for case-mix adjustment, but these are insufficient, and more complex case adjustment classification systems are needed to adjust for differences in patient severity. For example, if one practice had all healthy young people and the other had old diabetics, it would not be surprising that the first practice would have better outcomes than the other.

P4P schemes differ between high and low income countries. In high income countries, particularly those with fee-for-service, the problem is to constrain the ever increasing demand for more and better health services. In many low income countries, with long-standing National Health Services (often referred to as being the Public-Integrated Model), where health personnel are civil servants, there is often underutilisation and lack of coverage of key public health interventions like immunisation and ante-natal care. The goal is to increase utilisation particularly for high priority services at higher quality. The classic example is the Rwanda P4P where the scheme paid for a list of priority services. Other example measures include rewarding physicians to work in the public sector instead of the private sector (*e.g.* Turkey) or to diagnose patients with tuberculosis (China).

In fact, any measure can be selected in a P4P programme from narrow vertical disease programme goals like increasing vaccination to broader goals like improving primary care. In P4P programmes like the Quality Outcome Framework (QOF) in the United Kingdom, many different disease specific goals are combined into a single composite measure.

7. Rewarding providers

The second box within Figure 4.1 is the basis for reward. The primary categories used to base the reward include the absolute level of the measure, a change in the level, or the relative ranking. First, the absolute level reward could be based on achieving a target, such as achieving an 80% vaccination rate, or based on a continuum (*e.g.*, in QOF, once the minimum threshold is reached). A target rate may not be optimal, because those who start near or are already above the target will receive a reward with little to no improvement. And those who begin far below the target will likely need a large incentive to exert effort to reach the target. Second, the reward may be based on a change in the measure over time, such as how a provider's breast cancer screening rate has changed over time. The magnitude of improvement is rewarded in this case. Third, there are examples of rewards being based on relative performance or rankings. A practice is given a reward for being in the top, for example, 10% ranking. This payment basis has some appeal because random variation that affects all providers is controlled for. For any of the reward bases, it is important to control for case mix differences, in order to reduce provider's incentive to avoid high-need patients and to better control for outcomes outside of the provider's control, thus reducing the required risk premium.

The third box within Figure 4.1 is the reward, which may be financial or non-financial, or a combination of both. The rewards are often a bonus or lump sum payment or they can be an increase in the rate of payment or reimbursement. A non-financial reward may be to publicise provider rankings based on different measures. Although public rankings are not directly financial, they can become financial if patients or insurers use the rankings to determine which provider to visit or contract with.

Figure 4.2 shows the two primary payment models to distribute payments. The first type involves the payer paying the medical group or institution (*e.g.*, hospital) directly, and these entities then decide how to distribute the payment to individual health care workers. The second type involves paying the individual workers directly. Most P4P programmes pay rewards to the medical group or institution, because they are better able to determine how to best distribute the payment among health care workers, because they have more information than the payer. In some cases, when a medical group or institution is paid by multiple payers, such as a public payer, private insurer, and individual patients, the incentives may not align because rewards are based on different measures.

Figure 4.2. **P4P payment models and implementation**

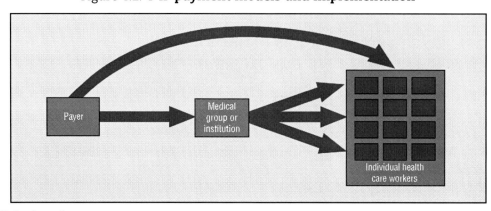

P4P: Pay for performance.
Source: Adapted from Scheffler (2008).

Under either payment model, the direct reward to individual health care workers is harder to structure, because of case mix differences, higher monitoring costs, and lower reliability when a particular individual treats a small number of patients for a given measure. For example, particular individual providers may see an above-average share of patients with complex conditions or patients that require intensive treatment. Adjustments are often difficult to make, because of the lack of data and the cost to collect the data. When the effort of each worker cannot be monitored or measured individually, a worker might tend to reduce his effort, because his reward is mostly based on the efforts of the other workers – the shirking problem. This will be particularly true when the reward is equally distributed among workers.

Another concern about P4P schemes is equity. Often, the best practices with the best physicians are located in wealthier areas serving wealthier and more educated populations. These are the types of people who immunise their children, do not smoke, are not overweight, and follow medical advice. In poor areas, patients are less educated and often do not come to the doctor's office and yet have greater health needs. One of the concerns about paying for performance is that it could reward the practices that are already doing well and increase inequities in the health system. It is important to monitor equity for any P4P scheme and to pay attention in the design to avert unintended consequences for equity whilst promoting efficiency.

8. P4P programmes in OECD countries

P4P programmes are common within many OECD countries, and Table 4.2 reports the P4P programme results from the 2008-09 OECD Survey on Health System Characteristics. Pay-for-performance programmes were reported to exist in 19 OECD countries, including measures in the following categories: primary care physicians (15), specialists (10), and hospitals (7). For primary care physicians and specialists, most bonuses are for quality of care targets such as preventive care and management of chronic diseases. For hospitals, most bonuses were for processes, but some were also for outcomes and patient satisfaction.

As might be expected, there is significant variation among countries. Countries such as Belgium, Japan, Turkey, United Kingdom, and United States report P4P in all three sectors (primary care, specialists, and hospitals). In contrast, Austria, Denmark, Finland, France, Germany, Greece, Iceland, Norway, and Switzerland do not report having any P4P programmes, which may be due to underreporting.

The proportion of physicians and hospitals participating in P4P programmes was only reported for a few countries. The proportions for each sector were as follows: primary care: Belgium (90%), Poland (80%) and United Kingdom (99%); specialty care: Poland (5%) and United Kingdom (68%); and hospitals: Luxembourg (9%). The share of the physician and hospital earnings represented by the bonus payment was only reported for a few countries, and they were generally 5% or less, except for the United Kingdom. The bonus shares for each sector were as follows: primary care: Belgium (2%), Poland (5%) and United Kingdom (15%); specialty care: Poland (5%); and hospitals: Belgium (0.5%) and Luxembourg (1.4%). These data are a beginning, but clearly, more data is needed in order to understand the attributes of these P4P programmes.

United States: California Pay-for-Performance Programme

One of the largest P4P programmes is the California Pay-for-Performance Programme, which began in 2003 (Robinson et al., 2009; Rebhun and Williams, 2009). As of 2009, it included

Table 4.2. **P4P programmes and measures in OECD countries**

	Bonus for primary care physicians	If so, targets related to:		Bonus for specialists	If so, targets related to:		Bonus for hospitals	If so, targets related to:			Financial incentives
		Preventive care	Chronic disease		Preventive care	Chronic disease		Clinical outcome	Process	Patient satisfaction	
Australia	X	X	X								X
Austria											
Belgium	X		X	X		X	X				
Canada											
Czech Republic	X	X		X							
Denmark											X
Finland											
France	X	X	X								X
Germany											
Greece											
Hungary	X										
Iceland											
Ireland											
Italy	X	X	X								
Japan	X	X	X	X	X	X	X	X			
Korea							X	X	X		X
Luxembourg							X				
Mexico											
Netherlands											
New Zealand	X	X	X								
Norway											
Poland	X	X	X	X	X	X					
Portugal	X	X	X								
Slovak Republic				X			X	X	X	X	
Spain	X	X	X	X							
Sweden	n.a.			n.a.			n.a.				
Switzerland											
Turkey	X	X		X	X		X		X		
United Kingdom	X	X	X	X	X	X	X	X	X	X	X
United States	X	X	X	X	X	X	X	X	X	X	X

P4P: Pay for performance.
n.a. not available.
Source: Paris et al. (2010); update with information from July 2010, and authors' estimates for the United States.

StatLink ᴍ⊑ᴾ *http://dx.doi.org/10.1787/888932319782*

eight commercial HMO health plans, covering 11.5 million enrolees, and approximately 230 physician groups with 35 000 physicians. Between 2003 and 2007, the plans paid USD 264 million in bonuses, which represented only 2% of the physician groups' revenues. The goal was for the payment levels to be 10%; however, plans have been reluctant to increase the percentage until there is stronger evidence on improved quality. The programme started with 13 measures in three domains, and has expanded to 68 measures in five domains, including the following with their associated weights: clinical quality (40%), patient experience (20%), IT-enabled systems (20%), co-ordinated diabetes care (20%) and resource use and efficiency (with a separate incentive pool).

Clinical performance improved an average of 3 percentage points per year, with groups who had the lowest baseline improving the most, particularly for HbA1c screening for diabetics – a good measure of diabetic control. The largest change was groups adopting specific IT activities, which increased an average of 7 percentage points per year. The non-financial incentives included the publicising of rankings, such as for the top 20% and the most improved. These amount to indirect financial incentives, because public recognition has been used by physician groups in their advertising and marketing materials. In summary, provider groups are still motivated to participate, but health plans are less motivated because quality improvements are not large, which is likely due in part because of the low P4P payments which are only 2%, and this may not be sufficient to motivate providers.

United States: Medicare

The Centers for Medicare & Medicaid Services (CMS) are involved in many P4P demonstration projects. However, as compared to its approximate USD 420 billion budget in FY2009 for Medicare, the P4P programme payments of approximately USD 40 million are very small (Tanenbaum, 2009). Two of these programmes are addressed here.

In order to increase the collection and reporting of quality measures, Medicare's Physicians Quality Reporting Initiative began in 2007 and pays physicians an additional 2% of their allowed charges for reporting quality measures to CMS (CMS, 2009). In 2007, the physician participation rate was 16% (Porter, 2008).

The Physician Group Practice (PGP) Demonstration began in 2005 and included ten PGPs as well as control groups (Trisolini *et al.*, 2008). The demonstration included both quality and efficiency measures. The 32 quality measures were drawn from CMS's Doctor's Office Quality (DOQ) project, focusing on measures from five condition modules: coronary artery disease, diabetes, heart failure, hypertension, and preventive care. One of the diabetes measures, for example, is the percentage of diabetics who received an HbA1c (blood sugar) test at least once per year. For each quality measure, PGPs must satisfy at least one of three targets: 1) the higher of either 75% compliance or, where comparable data are available, the mean value of the measure from the Medicare Health Plan Employer Data and Information Set (HEDIS); 2) the 70th percentile Medicare HEDIS level (again, where comparable data are available); or 3) a 10% or greater reduction in the gap between the level achieved by the PGP in the demonstration's base year and 100% compliance in Year 1. The first two targets are threshold targets, while the third is an improvement-over-time target. The initial results show some promise. All groups achieved target performance levels on at least seven of ten diabetes quality measures.

The PGP can also receive a payment based on efficiency or cost savings. For each PGP, Medicare savings from the Demonstration are calculated by comparing actual spending to a target: the PGP's own base year per capita expenditures trended forward by the comparison group's expenditure growth rate. The PGP and comparison groups' case mixes are adjusted to account for differences in the type of patients treated. The PGP is eligible to receive 80% of the savings that are above a 2% savings threshold. Two out of ten physician groups had at least 2% lower Medicare spending growth rates as compared to control groups.

United Kingdom: Quality and Outcomes Framework (QOF)

The QOF is the largest P4P scheme in the world. It began in 2004, and is a voluntary incentive pay programme for general practitioners with almost universal participation with 99.8% of patients registered in England enrolled in GP practices participating in the programme. The objective of the QOF is to reward GP practices for how well they care for patients, not just how many patients they have on their list.

The QOF contains four main areas known as domains: clinical, organisational, patient experience and additional services. Each domain contains indicators that define the specific process or outcome that practices participating in the QOF are asked to achieve for their patients. For example one of the clinical indicators in coronary heart disease (CHD) is: *The percentage of patients with CHD who are currently treated with a beta blocker (unless a contraindication or side effects are recorded)*. Clinical indicators are based on the best available evidence of the effectiveness of interventions in primary care. There are currently 146 indicators used to determine 1 000 points covering clinical quality, organisational quality, and patient experience.

The points are converted into monetary incentives by a conversion factor. In 2004, there were 1 050 points and each was worth GBP 76 (USD 133). Currently, there are 1 000 points and each is worth GBP 126.77. To illustrate how the QOF works, consider the example of the quality indicator for asthma, which is based on the percentage of patients with asthma who have had an asthma review in the previous 15 months. No points are awarded until the review rate reaches 25%, and the maximum number of points, 20, is awarded once the review rate reaches 70%. For review rates between 25% and 70%, the number of points earned linearly increases as the review rate increases. In 2004-05, the median general practitioner earned 1 003 points of the 1 050 points available, or 95.5%.

The number of points that GP practices achieved was much higher than expected. When QOF was negotiated, it was presumed that the average would be approximately 75% but it ended up at over 90%. QOF increased the gross average income of general practitioners by GBP 23 000 (USD 40 200); before QOF, general practitioners typically earned GBP 70 000-GBP 75 000 (USD 122 000-USD 131 000) (Doran *et al.*, 2006). Because of the large payout, the 2006/07 minimum thresholds were all increased, and some of the maximum thresholds were increased as well.

It is difficult to determine whether health care quality improved as a result of the QOF, because there were no control groups. It fact, almost everyone participated, so there was no natural experiment. However, Campbell *et al.* (2009) analysed data before and after the QOF was initiated and found the rate of improvement in the quality of care initially increased for asthma and diabetes, but not for heart disease, and by 2007, the rate of improvement had slowed for each condition. There is also some evidence that the programme has improved equity of outcomes. However, importantly, they also found that quality of those aspects of care that were not linked to an incentive had declined for asthma or heart disease.

One of the criticisms of the QOF was the process for determining which diseases and interventions would be included in the QOF. It was felt that this should not be political, but a technical exercise, and responsibility was shifted to the National Institute for Health and Clinical Excellence (NICE), which began overseeing a new independent and transparent process for developing and reviewing QOF health and clinical improvement indicators beginning 1 April 2009. The relative priority of these topics for inclusion in QOF would then be considered by an independent advisory committee, formally known as the Primary Care Quality and Outcomes Framework Indicator Advisory Committee. Each recommended indicator will be accompanied by a suite of supporting information – for example, on when new and renewed indicators should be reviewed and on the cost-effectiveness evidence to inform their financial value.

New Zealand: Performance-based Management

New Zealand started its Performance-based Management (PBM) programme in 2006 within its Primary Health Organisations (PHOs), which are non-profit organisations that provide primary health care services (Buetow, 2008). By January 2007, 81 PHOs, which represented over 98% of New Zealanders, enrolled in the PBM programme. The PBM setup payment was NZD 20 000 per PHO plus 60c per enrolled member. There was a guaranteed minimum payment of NZD 1.00-1.50 per enrolee for PHOs entering the PBM programme before December 2007. A maximum payment of NZD 6 per enrolee could be obtained if all targets were achieved, which include clinical indicators (60%), process indicators (10%), and financial indicators (30%). The clinical indicators include, for example, vaccinations for children and elderly, cervical smears, and breast cancer screening. The process indicators include, for example, ensuring access for those with high needs. Last, the financial indicators include, for example, pharmaceutical and laboratory expenditures. The payments are made to the PHO, who then decide how to distribute funds to individual health care workers. Based on a survey of 29 PHOs, they reported better clinical care co-ordination and data management as a result of PBM.

Australia

The Australian Government provides financial incentives to both immunisation providers and parents to encourage child immunisation. The General Practice Immunisation Incentive Scheme (GPII) was introduced in 1997 to reward general practitioners with bonus payments for childhood immunisation services. The pay-for-performance scheme for immunisation is part of a wider incentive scheme, Medicare's Practice Incentives Program (PIP), which has been using financial incentives to achieve wider health system goals. For a GP practice to be eligible to receive incentive payments, it must either be accredited or working towards accreditation of the Royal Australian College of General Practitioners Standards for General Practice. There are currently 13 broad elements including: after hours care; care for chronic conditions such as asthma and diabetes; indigenous health; domestic violence; eHealth, etc.

The aim of GPII was to encourage at least 90% of GP practices to fully immunise at least 90% of children under 7 years of age. In addition to incentives to GPs, there are also complementary incentives for parents. This includes the Maternity Immunisation Allowance which provides a bonus to parents for ensuring that their child's immunisation coverage is up-to-date for age and a Child Care Benefit which requires families to demonstrate that their child's immunisation coverage is up-to-date for age. The latter approach ensures that parents are reminded of the importance of immunising their children at each of the milestones. Since the introduction of this programme (PIP), the average practice immunisation coverage has increased from around 76% to around 92%. Data on immunisation rates from the Australian Childhood Immunisation Register continue to be published regularly in *Communicable Diseases Intelligence Journal* (CDI).

Brazil

In Brazil, there are several different P4P schemes including both demand and supply side. Brazil like many other Latin American countries has moved more rapidly in introducing demand-side P4P with: *Bolsa Escola* school cash transfer; *Cartao Alimentacao* food cash transfer; *Auxilo* gas-cooking gas compensation; and expanding conditional cash transfers to the poors (*Bolsa Familia*) and these include health outcomes as one of the criteria for the cash transfer. On the supply side, a private insurance company, UNIMED-Belo Horizonte, is implementing the largest scheme and its success has led to a new scheme for public providers of primary care. The UNIMED scheme is being implemented in Belo Horizonte, the third largest city in Brazil and includes a network of 258 providers serving 800 000 people.[2] The objective is to improve treatment and outcomes for patients with cardiovascular disease, diabetes, childhood asthma, and well child care. These conditions are managed by evidence-based clinical guidelines. Preliminary results indicate improved health status among patients enrolled in the P4P scheme with increased number of patients with cardiovascular disease and diabetes with better blood pressure control, reduced serum cholesterol and more optimal glucose control. There was also a drop in admissions for children with asthma.

The UBIH scheme is an example of cross-country learning. In 2007, UNIMED's director contacted and began working with Kaiser Permanente in California that has been a leader in the development of new methods of measuring and paying for quality. Together they worked with Integrated Health Care Association which hosts P4P summits to disseminate the positive experience of P4P in California outlined above. UNIMED modified the California scheme to the Brazilian context, where it is proving successful.

Although there appears to be great success, the evaluation of both the California and Brazilian schemes has been limited. In both schemes, there is no control group and it is presumed that one can compare before and after to capture the effects of P4P. Although the current schemes are very promising, they would benefit from better evaluation, allowing one to isolate the effects of P4P compared to other effects. Also, many of these schemes do not measure adequately the costs of implementation, so one has to wonder about the cost effectiveness of P4P, whether it improves quality sufficiently given the additional costs.

Korea

Korea has a long tradition of performance-related pay in several sectors. A recent survey reports that 45.2% of Korean firms with more than 100 employees have implemented compensation methods based on individual performance (Park and Yu, 2002). However, pay for performance in health care is relatively recent, and is a response to growing concerns about value for money achieved by increased health spending. Although Korea still has relatively low spending on health compared to other OECD countries (6.5% of GDP in 2008), the growth rate in real health expenditure per capita between 1995 and 2008 has been the highest in the OECD, reaching 8% an average per year.

There have been considerable health reforms in Korea since 2000 with integration of numerous health insurance funds into a single payer system. The Korean Health Insurance Review Agency (HIRA), founded in 2000, is an independent government body responsible for reviewing the medical fee schedule and evaluating whether health care services are delivered at appropriate level and cost. It has initiated a national quality assessment programme that led to considerable improvement in quality of care including reducing variation in quality. Linking quality of care to financial incentives is the latest step Korea is using to improve quality.

In 2007, the Ministry of Health and Welfare and HIRA launched the Value Incentive Programme, a pay-for-performance scheme covering 43 tertiary hospitals providing secondary care services. The scheme focuses on two important conditions: quality of treatment for acute myocardial infarction (AMI) and caesarean deliveries, whose rate is very high. HIRA developed synthetic quality measures. For myocardial infarction, there are seven indicators: process indicators (timeliness of reperfusion therapy, administration of aspirin) and outcome indicators (case fatality). For the caesarean section rate, there are 16 clinical risk factors. Bonus payments were made to providers based on quality improvement from a 2007 baseline survey of the indicators, where hospitals were ranked in five levels (see Figure 4.3). In 2009, high performers and performance improvers received bonuses amounting to 1% of reimbursements from National Health Insurance Corporation (USD 375 million) while performers below the 2007 baseline were penalised 1% of payments as well.

Figure 4.3. **Value Incentive Programme mechanisms in Korea**

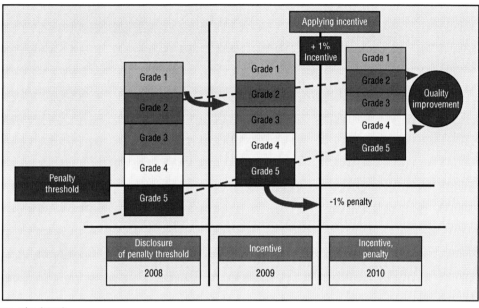

Source: Kim (2010).

The results of the Value Incentive Programme showed a 1.55% increase in total scores of the myocardial infarction measure between 2007 and 2008 while the caesarean section rate dropped by 0.56%. There was also a decrease in variance of quality among providers and a marked improvement in lowest performing group (see Figure 4.4).

Figure 4.4. **Composite quality score of AMI**

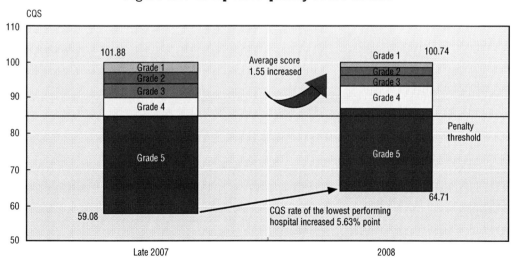

Source: Kim (2010).

Though the progress made has been substantial, the next step is to include more hospitals into the scheme (including general hospitals), to broaden the clinical areas covered, as well as increasing the incentive rate to 2%.

9. Conclusions

P4P programmes have been widely introduced across OECD countries, yet the research designs to evaluate them are often inadequate to provide a definitive answer about the effect of P4P programmes on quality and costs (Rosenthal and Frank, 2006).

There is one example of a properly-evaluated P4P programme, though it comes from a surprising source: the Rwandan P4P programme (see Box 4.1). The lesson from the Rwanda P4P is not the type of incentives used, but rather the proper approach to evaluation which allows the isolation of the effect of P4P from other reforms. Indeed, as the Rwandan experience is replicated in other countries, it is likely that soon there will be much better evidence on "what works" in P4P in developing countries than in OECD countries.

However, even with limited evaluation in OECD countries, the initial results of P4P programmes appear promising and have galvanised payers and providers to measure health care quality (Rebhun and Williams, 2009). There appears to be growing evidence that incentivising priority public health interventions like cancer screening works and also P4P works in getting physicians to follow evidence-based guidelines for chronic conditions like diabetes and cardiovascular disease. But there are still challenging measurement and design issues. Measures of quality of care will continue to improve, but this will continue to be a difficult area, since quality is multidimensional, includes clinical effectiveness but also patient experience, and outcomes are difficult to measure particularly for individuals, and often do not appear for a long time. Given these constraints, paying for quality will continue to require better methods of measuring quality of care. Furthermore, the impact of P4P schemes has often been limited because, aside from a few notable exceptions such as UK QOF, the size of the incentives has been small.

P4P schemes are not the only way of delivering improvements in technical and allocative efficiency in the health sector. In some areas, an alternative to supply-side incentives is to affect the demand for services. Patient-incentive programmes are becoming more prevalent, growing out of conditional cash transfer programmes developed in education such as those used to encourage school attendance.

There is still a lot to learn about how and when these programmes work. What is the ideal level of payment incentive to change provider behaviour? How should payments be distributed? If OECD countries currently implementing P4P schemes can organise proper evaluations, then other countries can learn what works, and all countries can benefit from real improvements in health care quality and efficiency in the future.

Box 4.1. Overcoming limitations in P4P assessment: the surprising case of Rwanda

Rwanda has perhaps the best evaluated pay-for-performance scheme in the world. Rwanda started experimenting with pay-for-performance schemes in 2002 to address underlying poor performance by public sector providers who were paid on salary and had little motivation to increase outputs. The providers were paid by inputs rather than outputs, and there was low coverage of key public health interventions such as vaccination, ante-natal care, and deliveries in health centres. Several pilot projects were established with different donor support (Dutch, Belgian, Cordaid) to set up pilot projects that used a fee schedule to pay bonuses for key interventions and also included contracting to private providers. The pilot projects were transformed into a national scheme with support from the World Bank beginning in 2005.

The national scheme includes a set of priority services and a unit weight for each service similar to a traditional fee schedule as in Germany or the US Medicare. It also has a synthetic measure of quality of care in health centres measured by structure and process indicators. This includes things like cleanliness of facility and also availability of services like family planning and process measures such as growth monitoring of children. There were several difficulties in the evaluation scheme. First and foremost was the problem of additional resources and trying to isolate the effect of incentives. In many schemes, there are additional resources used to fund the scheme, so it is not clear if the improvement is due to more resources or to the incentives. In the case of Rwanda, they took advantage of rollout of the national scheme, using those that first implemented the P4P scheme compared to the controls who had not yet implemented it. Those that implemented the scheme first were chosen by random assignment.

There were also several other reforms occurring in Rwanda at the same time, including the rapid expansion of community-style insurance through the Mutuelle system which grew from less than 5% of population in 2002 to 85% of the population by 2008. Coverage by insurance meant that there was increased demand for use of health centres because people no longer had to pay directly out-of-pocket and this fueled greater demand for health services. In addition, the government introduced performance contracting as part of their programme of decentralisation. Known as the Imihigo, this programme provided block grants from the central government to the district, where mayors of districts had to sign contracts with the President to improve important public services such as health. Decentralisation of funding to districts was dramatic with the districts' share of health funds increasing from 37% in 2003 to 85% in 2007. Health spending quadrupled from 2005 to 2008, increasing from USD 7.5 million to USD 30.3 million.

Given the rapidly changing context in Rwanda, it was difficult to disentangle the effects of P4P from other effects such as rising health spending, increased increase coverage, and decentralisation. However, the impact evaluation included cross-over control districts that had no P4P, but had all the other changes. P4P increased deliveries in health centres; increased prevention interventions in children such as immunisation. It also led to reduced child mortality and taller children. The size of the change observed is larger for most interventions showing that P4P works. Given the success, many low income countries are learning from the experience of Rwanda and developing variants of the scheme they piloted.

Notes

1. Pay for performance is a subset of a wider set of policy interventions often known as results-based financing which also includes demand-side incentives such as conditional cash transfer programmes like *Opportunitades* in Mexico. In addition, decentralised health systems are increasingly using incentive schemes between levels of government (*e.g.* federal government to state government) such as Plan Nacer in Argentina. These other methods are not included in this chapter, which focuses on incentives to providers for quality, but these other schemes, which are included in the broader definition of results-based financing, are also promising avenues for improving health system performance.

2. UNIMED in Belo Horizonte (UBH) is both a health insurance company and medical co-operative operating in a highly competitive market for private health insurance. UNIMED serves 800 000 out of a total population of 5.4 million in the metropolitan area. Currently, 4 700 physicians are part of the co-operative and UBH owns and operates seven facilities. UNIMED has contracts with an additional 258 facilities.

Bibliography

Agency for Healthcare Research and Quality (AHRQ), *Evaluation of the Use of AHRQ and Other Quality Indicators*, undated, accessed 17 February 2010 at *www.ahrq.gov/about/evaluations/qualityindicators/qualindsum.htm*.

Buetow, S. (2008), "P4P in New Zealand Primary Health Care", *Journal of Health Organization and Management,* Vol. 22, No. 1, p. 36.

Campbell, S.M., D. Reeves, E. Kontopantelis, B. Sibbald and M. Roland (2009), "Effects of Pay for Performance on the Quality of Primary Care in England", *New England Journal of Medicine,* Vol. 361, pp. 368-378.

Casalino, L.P., G.C. Alexander, L. Jin and L.T. Konetzka (2007), "General Internists' Views on Pay-for-Performance and Public Reporting of Quality Scores: A National Survey", *Health Affairs,* Vol. 26, No. 2, pp. 492-499.

Centers for Medicare and Medicaid Services (2006), "State Medicaid Director Letter", No. 06-003, 6 April 2006.

CMS (2009), "Physician Quality Reporting Initiative (PQRI)", accessed January 2010 at *www.cms.hhs.gov/pqri/*.

Deming, W.E. (1986), "Out of the Crisis", MIT Press.

Donabedian, A. (2005), "Evaluating the Quality of Medical Care", *The Milbank Quarterly,* Vol. 83, No. 4, pp. 691-729, reprinted from *The Milbank Memorial Fund Quarterly,* Vol. 44, No. 3, pp. 166-203.

Doran, T., C. Fullwood, H. Gravelle, D. Reeves, E. Kontopantelis, U. Hiroeh *et al.* (2006), "Pay-for-Performance Programs in Family Practices in the United Kingdom", *New England Journal of Medicine,* Vol. 355, No. 4, pp. 375-384.

Eichler, R. and S. De (2008), *Paying for Performance in Health: Guide to Developing the Blueprint,* USAID/Health Systems 20/20 Project, May 2008, accessed 17 February 2010 at *http://pdf.usaid.gov/pdf_docs/PNADN760.pdf*.

Glassman, A., J. Todd and M. Gaarder (2007), *Performance-based Incentives for Health: Conditional Cash Transfer Programs in Latin America and the Caribbean,* Center for Global Development, Washington, DC.

Herd, R. *et al.* (2010), "Improving China's Health System", OECD Economics Department Working Paper, No. 751, OECD Publishing, Paris.

Institute of Medicine (2001), "Crossing the Quality Chasm: A New Health System for the 21st Century", Committee on Quality of Health Care in America, Institute of Medicine, National Academy Press, Washington, DC.

Juran, J.M. (1951), *Quality Control Handbook,* McGraw-Hill, New York.

Kelly, T., V. Gray and M. Minges (2003), "Broadband Korea: Internet Case Study", International Telecommunication Union.

Kim, B.Y. (2010), "Quality Assessment and Pay for Performance in Korea", HIRA, Korean Health Insurance Review Agency, May.

Kohn, L.T., J.M. Corrigan and M.S. Donaldson (2000), "To Err is Human: Building a Safer Health System", Committee on Quality of Health Care in America, Institute of Medicine, National Academy Press, Washington, DC.

OECD (2009), *Achieving Better Value for Money in Health Care*, OECD Health Policy Studies, OECD Publishing, Paris.

Oxman, A.D. and A. Fretheim (2008), *An Overview of Research on the Effects of Results-based Financing*, Report No. 16-2008, Nasjonalt kunnskapssenter for helsetjenesten, Oslo, accessed 17 February 2010 at *http://hera.helsebiblioteket.no/hera/bitstream/10143/33892/1/NOKCrapport16_2008.pdf.*

Paris, V., M. Devaux and L. Wei (2010), "Health Systems Institutional Characteristics: A Survey of 29 OECD Countries", OECD Health Working Paper, No. 50, OECD Publishing, Paris.

Park, W. and G. Yu (2002), "HRM in Korea: Transformation and New Patterns", in Z. Rhee and E. Chang (eds.), *Korean Business and Management: The Reality and the Vision*, Hollym Corp., Seoul.

Paul-Ebhohimhen, V. and A. Avenell (2008), "Systematic Review of the Use of Financial Incentives in Treatments for Obesity and Overweight", *Obesity Reviews*, Vol. 9, No. 4, pp. 355-367.

Porter, S. (2008), "Preliminary Report Offers First Glimpse of Quality Reporting Progress", AAFP, available at *www.aafp.org/online/en/home/publications/news/news-now/practice-management/20080305pqrireport.html.*

RAND Corporation, RAND COMPARE Glossary, accessed 17 February 2010 at *www.randcompare.org/glossary/16/letterp.*

Rebhun, D. and T. Williams (2009), *The California Pay For Performance Programme: The Second Chapter Measurement Years 2006-2009*, Integrated Healthcare Association, Oakland, California.

Robinson, J.C., T. Williams and T. Yanagihara (2009), "Measurement of and Reward for Efficiency in California's Pay-for-Performance Programme", *Health Affairs*, Vol. 28, No. 5, pp. 1438-1447.

Rosenthal, M.B. and R.A. Dudley (2007), "Pay for Performance: Will the Latest Payment Trend Improve Care?", *JAMA*, Vol. 297, No. 7, pp. 740-744.

Rosenthal, M.B. and R.G. Frank (2006), "What is the Empirical Basis for Paying for Quality in Health Care?", *Med Care Res Rev*, Vol. 63, pp. 135-157.

Scheffler, R.M. (2008), *Is There a Doctor in the House? Market Signals and Tomorrow's Supply of Doctors*, Stanford University Press, Palo Alto, California.

Tanenbaum, S. (2009), "Pay for Performance in Medicare: Evidentiary Irony and the Politics of Value", *Journal of Health Politics, Policy and Law*, Vol. 34, No. 5, pp. 717-746.

Trisolini, M. *et al.* (2008), *The Medicare Physician Group Demonstration: Lessons Learned on Improving Quality and Efficiency in Health Care*, Commonwealth Fund, New York, February.

Wagstaff, A. *et al.* (2009), *Reforming China's Rural Health System*, World Bank, Washington, DC.

World Bank (2008), *Health Systems and Financing: Results-based Financing (RBF)*, accessed 17 February 2010 at *http://web.worldbank.org/WBSITE/EXTERNAL/TOPICS/EXTHEALTHNUTRITIONANDPOPULATION/EXTHSD/0,,contentMDK:21840544XXXmenuPK:5364481XXXpagePK:148956XXXpiPK:216618XXXtheSitePK:376793,00.html.*

Chapter 5

Improving Co-ordination of Care for Chronic Diseases to Achieve Better Value for Money

Health care systems in OECD countries have become increasingly complex: multiple providers, lack of adherence to care protocols, inconsistencies in reimbursement and decentralised medical records are still the status quo in most OECD health systems. The problems that health systems have to deal with have evolved too: with more patients receiving care from multiple providers for chronic conditions, there is a growing problem of fragmentation within health systems. This results in poor patient experiences, coupled with ineffective and unsafe care. Can better co-ordination contribute substantially to solving these problems? What tools can be used to improve the co-ordination of care? This chapter explores the barriers to good co-ordination and looks at what can be done to improve the co-ordination of care in health systems across the OECD.

1. Introduction

Health care systems in OECD countries have become increasingly complex. Gone are the days when the midwife and local doctor were the only medical personnel most people would ever encounter. Health systems now encompass dozens of different job classifications from nurses to technicians to specialist surgeons, plus a whole management class of directors, administrators, accountants and others. Health care takes place in many different types of settings – from home visits to clinics to large hospitals – and is paid for through a complex combination of public and private insurance funds.

The health problems systems have to deal with have evolved too. Chronic diseases, including cardiovascular diseases, cancers, respiratory conditions, diabetes, and mental disorders, now account for the largest segment of the burden of disease and a large percentage of health care costs. The WHO estimated that 60% of deaths around the world were due to chronic diseases (not including HIV/AIDs) and for 86% of deaths in the European Region (WHO, 2004). The economic and medical progress that have extended lifespan have accompanied certain lifestyle trends that contribute to the development of chronic diseases such as diabetes, heart disease and cancer. In essence, health care has become good at keeping people alive with diseases that would in the past have killed them, and even in the recent past, as with HIV/AIDS.

With more patients receiving care from multiple providers for chronic conditions, there is a growing problem of fragmentation within health systems. This results in poor patient experiences, coupled with ineffective and unsafe care. Patients with chronic diseases receive a wide range of clinical inputs from different specialities including allied health professionals. The growing specialisation of medical knowledge, partly reflecting the ever increasing complexity of medical science, has given specialists an important role in managing complex cases of chronic diseases. However, ongoing care for chronic diseases still takes place in primary care. This separation leads to a problem of co-ordination between the two settings in that they are generally organised and paid differently. Not only that, but the two systems often operate under incentive structures (relative to cost control and quality) that are not aligned, or even at odds with each other and often operate under different budgetary regimes and often they are under the responsibility of different levels of government.

Beyond health care, there is the difficulty of co-ordinating hospital care with long-term care for the elderly with multiple chronic conditions; and the co-ordination problem between health care and social care which are usually organised and financed in dramatically different ways. In order to address patients' expectations for seamless care regardless of the system, it will be increasingly important to consider co-ordination of care in a broader perspective beyond health care.

The role of patients in the care process has also taken on much greater importance in recent years. There is growing recognition that patients play a critical and under-utilised role in managing their own chronic diseases. Whether patients take responsibility for their treatment can have a significant impact on their health outcomes. Many investments in co-ordination indeed depend on how much patients make use of the services and support provided. Yet it has been very difficult to determine the best way to involve patients in their own care, not least because people vary greatly in their responsiveness to information, advice and treatment guidelines.

Multiple providers, lack of adherence to care protocols, inconsistencies in reimbursement and decentralised medical records are still the status quo in most OECD health systems. All of these factors add up to a fragmented structure that impedes good co-ordination, and makes it more difficult for the chronically ill to find their way through the system. Given the sheer size and diversity of health care systems, co-ordination is indispensible. Doctors typically ask what other care a patient might have received from another provider. Insurance systems have to make decisions on whether or not they will reimburse a medical act, and so must obtain some kind of information from the care provider. Efficient co-ordination does not arise naturally as systems grow more complex, and no one has yet found a magic bullet to solve the problem of co-ordinating the web of existing structures of health provision, each with its own culture and way of working. What is needed is timely care that is accessible, effective, safe, integrated and centred around the patient.

In response to the challenges of managing health systems dominated by chronic disease, OECD countries (and private providers within countries) have been trying out various approaches to improving co-ordination. Essentially, the task of co-ordinating health care efficiently involves connecting the different parts of the health puzzle – doctors (primary and specialist), other health professionals such as nurses, counsellors and home care providers across multiple health care institutions such as hospitals, primary care practices, nursing homes, and patient homes. As we will see in this chapter, some systems, primarily in the United States, have implemented a completely integrated model, often called "managed care", one that fuses primary care with specialist hospital care into a single organisation, with a common IT system, common culture, and aligned incentives. Many countries have begun to use programmes that integrate some part of the health system in an attempt to reap the benefits of better co-ordination without making a radical change to the entire system.

Care co-ordination offers the potential to improve value for money in health systems. First, it has the potential to improve quality of care particularly for patients for chronic illnesses. For patients with diseases like diabetes, it is critically important they adhere to their medications, alter their diet to ensure better control of their disease. In addition, they need to undertake preventive measures like foot care and eye exams. If these happen, they will have better clinical outcomes including living longer with fewer complications. In addition, better control of their disease has the potential to save money. They are less likely to be hospitalised for complications and these complications are very expensive. For example, better control would mean they are less likely to develop renal disease and require expensive kidney dialysis. They are less likely to develop vascular disease and require amputation. They are also less likely to have high blood sugar and even diabetic coma requiring expensive emergency hospitalisation. The experience from integrated delivery systems like Kaiser show that one can achieve these good outcomes with much fewer and shorter hospitalisations than most health systems current achieve.

A variety of new instruments have been developed to improve the co-ordination of care. These range from narrow disease management programmes for specific conditions like diabetes and heart disease to integrated care co-ordination models that provide multiaxial assessments linking health and social care. Programmes typically include measures to rationalise the various elements in the health care provision chain: evidence-based guidelines, decision support for clinicians, better information systems and support for patient decision making and empowerment.

The idea that care co-ordination should improve the quality of health care and possibly lower costs seems like common sense: avoiding duplication in care, reducing errors, helping patients make full and proper use of the care they receive are all obvious goals that seem likely to be useful in controlling costs. Yet so far, the evidence on whether care co-ordination programmes yield the expected benefits is limited, particularly in lowering costs. Fully integrated systems like Kaiser appear to have less hospital admissions and shorter lengths of stay, hospital stay being the most expensive part of health systems. Improved efficiency in hospital care should therefore result in cost savings. Results from models of partial integration, mostly in the form of disease management programmes, have been less conclusive; they appear to improve quality of care, but do not necessarily lower costs. Some have shown promising results in increasing value for money in such cases as Germany and Austria.

Chronic diseases will continue to increase and health systems are likely to grow even more complex. It is therefore important for OECD countries to further explore promising methods for improving the efficiency and effectiveness of health care through better co-ordination. This chapter looks at different types of care co-ordination and how they have – or have not – shown expected benefits in value and efficiency, and examines the ways in which care management/co-ordination should be able to improve health care delivery and make efficient use of resources. The key questions that emerge then are: What kind of co-ordination is the most useful? What improvements can help to deliver higher quality? Can better co-ordination make health care more efficient? What results do we expect from the system that we are trying to manage? Can better chronic disease management increase value for money? What evidence do we have so far that it does?

2. Changing burden of disease in OECD countries

Unprecedented improvements in population health have taken place in OECD countries over the course of the past century. Life expectancy has increased on average by as much as 25-30 years. Most major infectious diseases have been greatly reduced. Infant mortality rates have fallen dramatically as has maternal death. Fertility has also fallen. This combination of falling childhood mortality and decreased fertility are often referred to as the epidemiological transition, where the structure of the population shifts towards an ageing population, and people live longer with chronic diseases.

Mortality may have fallen dramatically, but the incidence of disease has not. When combined with the general increase in longevity, the result has been a substantial growth of morbidity associated with chronic diseases. As people live longer, they also accumulate chronic non-communicable diseases which are now are now the main cause of both disability and death in OECD countries. Co-morbidities also increase with age, and populations are ageing rapidly in the OECD area. In western Europe, the number of people aged over 64 has more than doubled in the last 60 years, while the number of those aged over 80 has quadrupled. As a consequence, many people have to live with several chronic diseases. At least 35% of men over 60 years of age have two or more chronic conditions (WHO Europe, 2006).

3. Adapting health systems to meet the needs of the chronically ill

There is consensus on what basic elements should be part of a good co-ordination model

Key to the advent of care co-ordination was the development in the 1990s of a chronic care model by Edward Wagner and colleagues at Group Health in Washington, United States, one of the early managed care systems. Their model identified the key elements needed to improve health care services to patients with chronic illnesses and has become widely used as a heuristic for more widespread reflection on the subject (see Figure 5.1). It has been used throughout the OECD in comprehensive reviews of clinical care and as a guide to policy.

Figure 5.1. **Improving outcomes in chronic illness**

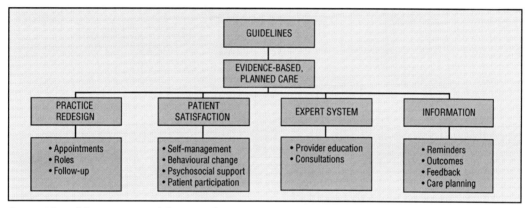

Source: Adapted from Wagner *et al.* (1996, 2001).

Evidence shows that most health systems are still struggling to implement co-ordination programmes

In spite of wide recognition of the merits of this approach, most health systems fail to deliver most of the attributes of good co-ordinated care for chronic diseases. A comprehensive review of chronic care patients across selected OECD countries carried out by the Commonwealth Fund shows systematic failures across most of the countries studied on co-ordination of care (see Table 5.1). This is a household survey of chronic disease patients and is one of the first studies to develop cross-country comparative information on chronic diseases (Schoen *et al.*, 2008).

For almost all countries, there are systematic problems with co-ordination of care for patients with chronic illness. The survey documents the problems with patient experience – having to wait long periods of time between appointments from primary care to specialist care. It also shows significant rates of waste including medication errors, duplication of tests, etc.

4. OECD care co-ordination survey

The OECD questionnaire (see Box 5.1) to national health authorities indicated that policy makers in virtually all responding countries were concerned about inadequate care co-ordination and almost 80% of respondents see patients with chronic conditions and the elderly as being the population groups likely to be most affected by inadequate co-ordination of care.

Table 5.1. **Problems with care co-ordination in OECD countries**

Percentage of adults with any chronic condition	Australia	Canada	France	Germany	Netherlands	New Zealand	United Kingdom	United States
Failure to discuss medication at discharge[1]	39	42	44	23	41	45	35	30
Test results/records not available at time of apt	16	19	15	12	11	17	15	24
Duplicate tests ordered by doctors	12	11	10	18	4	10	7	20
Pharmacist alerted patient of harmful medication[2]	30	23	12	15	38	20	17	20
Adults with a chronic condition								
Saw more than four doctors in the past two years	38	32	31	50	34	34	50	48
Taking more than four prescriptions regularly	33	41	38	39	39	35	50	48
Doctors did not regularly review medecines in two years co-ordination of care[2]	41	40	68	49	62	48	48	41
Diabetics who received preventative care services	36	39	31	40	59	55	67	43
Perception of care								
Doctor recommended treatment had no benefit	22	22	35	24	14	19	15	27
Wasted time due to poorly organised care	26	29	20	31	21	23	18	36
Waiting time for an appointment with a specialist								
Less than four weeks[3]	45	40	55	68	69	45	42	74
Two months or longer[3]	29	42	23	20	25	33	33	10
Medical, medication, lab test errors in past two years								
Wrong medication or dose	13	10	8	7	6	13	9	14
Incorrect diagnostic/lab test results[4]	7	5	3	5	1	3	3	7
Delays in abnormal test results[4]	13	12	5	5	5	10	8	16
Patient engagement in care								
Doctor *always* gives treatment options[5]	58	56	43	56	63	62	51	53
Given written plan to manage care at home[5]	42	47	34	31	35	43	35	66
Access to doctor when sick or needed care								
Same-day appointment	36	26	42	43	60	54	48	26
Usage of emergency room in past two years	53	64	41	39	26	45	40	59

1. Percentage of adults with chronic condition hospitalised in past two years and given new medication.
2. Percentage of adults with chronic condition and taking Rx medications regularly.
3. Percentage of adults with any chronic condition who needed to see a specialist in past two years.
4. Among those who had blood test, x-rays, or other tests.
5. Among those with regular doctor or place of care.

Source: 2008 Commonwealth Fund International Health Policy Survey of Sicker Adults.

StatLink 🔗 *http://dx.doi.org/10.1787/888932319801*

Analysis of questionnaire results – and of the literature more generally – suggests that concern over care co-ordination issues is widespread among policy makers, health care providers and the public at large. These concerns appear to be more intense in countries with high levels of health care spending in GDP. Country replies to the questionnaire also overwhelmingly indicate that policy discussions about care co-ordination are most closely linked to issues of *quality of care* (i.e. impact on health outcomes and responsiveness to patient needs), of *cost efficiency* and, to a lesser degree, of *ensuring access to care*. Co-ordination of care represents one possible way to improve the delivery of quality health care through greater coherence, leading in turn to greater adherence to "best-practice" medicine.

The analysis of questionnaire results suggests that there are a number of common features of care co-ordination practices across the OECD and the European Union:

● Irrespective of whether there are gate-keeping arrangements, nearly all countries have some form of regulatory or behavioral constraint on referrals. In the view of the questionnaire respondents, first contacts with the health care system almost always occur at the primary-care level and patients do not see specialists without a referral.

> **Box 5.1. OECD co-ordination-of-care questionnaire**
>
> With consistent cross-country information on care co-ordination largely absent, the Secretariat has used a questionnaire to canvass views and gather information on current care co-ordination concerns, problems and practices in OECD and EU countries. This questionnaire – for which responses were received from 26 OECD and EU countries – requested that national experts reply to questions in four areas: the importance of co-ordination issues and population groups affected; co-ordination practices; impediments to care co-ordination and the importance of "targeted" programmes in their country. Responses to specific statements or questions in the questionnaire use a Likert scale which is used to capture the *intensity* of concerns or the frequency of occurrence of certain problems, policies or events. In this case, a scale of 1 to 3 was used with a label attached to each level (*e.g.* seldom, moderately frequent, often).
>
> Given the range of government departments, agencies and professional bodies involved in monitoring and promoting care co-ordination, countries were encouraged to enlist the help of a range of stakeholders at different governmental and professional levels in answering the questionnaire. For federal countries, the Secretariat recommended that the federal or central authorities prepare the questionnaire, drawing on expertise at the sub-national level where available. (For further information see Annex 2 of Hofmarcher *et al.*, 2007.)

- More than half of countries see primary-care providers as "often" giving patients guidance as they move through the health care system and thereby act – to some degree at least – as care co-ordinators for the system. However, the role of the primary-care physicians in guiding the patient appears to decline in many countries as patients move towards hospital and institutional care.[1]

- Replies by respondents suggest that referrals from hospitals back to primary care providers appear widespread, possibly reflecting the importance attributed to primary-care providers in ensuring patient follow-up and care co-ordination.[2] Referrals from hospitals back to ambulatory care specialists are less frequent, this pattern of referrals and the resulting provider behavior seem to be a key source of concern for national authorities with respect to co-ordination of care.

- Particular problems in co-ordination appear at the interfaces between levels of care, especially at cross-over points to long-term care. Around two-thirds of countries "agree" that difficulties exist at transitions from ambulatory care and four-fifths at the level of transitions from acute care. In spite of the fact that other health care professionals are managing transitions into long-term care, these services do not appear adequate or appropriately formulated to meet the challenge of care co-ordination. These problems seem to prevail in spite of widespread efforts in many countries to improve continuity between hospital and community care (Leichsenring *et al.*, 2004).[3]

- In comparison, problems *within* care settings seem less important. For example, care co-ordination within hospitals is carried out most of the time at the specialist level. Nonetheless, 30% of countries indicate problems of care co-ordination within this setting suggesting that there is also potential to improve the organisation of care delivery in hospitals.

- Financing of care from multiple sources that are tied to individual silos can make care co-ordination more difficult and encourage costs shifting between provider levels; and,

● Co-ordination of care may be hampered where strong limitations exist on scope of practice rules of different health care professionals and where there is a lack of mutual professional esteem between them.

In sum, replies to the questionnaire provide a fairly consistent picture across countries of some form of care co-ordination in which health professionals help guide patients across institutional transitions and within individual sectors. However, country replies to the questionnaire also suggest that the health care "co-ordinator" can, and often does, differ at each transition, such that there is no assurance that patients are followed by a sole health care professional through any single episode of care.

In many cases, current arrangements do not appear to encourage the development of skills aimed at chronic-care management, communication with patients, patient support and networking with other providers, particularly in the social- or long-term care sectors. Some studies suggest that time allocated to see patients can differ significantly across countries and between the predominant payment schemes in use.[4] Only a small fraction of countries has given their primary-care co-ordinators budgets to purchase care for their patients.

Despite the recognised importance of co-ordination of care, few countries encourage care co-ordination on a contractual basis. Survey results show that only 31% of countries "often" have explicit payment for care co-ordination at the primary-care level. Care co-ordination objectives or stipulations regarding care quality are even less frequent. Thus, there is little financial encouragement for improved care co-ordination even though co-ordination takes time and needs to be rewarded if it is not to be "crowded out" by activities which are remunerated.

5. Models of care co-ordination

There is a continuum of care co-ordination models ranging from the integrated delivery systems to more narrow approaches like disease management. An integrated delivery system generally combines primary and hospital care into a single integrated delivery system. The system is generally paid a fixed fee for managing all of the health care needs of a person. Disease management is a more narrow approach to providing greater co-ordinated care for chronic diseases. It usually consists of a care co-ordinator who manages patient cases (this can be the primary care provider or a third party) and includes clinical protocols for treatment of chronic disease and support for patient management. All of the models of clinical care co-ordination include the key components of chronic disease model: evidence-based guidelines; support to clinical decision making, information systems, patient education, and some degree of integration.

Kaiser Permanente – a model of managed care integrating health financing and service delivery primary ambulatory care and specialist hospital care

Kaiser Permanente is the most well known example of integrated/co-ordinated care for delivering more efficient care particularly for chronic disease. Kaiser is the largest "managed care" organisation in the United States which bridges the divide between primary ambulatory care and specialist care hospital care into a fully integrated system. Its *integrated* model and use of data allows it to achieve high performance and particularly co-ordinated management for *chronic care* that achieves good outcomes for lower costs. Dr. Yan Chow, director of Kaiser's innovation and advance technology group, says "Health care should not be a crisis management care model but should much better be a preventive care model, with the implication that the relationship between the patient and the health care provider is a lifelong relationship. Working from the principle that unplanned hospital admissions are a sign of system failure, Kaiser focuses on keeping people healthy, and ensuring effective links between hospitals and the community, so when patients do go in for treatment the right help is available as soon as they are ready to come out."

Kaiser has 8.6 million members – over 6.5 million of these are in California, the remainder across six other US regions. In 2009, the Kaiser Foundation Health Plan and Hospitals reported operating revenues of USD 42.1 billion. Although a small fraction of US health spending, its population and revenue make it larger than health systems in many smaller OECD countries. As in all examples from the United States, it is complex to match the complexity of the US health system including US federal structure. Kaiser consists of a tripartite structure of health plan, hospitals and autonomous doctors' groups.

Integration

Three aspects of integration contribute to Kaiser's performance:

- *Integration of financing and provision.* Hospital managers and doctors know they have to work within a set financing envelope, and work together to do this.

- *Integration of primary care and secondary hospital care.* The common distinction between primary and secondary care is not recognised by Kaiser employees (see Box 5.2). Specialists work both in Medical Centers and out in local Medical Offices. There is a creative model of interaction between specialists and primary care physicians. For example, primary care physicians may ring specialists and have a three-way consultation with the patient on the spot, rather than referring and waiting for a further appointment.

- *Integration of prevention, treatment and care.* In particular, people with chronic disease receive care from multidisciplinary teams in the community, and teams are bigger than traditional GP practices.

Box 5.2. **Integrated Care Pilots in England**

The National Health Service (NHS) has been committed for some time to improving care for those with chronic long-term conditions – shifting care into the community and closer to home, making care more personalised and supporting people living independently for longer. Yet is clear that the health system continues to fall short of its ambitions. One could argue that the organisational separation between general practice and hospital care is a design flaw in the NHS that renders such goals difficult to attain.

Lord Darzi's NHS Next Stage Review introduced the concept of Integrated Care Organisations (ICOs), intended to encourage primary care and other clinicians to take responsibility for designing, delivering, and ultimately managing the budget for integrated clinical services. Sixteen pilots in integrated care began in April 2009, designed to explore whether better care co-ordination can reduce utilisation and ultimately health care costs. The pilots take many different forms with most creating networks of providers operating under an integrated budget ("virtual integration"), and covering a range of chronic conditions including cardiovascular disease, chronic obstructive pulmonary disease, dementia, mental health, and substance abuse. The pilots are to be independently evaluated after two years.

Chronic care

Kaiser has a strong focus on members who have, or are at risk of developing, a chronic condition. Members are stratified into three levels of care (see Figure 5.2 below – the "Kaiser triangle").

Figure 5.2. **Population management: more than care and case management**

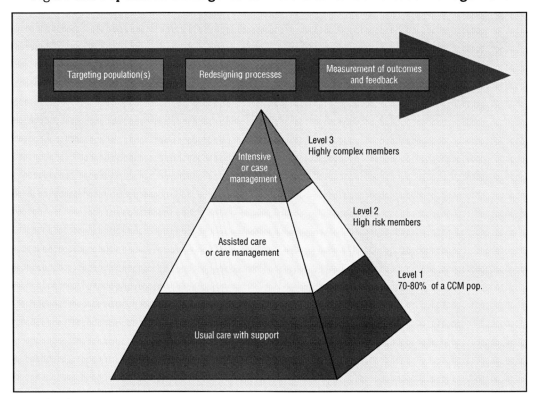

CCM: Chronic Care Management.
Source: The "Kaiser Triangle", adapted from Singh and Ham (2006).

Kaiser's population management approach includes an emphasis on prevention, self-management support, disease management, and case management for members with highly complex conditions. Self-management support includes providing information and education programmes, increasingly supported by IT. There is a strong focus on patient empowerment.

In-patient management

In international comparisons, Kaiser hospitalise patients much less frequently and with shorter lengths of stay compared to the UK NHS (Feachem, 2002; Ham, 2008). In comparison with the NHS, Kaiser used approximately one-third of the hospital beds and had higher rates of use of preventative measures for chronic diseases like diabetes and heart disease. The lower use of beds is driven by Kaiser's strong focus on active management of in-patients, using care pathways, discharge planners, and step-down rehabilitation facilities. Kaiser also employs general physicians ("hospitalists") as case managers in hospitals, to co-ordinate inputs from different specialists. The relative low use of hospital beds by Kaiser is the key factor that accounts for its cost effectiveness, and if its rate of use is applied to other health systems, like the NHS, then significant cost savings are possible (Feachem, 2002; Ham, 2008).

ICT

Kaiser is seen as a leader on IT and has a long history of using IT to support both administrative and clinical functions. Kaiser put USD 4.5 billion into developing and disseminating a new sophisticated health information system, HealthConnect, which includes advanced medical records, clinical decision support tools, and a robust on-line patient support. The system includes:

- Electronic prescribing and test ordering.

- Electronic referrals.

- Population management tools such as needed preventative measures treatments like screening tests.

- Clinical decision support tools such as medication safety reminders.

- Patient registration and billing.

- Performance monitoring.

The IT system allows patients to email securely their doctors with a 30% reduction in face-to-face appointments The IT system "nudges" staff to act in certain ways. For example, if new joiners to Kaiser are smokers, it will suggest a referral to smoking cessation support. Kaiser also has an extensive system for patient self-management of chronic diseases. The IT system allows patients to access their own medical records. It provides a wide range of support tools for patients with chronic diseases.

The IT system allows doctors to run "virtual clinics" between the primary care physicians and specialists like interpreting an x-ray or other diagnostic tests.

Kaiser has achieved real integration through partnerships between physicians and administration that allows it to exercise control and accountability across all components of the health care system. This allows it to manage patients in the most appropriate setting, implement disease management programmes for chronic disease that increase the uptake of prevention, and make trade-offs in expenditures based on appropriateness and cost effectiveness. Kaiser configures care according to the needs of the patient throughout an episode of illness, and for chronic illness throughout the patient's life. Kaiser achieves lower costs and superior performance though its enormous capacity to help to manage a constructive patient journey from out-patient services to hospital and to speciality services and back.

6. Disease management: a yet unproven tool for bending the cost curve

"The cost of avoiding costs is about equal to the avoided costs – at best."

During the 1990s in the United States, commercial health insurers widely adopted disease management programmes to improve outcomes and to decrease mounting health care costs due to chronic illness. Managed care, where service delivery functions were integrated like Kaiser, had shown that it was possible to provide lower health care costs for those with chronic illness, with fewer hospitalisations, if there was greater co-ordinated care. However, models like Kaiser are unique and difficult to replicate especially in a more heterogeneous health care system dominated by fee-for-service and a split between ambulatory primary care and specialist hospital care. Disease management is a way of achieving similar aims of care co-ordination for chronic diseases, but without formal integration and without major structural changes in the system.

In the US setting, this meant disease management programmes were often achieved through a third-party care co-ordinator. Often, the care management is done by nurses telephoning patients. There role includes ensuring care co-ordination, but also the use of clinical protocols based on evidence-based medicine, and also working on patient adherence to medications, ensuring patients get preventative services like eyes exams and foot care for diabetics. Disease Management Programmes (DMPs) initially focused on chronic diseases like diabetes, chronic obstructive pulmonary disease/asthma; heart failure; and other chronic conditions. The assumption is that this type of care co-ordination can prevent expensive hospitalisation and also that it is less expensive because it replaces physicians with lower-level health personnel using protocols.

What is disease management? Disease management as defined by its own professional organisation is "a system of co-ordinated health care interventions and communications for populations with conditions in which patient self-care efforts are significant". DM has been held out as a means of bringing the care of patients with chronic illness in line with evidence, thereby improving outcomes and reducing costs. A wide variety of interventions, settings, and target populations are feasible under this definition.

The Robert Wood Johnson Foundation categorised the burgeoning field of disease management and care co-ordination which can occur in many settings:

● *Primary care* is the logical setting for care management. However, many primary care practices are small and lack the financial and organisation capacity to implement care management.

● *Large multispecialty practice.* Some large practices have separate care management departments.

● *Vendor supported.* Under the commercial disease management model, care management is performed by nurses remotely via telephone.

● *Hospital to home.* Care managers meet with patients prior to discharge from the hospital and follow-up with home visits after discharge.

● *Home.* Care managers provide all services in patient's homes.

German health insurance defines it in law as: an organisational approach to medical care that involves the co-ordinated treatment and care of patients with chronic disease across boundaries between individual providers and on the basis of scientific and up-to-date evidence (Bundesministerium der Justiz, 2008).

Experience of disease management in US Medicare: it does not save money and has limited effect on quality of care

The most systematic evaluation of disease management and care co-ordination has been carried out in the United States by the Centers for Medicare and Medicaid Services (CMS) which administers the US Medicare and Medicaid public insurance programmes. Medicare costs have continued to rise more rapidly than the rest of the economy and make up an increasing larger share of the federal budget. There is an overriding goal of controlling Medicare spending and disease management programmes for chronic diseases were touted as a policy tool that would help save Medicare money. Beginning in 1999, Medicare began systematically experimenting with disease management programmes in many different guises to see whether they would help control Medicare spending by targeting Medicare patients with chronic diseases, especially high users of hospital services.

Table 5.2 summarises the disappointing findings of seven large scale demonstration projects with 35 programmes, testing a wide variety of DMP policy instruments. Almost none of the programmes saved Medicare money. Sometimes they decreased hospitalisations, but the costs of the disease management programme were more than the hospitalisations they averted. It is important to remember that co-ordinating care costs money and often theses costs are more than the costs they avert.

Most recently, researchers began publishing the results of Medicare Co-ordinated Care Demonstration (MCCD) which included 15 Randomised Controlled Trials on the effect of DMPs. Again, the findings are similarly negative, with no effect on saving money for Medicare and little improvement in any of the quality indicators. The 15 RCTS included a wide range of providers not only third party purveyors of disease management: five disease management organisations; three academic medical centres; one integrated delivery system; one hospice; one long-term care facility. A statistically significant improvement in clinical care was found in only one of the 15 demonstration projects. One of the important findings from the MCCD is that it is very difficult to get patients to change their behaviour. Most of the pilots struggled to get patients to exercise, improve their diet, stop smoking, and make other lifestyle changes to improve health and reduce costs. There may be scope for coupling to financial incentives – a promising idea of demand-side P4P.

The CMS demonstrations offer rich experience of the results of disease management in the context of Medicare patients. It must be stressed this is a very particular situation, where Medicare represents elderly patients. It also occurs not in the competitive insurance market, where disease management programmes are common place, but in the traditional fee-for-service Medicare environment. Still, the results are very sobering, given the early promise raised by disease management. The theory that evidence-based guidelines and care co-ordination would save money is intuitively appealing, the case appears strong, but the evidence that it works effectively continues to elude us.

Reflecting on almost two decades of experience, Medicare officials write: "Results from the CMS demonstration have not shown widespread evidence of improvement in compliance with evidence-based care, satisfaction for providers or beneficiaries or broad behaviour change. Only a few programmes have produced financing savings net of fees. … Unfortunately, no single measured programme or intervention characteristic, or even a small subset of them, stands out as a clear and consistent determinant of overall programme success in the evaluation."

It is accepted that care management programmes need time to bed down and show their value in the health system. Co-ordinating care in a complex system often requires a long-time particularly when there is not a common culture like Kaiser where everyone is committed to higher quality care at the lowest possible cost. There are also significant upfront investments, and the benefits often take many years to show up. Medicare continues to develop new demonstrations and refine old ones. OECD countries can learn from this rich experience.

Experience of incorporating chronic diseases into fee-for-service primary care: Germany and Austria

The innovations of managed care in the United States were closely studied by other health systems like Germany, United Kingdom and Australia. For systems with a long-standing divide between primary care/general practice and hospital specialist care,

Table 5.2. **Evaluation of US Medicare disease management initiatives**

Demonstration	Sites	Population	Intervention	Results
IdeaTel Informatics, telemedicine, and education demonstration	1	1 093	Home telemedicine "visits" with Nurse Case Manager	Improved patient satisfaction Improved clinical outcomes *Net increase in Medicare costs*
Case management Case management demonstration for heart failure and diabetes Mellitus	1	257	Case manage with in-person assessments and telephonic monitoring	Improved quality of care Reduction in hospitalisation *Costs savings less than programme costs*
Co-ordinated care Medicare Co-ordinated Care Demonstration	15	13 379	Case management, telephonic management, telemonitoring	Improved quality of care *Increased Medicare costs by 11%*
DIPA DM Medicare Disease Management for Severely Chronically Ill	3	18 165	Telephonic disease management and prescription drug benefit with remote monitoring of heart failure patients	One programme improved quality of care *Medicare cost increase*
DM Dual Eligibles Disease Management for Dual Eligible Beneficiaries (Medicare + Medicaid)	1	30 000	Predominately telephonic disease management by nurses, supplemented with in-home case management	First phase cost increasing, *Second phase re-design with targeted population is recouping costs*
High cost Care Management for High Cost Beneficiaries	6	47 000	Each programme tests different intervention. Interventions include physicians, nurse home visits, in-home monitoring devices, caregiver support and education, preventive care tracking and reminders, 24 hour nurse telephone lines	*Two of six saving costs*
MHS Medicare health Support (Chronic Care Improvement Programmes)	8	206 000	Care and disease management telephonic health coaching also telemonitoring	*Medicare costs increase of 5-11%*

Source: Botts *et al.* (2009).

integrated solutions like Kaiser were infeasible. Disease management offered promise of solving the co-ordination between primary and secondary care for chronic disease management. They looked to the United States experience on disease management and adapted to their health systems.

The US experience is quite different from other countries because it relies on the use of third party for-profit firms to provide disease management. In Germany and Austria, the idea is to embed disease management into primary care. In these systems, disease management means making additional payments in a fee-for-service system to pay GPs to co-ordinate care. In a traditional fee-for-service system, GPs have little incentive to prioritise prevention or co-ordination of care. Therefore additional payments are made to take on this role along with clinical guidelines, improvements in IT, and patient support.

The German case is of particular interest because the driving force behind the changes was a profound change in the funding formula to German insurance funds. The change in the risk equalisation scheme meant that insurance funds received additional capitated funds for patients enrolled in disease management programmes. This meant it was now worth their while to enrol patients with chronic diseases and also to improve the efficiency of their care.

The German insurance funds forced the medical profession to accept case management principles. In 2002, the government formally introduced structured disease management into the statutory health insurance system, where it was defined legally as "an organisational approach to medical care that involves co-ordinated treatments and care of patients with chronic disease across boundaries between individual providers on the basis of scientific up-to-date evidence". This includes a fixed payment to primary care for specific disease management. DMP were introduced for breast cancer, type 2 diabetes, coronary artery disease (2004), asthma (2006) and COPD (2006). By June 2007, there were more than 14 000 contracts for DMP. By 2005, over 2 million people were enrolled in DMPs (see Figure 5.3). It is estimated that almost 70% of diabetics are registered in DMPs (Nolte, 2009).

Figure 5.3. **Disease management programmes in Germany**

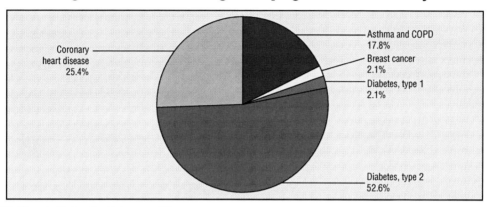

COPD: Chronic Obstructive Pulmonary Disease.
Source: Adapted from AOK Bundesverband (2009b).

StatLink ⟨⟨⟩⟩ *http://dx.doi.org/10.1787/888932319516*

The introduction of DMP in Germany came as a response to a report (from the Advisory Council on the Assessment of Developments in Health Care, SVR) indicating that the German health system had not adapted to the shift of the burden of disease towards chronic illness. The report highlighted the dominance of acute care, the lack of preventive services, and the passive status of chronic disease patients as recipients of medical services. It also pointed to the strict separation between ambulatory and hospital care, the lack of incentives, and lack of evidence-based clinical guidelines. All of these factors contributed to poor co-ordination and low quality of care for the chronically ill.

The primary aim of DMP introduction was the improvement of quality of medical care for patients with chronic diseases and not simply cost saving. The DMPs in Germany contain the following key elements:

State-of-the-art medical treatment according to the best available evidence and evidence-based clinical guidelines.

● Quality assurance measures.

● Standardised criteria and procedures for in- and exclusion of patients.

● Structured education/training for care providers and especially for patients.

● Monitoring of performance measures.

● Evaluation of efficiency and costs.

The DMPs also contain specific regulations for the co-ordination of care to overcome the barriers between the different health care sectors. The treatment recommendations urge physicians to improve interdisciplinary co-operation (between physicians of different specialties, hospitals, and rehabilitation). Indications when to transfer the patient to the qualified specialists are foreseen in the programmes in order to ensure the comprehensiveness of care.

DMPs seem to have had a positive impact on improving the quality of care particularly for diabetes. The German Federal Doctors Association ("Kassenärztlichen Bundesvereinigung") reported that overall quality targets for the DMPs on type 2 diabetes could be fully achieved in five of nine specified clinical parameters (Kassenärztlichen Bundesvereinigung, 2009). Another study showed improved quality of life for those enrolled in DMPs (Ose et al., 2009). Yet another study found a significant improvement in the quality of care between patients enrolled in the national DMP compared to those not enrolled. The biggest improvements were for care co-ordination including follow-up and greater involvement of patients in their own care.

One study reported that participation in DMP type 2 diabetes reduced mortality after three years (Miksch et al., 2010). The overall mortality rate was 11.3% in the DMP and 14.4% in the non-DMP group. Another study found that participants in a DMP type 2 diabetes had significantly fewer strokes and amputation (Graf et al., 2009). Overall, it appears that the DMPs for diabetes significantly improved the quality of care for patients with chronic diseases.

The issue of whether DMPs in Germany save money remains unclear (see Figure 5.4). There is some evidence that patients in DMPs appear to have less hospitalisation compared to the unenrolled. Not surprisingly, the costs for ambulatory care increased, since there was a greater number of visits in primary care. Drug cost remained the same. On balance, there appears to be scope for efficiency gains from disease management due to reduction in hospitalisation.

Austria is following the path of Germany and has begun to introduce disease management programmes. In 2007, a DMP for type 2 diabetes was launched ("Therapie Aktiv") and is growing rapidly (see Figure 5.5). In Salzburg, a cluster randomised, controlled intervention study was conducted involving 98 physicians (48 interventions, 50 controls) and 1 494 patients (654 interventions and 840 controls). The Salzburg study, one of the largest randomised controlled studies in the field of disease management, showed improved diabetes control (a significant reduction of HbA1c levels), improved control of hypertension (reduction in blood pressure), and increased uptake of preventive measures (eyes and feet examination). The study will continue to follow patients and will provide information on long-term effects of disease management (Sönnichsen et al., 2008).

The German and Austrian cases appear to provide promising evidence on the effectiveness of disease management programmes particularly for diabetes. This suggests that the US context and experience may not always be applicable to other countries and that disease management has the promise to improve care co-ordination and potentially improve the efficiency and effectiveness of chronic care management.

One might speculate that the results for Germany and Austria would differ from the United States because they use primary care as the care co-ordinator. This may be less expensive than the use of a separate care co-ordinator. Relying on primary care for co-ordination also avoids the burden of creating a new organisation. Furthermore, in Germany and Austria, DMPs constitute one of the first significant attempts to introduce clinical guidelines. In addition, the US co-ordinated care trials were only for patients over 65 who may be less prepared to change their behaviour in response to DMPs.

Figure 5.4. **DMPs for type 2 diabetes programmes reduce hospital cost**

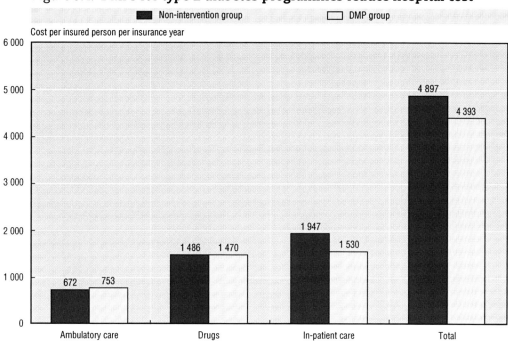

DMP: Disease Management Programmes.
Source: Adapted from AOK-Bundesverband (2009a).

StatLink http://dx.doi.org/10.1787/888932319535

Figure 5.5. **Enrolment in DMP type 2 diabetes in Austria, May 2010**

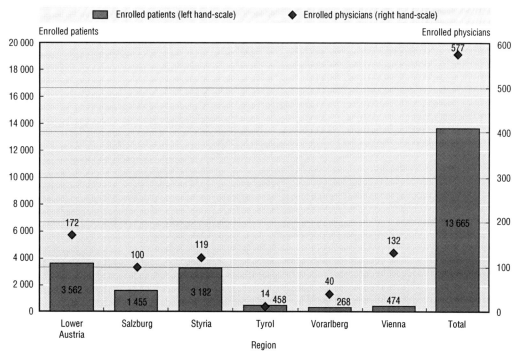

Source: Adapted from *http://diabetes.therapie-aktiv.at.*

StatLink http://dx.doi.org/10.1787/888932319554

The effects on costs still remain speculative. The costs of setting up the programmes is high and that there is a cost to co-ordination. The question is whether this cost is offset by reductions in hospitalisations. In the Medicare Co-ordinated Care trials, the reductions were very small and did not offset the additional programme costs. Further evaluation is needed in Germany and Austria to see whether DMPs actually save money.

However, even if these investments do not generate cost savings for the health system, they may improve health in a cost-effective manner. Disease management programmes should be thought of as "technologies of care" similar to other interventions like drugs and should be perhaps measured on a similar metrics. Instead of thinking whether these interventions save money, we should ask whether they achieve value for money or achieve an improvement in outcomes commensurate with their costs. If this looser standard is used, many of these interventions would be considered cost-effective compared to other standard interventions.

Other countries

Some additional countries have begun to establish programmes of this kind and others are experimenting with such arrangements but they remain at a very early stage, often in the form of pilots: only one quarter of the reporting countries indicated programmes of this nature and these most frequently concern diabetes.

Assessing whether such programmes have the desired impact on performance is not straightforward. There are large differences between the programmes in terms of structure and intent. Evaluations differ due to the length of time of the trials and in the methodology used for evaluation. The bulk of the information comes from the United States, where the institutional environment for finance and provision of health care differs from most other countries. While it is probably too early to take a definitive view of their effects, it would appear, nonetheless, that these programmes have an impact on the *quality of care* although the impact can depend on the illness in question.

There are several possible reasons for this outcome: high costs of setting up programmes and running them; the fact that these programmes may reveal unmet needs; and, inadequate matching of care and follow-up with the degree of need. The latter can be technically difficult, particularly where there is only limited clinical or other information – such as the degree of family support – available for this purpose. To achieve consistently better performance of health care systems, such targeted programmes may need to be developed within broader efforts to improve care co-ordination and to make care delivery more patient-centred.

Lessons learned: what is good practice?

In terms of good practice, IGAS (2006) suggests three broad conditions that appear likely to increase the chances of a positive result:

1. Where providers are more integrated – either in physician group network models, in staff model HMOs such as Kaiser Permanente or in the US Veterans Hospital Administration.[5]

2. Where other medical personnel such as nurses or social workers and pharmacists are integrated into the care process and follow-up.

3. Where programmes encourage patients to change their behaviour through patient education and self-help. Indeed, programmes which combine both patient education

and a stronger role of other medical personnel than doctors seem to reinforce each other and have a stronger overall impact.[6]

In sum, disease management programmes have the potential to improve health outcomes and to raise system performance in terms of quality even if the impact on costs remains uncertain. However these models are only one approach to enhancing care co-ordination. Recent policies in a number of countries are also seeking to provide appropriate and safe care outside of hospitals by strengthening the role of ambulatory care delivery. In this context, more attention may need to be paid to ensuring that information flows, care capacity, incentives and patterns of provision in the ambulatory sector are adequate to support such changes.

7. Improving the cost effectiveness of disease management

Predictive modelling

One of the issues with Medicare co-ordinated care trials is that they were open to everyone with chronic diseases. If one could limit the intervention largely to those for whom it worked, then the cost effectiveness of the DMPs would be enhanced. In fact, it appears that in the United States, private insurance companies using DMPs already do this (Lewis, 2010). The question is whether one could identify patients for whom case management would work. In essence, you are doing exactly the opposite of a randomised controlled trial and using the information on characteristics of patients who benefit as a way of predicting who will benefit.

Impact models are tools that are designed to identify systematically the subset of at-risk enrolees in whom preventive care is expected to be successful (Weber and Neeser, 2006). It predicts who will acquire a disease, an adverse event related to a disease, or change from one health (functioning) state to another, where these outcomes are impactible with some specific intervention such as taking or stopping a medication, doing a test, reducing avoidable medical costs, making a behavioural change, or changing the person's environment (Duncan, 2004).

Impactability models build on predictive models and can be used to identify people at high risk of unplanned hospitalisation. However, predictive hospitalisation models identify patients at-risk for hospitalisation, but some of these high risk patients identified may not be amenable to preventive care. Impactability models aim to identify the subset of at-risk patients in whom preventive care is expected to be successful. They also can exclude patients who are least likely to engage in preventative care. They can also be used to match preventative care interventions to the characteristics of the patient that are most likely to work.

Since the 1980s, risk adjustment tools have become more widely used in health care. They are at the heart of capitation systems particularly the new competitive insurance model in the Netherlands and Germany which use risk adjustment to determine payments to insurance funds for different patients. Risk adjustment is one of the key building blocks on this new model of competitive health insurance funds (Bevan and Van de Ven, 2010).

Risk adjustment methods can be used to predict future hospitalisations, but these predictions are unreliable. High cost patients have markedly lower costs in the future even without intervention, a phenomenon called "regression to the mean". This means that disease management programmes should not focus on patients who are currently experiencing multiple hospital admissions. Instead, the focus should be on predicting those who are at higher risk for being hospitalised in the future. This type of predictive modelling is being used in English "virtual ward" projects which show some promise in reducing hospital admissions. It uses productive models to generate predictions and then uses multiaxial teams including health and social care to carry out virtual rounds on the patients (Lewis, 2010).

Another promising approach is using modelling to predict receptivity to behavioural change. Although it is well accepted that prevention would improve health outcomes like getting a patient to stop smoking or lose weight, often the patient is not ready to change. Some predictive modelling techniques predict whether a patient is likely to be ready to change their behaviour. There are many different methods being used to predict patients' receptivity and expected engagement with preventative care using concepts such as "patient activation" or "co-operability". Some standard instruments have been developed such as Patient Activation Measures (Hibbard *et al.*, 2004), or using patient characteristics such as previous non-compliance or similarity to other successful patients.

Predictive modelling and impactability tools may significantly increase the cost effectiveness of disease management tools. If the expensive intervention could be targeted, similar to a drug, to those who would respond, then its effectiveness could be enhanced. It still might not be cost savings, but it may make disease management programmes a good purchase based on value for money.

Collaborative care model – lessons from mental health

One area where disease management appears to work is mental health. There are numerous clinical trials in mental health showing that care co-ordination improves outcomes. A comprehensive meta-analysis of effectiveness of the collaborative care model in mental health showed that it significantly improved health outcomes. It showed 25% improved quality of life at six months and 15% at five years. UK studies show even higher effectiveness. These are very substantial gains compared to common medical treatments.

Based on extensive RCTs, the collaborative care model in treatment of depression includes the following important elements:

- Physician time.
- Care manager services.
- Specialty consultation.
- Registry-decision support.

Figure 5.6 presents eight studies of the cost effectiveness of the collaborative care model. Each of the points shows the relative effectiveness of collaborative care model for the treatment of moderate depression. The chart shows that there is vast number of studies demonstrating the effectiveness of the intervention (*e.g.* all of the studies show that it improves clinical outcomes). The vast majority of the studies show that the improvement in outcomes is at a relatively low cost, and it is below the traditional threshold used by UK NICE for evaluating new drugs (approximately USD 50 000 per QALY).

Even if one is fairly conservative in making assumptions about effectiveness, it still appears to be good value for money. It is important to emphasize that the cost effectiveness of DMP for depression does not necessarily mean that it will save money. However, it is highly cost effective and more cost effective than treatments in other disease areas. Furthermore, the cost effectiveness would be enhanced if it included a wider

Figure 5.6. **Primary care depression**

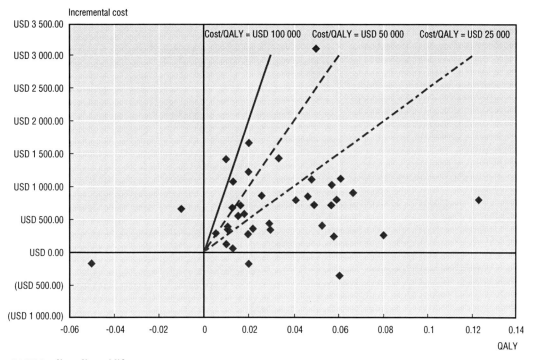

QALY: Quality adjusted life years.

Note: Data points represent randomised controlled trials.

Source: Adapted from Glied *et al.* (2010).

definition of costs included the costs of employment. Treatment of depression means people are more likely to return to work and not to be on the disability system. Addition of these costs into the equation would further enhance the cost-effectiveness ratio and perhaps even shift the balance to cost savings.

The collaborative care models that use stepped care are even more cost effective. This is when the intensity is stepped up only when proven necessary. Patients are first offered an intervention that while likely to be effective is relatively easy to implement and carries relatively low cost or side effects. If the effect turns out to be insufficient, treatment is stepped up to a more complex costly or taxing level. The aim is to ensure that all eligible patients have access to appropriate care, while reserving the most complex treatments for those that have demonstrated not to benefit from more simple treatments.

Disease management for mental illness appears to be more cost effective than many other diseases. Perhaps, this is because the co-ordination plays such as a central role in management of the disease. First, adherence to medication and psychotherapy plays critical role in achieving good outcomes. DMPs can assure better standardisation of psychotherapy. It can also play an important role in better medication adherence by ensuring that patients have more regular discussions on side effects and changing treatment as needed. In addition, it can also ensure better co-ordination between mental and physical illness which is often a critical co-ordination problem for people with mental diseases. Finally, early detection and treatment of mental disorders is likely to prevent expensive hospital stays.

Palliative care

Palliative care describes the type of patient-centered and responsive care provided to patients with chronic or severe and life-threatening illnesses. In contrast with curative care often geared toward infectious or acute diseases, this approach is primarily focused on reducing pain and improving the quality of life through life prolonging treatments and therapies. Holistically incorporating the physiological and psychosocial needs of the patient, palliative care also seeks to involve the family and social networks of the patient. Informed medical decision making is made taking into consideration the practical needs as well as the personal goals of the patient through the administration of high quality care.

Palliative care can be provided in a variety of settings from the hospital to home to hospice. Administered through the continuum of care, palliative care can be integrated in the hospital or home through co-ordination with conventional health care professionals or through specialists trained in palliative medicine. With the focus of palliative care being on the patient and providing family support, innovative approaches are employed with health care professionals receiving specialised training for managing and caring for the patient through this care pathway. For advanced stage diseases including cancer and dementia, the approach appears to improve quality of life and patient empowerment through control of symptoms. Patients and families generally report better higher quality and satisfaction with the care received. Although limited data is available from effectiveness research, results show that palliative care improves quality of care and quality of life through reduced symptom distress and improved satisfaction for the patient and family members (Gelfman, 2008).

Recent studies of hospital-based palliative care programmes have found these to be highly cost effective and even cost saving. Palliative care consultation services in hospital show reported improvements in clinical care and reductions in the utilisation of costly intensive care unit services (Morrison *et al.*, 2008). Palliative care consultations have been associated with reduced length of hospital stay (Smith and Cassel, 2009).

Where other care approaches may be centered on treating the disease with high-cost technology and effective therapies, with health care workers administering best practices of known treatments, palliative care offers a distinctly patient centered and patient empowering approach. When administered at end-of-life, palliative care responds most effectively to the goals of the patient and family and may avoid aggressive and costly care. Where chronic conditions requiring long-term care are on the rise in developed countries, palliative care in the home may have the potential to offer increases in the quality of care and patient satisfaction while reducing the strain of hospital resources. While some of the savings from palliative care in the home generally come from more informal care provided by the family, caregiver satisfaction is reported to be high (Carter *et al.*, 2010).

End-of-life care is very costly particularly for cancer. As survival rates increase, cancer services are placing greater strain on limited resources. End-of-life care is often considered the most costly phase of health care and a target for cost-effectiveness measures. Palliative care may offer alternatives to conventional hospital care that may be more effective (Garcia-Perez, 2009) and cost saving (Remonnay, 2005). Particularly for cancer patients, palliative care options may offer options for continued care in the home setting that may be preferred by patients and families. Palliative care appears to offer alternatives to conventional hospital-based therapies for the treatment of long-term care for chronic conditions, late-stage cancer care and dementia, some of costliest areas of health care for developed countries.

Care co-ordination and HIV/AIDS

With the advent of effective therapy, AIDS has changed from a terminal communicable disease to a chronic disease, where good care co-ordination is essential. Initially, care co-ordination for AIDS was an issue for largely for OECD countries, who could afford AIDS treatment, but with decreasing prices for AIDS drugs and concerted effort by the international community to improve access to antiretroviral therapy, there has been a large increase in the number of people on treatment for AIDS in low and middle income countries. There is a consensus on the need to shift from an exclusively acute care model to a chronic care model that includes antiretroviral therapy, but is wider. One of the drivers of new approaches to AIDS is the need to ensure strict adherence to complex medication regimes, as lack of adherence leads to the development of resistance to the drugs similar to antibiotics and multi-drug resistant HIV is increasing.

In terms of care co-ordination, a variety of medical and social needs are required by persons living with HIV/AIDS. Clinical care should focus on identifying opportunistic infections during the early part of clinical management to ensure better care co-ordination. For later stages of clinical management, palliative care should be combined with social support. There is also a need to ensure a continuing focus on prevention for those living with AIDS. Comprehensive approaches to care delivery also include case management, often through community health workers or patient navigators. In order to ensure the continuum of care (Praag and Tarantola, 2001), counselling services should be provided before meeting specific clinical needs of patients. Indeed, synergy exists between levels of health care (home and community, primary, secondary, tertiary) and calls for well-defined roles and functions within each element of the care continuum.

The core functions of case managers are quite similar to other diseases: needs assessment, development of a care plan, linking clients with services, monitoring patient progress, and advocacy or barrier removal (Piette *et al.*, 1992). There have been numerous studies showing that case management for AIDS leads to better outcomes (Katz *et al.*, 2001; Sherer *et al.*, 2002; Twyman and Libbus, 1994; Havens *et al.*, 1997). Most studies have found that case management is associated with better adherence to treatment, fewer unmet needs, and better health-related quality of life (Chernesky, 1999; Kushel *et al.*, 2006). There have also been studies comparing differences when case management is organised in the hospital versus through community-based case managers (London *et al.*, 1998; Payne *et al.*, 1992). In general, in OECD countries there is increasingly emphasis on managing patients in the community similar to other chronic disease management. According to several studies, the use of community health workers improves health outcomes and care for patients (Gary *et al.*, 2004; Fedder *et al.*, 2003).

8. Achieving better returns from care co-ordination

At the centre of the co-ordination challenge is the need to have coherent oversight of the various resources used for chronically ill patients. As we have seen in the cases described above, there are many different ways of going about that – but no single successful model that can be put forward to follow. Instead, we can draw lessons from the successes and failures to date – and suggest policies that are likely to increase the value health systems can get from better co-ordination. It is important to remember that there is a cost to co-ordination and this must be balanced by the gain. It is also important to emphasize the role of the patient and their family in managing their own care.

Incentives

Many OECD countries are increasingly using financial incentives to encourage providers to improve the quality of care for chronic diseases. Most P4P schemes incentivise the use of preventive services or adherence to evidence-based guidelines. The results on P4P have been similar to disease management programmes. They have not been systematically evaluated. Most of the evaluations suggest there may be an effect, but it is not dramatic. As in disease management programmes, there is a cost to the intervention itself. For example, the UK Quality Outcome Framework was very expensive and significantly increased the pay to primary care practitioners without large increases in the quality of care.

Although P4P schemes have not had dramatic effects, it is important to ensure that incentives are aligned to achieve improved outcomes. The performance of these models will strongly depend on contractual relations between the providers and payers (e.g. fee-for-service versus capitation). Payment systems should pay for the service of co-ordination, given its importance for chronic diseases. Incentives also need to be aligned to encourage the use of multiaxial teams who are co-ordinating information. Incentives also have a role in modifying provider behaviour such as adherence to evidence-based clinical guidelines.

ICT is a barrier

While Information and Communications Technology (ICT) appears to hold promise as a vehicle for this purpose, the penetration of information technology has remained weak to date in many countries despite increased government efforts in this area and significantly improved technology. Questionnaire results suggest that information on medical records and patient needs is "often" shared among providers in only half of the countries. We are a long way from Kaiser's HealthConnect and linked information systems that could decrease duplication of tests, medication errors, automatic prompts for preventative interventions, etc.

Supply-side constraints – workforce

Most countries have experienced a shift in the supply of care from an in-patient to an out-patient environment as technology has allowed more individuals to be cared for in ambulatory environments. Multidisciplinary teams involving medical and non-medical professionals are required to provide more coherent care for patients with multiple pathologies. Systems dominated by providers operating in solo practice and paid for on a fee-for-service basis may be less-well suited to meeting the care needs of the chronically ill. Instead, GP needs to become the hub of a multidisciplinary team of professionals working on similar patients.

Transition to long-term care

A European study found that the management of patients at transitions to long-term care was facilitated if the care models had included a clear statement that co-ordination/ integration is a task on its own, with respective skills and methods, i.e. "co-ordination as a profession" (Leichsenring et al., 2004). In this context, the promotion of a "shared culture" in teams has been found to mitigate some of the resistance of medical providers towards multidisciplinary work (Coxon et al., 2004). Thus, profiles of health care professionals and, in particular, of medical professionals involved in co-ordinating care need to be adapted to the multifaceted challenge of "curing" and "caring" for chronically ill patients.

9. Conclusions

The Medicare demonstrations are sobering, but then again, the story is similar to hope that prevention would save money. These investments do not generate cost savings for the health system, but they may improve health in a cost-effective manner. Disease management programmes should be thought of as "technologies of care" similar to other interventions like drugs and should be perhaps measured on a similar metrics. Instead of thinking whether these interventions save money, we should ask whether they achieve value for money or achieve an improvement in outcomes commensurate with their costs. If this looser standard is used, many of these interventions would likely be effective compared to other standard interventions. In fact, some of the CMS projects actually show small cost savings. If some of the programmes were better targeted, their cost effectiveness would improve.

The experience from integrated systems like Kaiser suggests that it is important to put together all of the elements of integration in order to achieve the results of better value for money. You need the structures, the technical components, but also the culture and strategy to achieve these results (Shortell, 2000). With only a couple of the components, the outcomes appear to be less. However, there do appear to be areas that are particularly promising such as mental health and palliative care.

It seems obvious that greater care co-ordination *should* lead to better health outcomes, for instance by making sure that one intervention does not nullify the contribution of another, that effort is not duplicated, or that the various actors, including the patient, are well-informed of what is being done, by whom, why, and (too often overlooked) when. However, there is a degree of dissonance between this intuition and many of the experiences described above. Results regarding the benefits of co-ordination have often been disappointing or unclear. Why has it proven to be so difficult to realise the potential of care co-ordination?

One robust conclusion seems to be that co-ordinated care works best when the system is designed in a co-ordinated manner to begin with. This includes the structures (hospital and ambulatory care), the technical components (evidence-based guidelines, decision aids, a common IT system) and aligned incentives, but also culture and strategy. As a number of studies (for example Shortell, 2000) show that attempting to impose co-ordination on a disparate collection of practitioners, payers, patients and pathologies is resource intensive, and, whatever the health outcomes, likely to save little if any money. Being less ambitious, by focusing on particular diseases or correcting the most incompatible parts of the unco-ordinated system, may yield higher returns. This may explain the success of the disease management programmes in Germany and Austria for example. Areas such as mental health and palliative care are also particularly promising for reaping benefits from partial integration, along with transition to long-term care.

As with nearly all aspects of health policy (and indeed policy in general), there are gaps and weaknesses in the evidence and in the tools used to analyse care co-ordination. For instance, the successful adaptation of disease management programmes from the United States to primary care in Germany shows the importance of cross-country lesson learning and offers lessons to other countries, particularly those where health care is purchased by insurance funds. In this regard, it would be useful if more common metrics were established to allow better cross-country learning. There is also a need to better understand the continuing challenge raised by chronic diseases for modern health systems, and to better understand which tools work best and under what circumstances before attempting to reproduce the success achieved in one set of circumstances elsewhere.

There is hope that health systems can move closer to the chronic care model envisaged by Wagner, but perhaps it is also time to revisit this model which was developed when physicians still dominated health care. Now, with patients' rights more central to health systems, the chronic care model is evolving towards a new model of patient empowerment. This means new tools like greater use of personal budgets and greater scope for patient user groups – virtually unexplored terrain for many OECD health systems, and one that offers promise for improving value for money in treating chronic diseases.

Notes

1. While almost three countries out of four see a GP managing patients at the interface between primary care and ambulatory specialists, the likelihood of guidance from the primary-care level declines at successive interfaces such that only one in five countries judged that guidance to patients is given "often" by a primary-care provider.

2. However, 30% of countries indicate that they infrequently refer hospital patients back to primary care providers, suggesting, for example, that problems of information transmission may be important in many countries.

3. In addition, countries that are particularly concerned with problems at these interfaces also appear to be those that are highly concerned about efficiency issues more generally (see Table 5.2).

4. For example, Boerma (2003) finds that home visits are more likely if providers are paid on a fee-for-service basis and that GPs spend less time with patients in countries where they work under a mixed capitation scheme (compared with countries with salary and fee-for-service).

5. Better performance was partly attributed to the strong ICT support systems in the last two institutions. In this context, payment-for-performance approaches were also seen as having a positive impact.

6. They also note that in the United States a number of other factors can reduce the impact of such programmes including: lack of insurance coverage; cultural barriers for ethnic minorities; proximity to care; co-morbidities and mental problems.

Bibliography

Advisory Council on the Assessment of Developments in the Health Care System (2007), "Cooperation and Responsibility, Prerequisites for Target-Oriented Health Care".

AOK-Bundesverband (2009a), "Chronikerprogramme lohnen sich", *Gesundheit und Gesellschaft*, Vol. 6/2009.

AOK-Bundesverband (2009b), "Disease Management Programme", *Gesundheit und Gesellschaft*, Vol. Spezial 9/2009.

Bevan, R.G. and W. Van de Ven (2010), "Choice of Provider and Mutual Healthcare Purchaser: Can the English National Health Service Learn Dutch Reform", *Health Economics, Policy and Law*, pp. 1-27.

Bodenheimer, T., E.H. Wagner and K. Grumbach (2002), "Improving Primary Care for Patients with Chronic Illness", *Journal of the American Medical Association*, Vol. 14, pp. 1775-1779.

Boerma, W.G.W. (2003), *Profiles of General Practice in Europe: An International Study of Variation in the Tasks of General Practitioners*, NIVEL, Utrecht.

Botts, D.M., M.C. Kapp, L.B. Johnson and L.M. Magno (2009), "Disease Management for Chronically Ill Beneficiaries in Traditional Medicare", *Health Affairs*, Vol. 28, No. 1, pp. 86-98.

Bundesministerium der Justiz (2008), "Verordnung über das Verfahren zum Risikostrukturausgleich in der gesetzlichen Krankenversicherung", Bundesministerium der Justiz, Berlin, available at *www.bundesrecht.juris.de/rsav/BJNR005500994.html*.

Carter, G.L. *et al.* (2010), "Caregiver Satisfaction with Out-patient Oncology Services: Utility of the FAMCARE Instrument and Development of the FAMCARE-6", *Support Care Cancer*, published online 28 March 2010.

Chernesky R.H. (1999), "A Review of HIV/AIDS Case Management Research", *Care Manag J*, Vol. 1, pp. 105-113.

Coxon, K. *et al.* (2004), "Inter-professional Working and Integrated Care Organizations", in J. Billings and K. Leichsenring (eds.), *Long-term Care in Integrating Health and Social Care Services for Older Persons, Evidence from Nine European Countries*, European Centre, Ashgate, Vienna.

Darzi, Lord (2008), "High Quality Care for All: NHS Next Stage Review Final Report", Department of Health, United Kingdom.

Duncan, I. (2004), "Dictionary of Disease Management Terminology", *Disease Management Association of America*, Washington, DC.

Feachem, R.G.A., N.K. Sekhri and K.L. White (2002), "Getting More for Their Dollar: A Comparison of the NHS with California's Kaiser Permanente", *BMJ*, No. 324, pp. 135-143.

Fedder, D.O., R.J. Chang, S. Curry and G. Nichols (2003), "The Effectiveness of a Community Health Worker Outreach Program on Healthcare Utilization of West Baltimore City Medicaid Patients with Diabetes, With or Without Hypertension", *Ethn Dis*, Vol. 13, pp. 22-27.

Garica-Perez, L. *et al.* (2009), "A Systematic Review of Specialised Palliative Care for Terminal Patients: Which Model is Better?", *Palliative Medicine*, Vol. 23, No. 1, pp. 17-22.

Gary, T.L., M. Batts-Turner, L. R. Bone *et al.* (2004), "A Randomized Controlled Trial of the Effects of Nurse Case Manager and Community Health Worker Team Interventions in Urban African-Americans with Type 2 Diabetes", *Control Clin Trials*, Vol. 25, pp. 53-66.

Gelfman, L.P. (2008), "Does Palliative Care Improve Quality? A Survey of Bereaved Family Members", *Journal of Pain and Symptom Management*, Vol. 36, No. 1, pp. 22-28.

Glied, S., K. Herzog and R. Frank (2010), "The Net Benefits of Depression Management in Primary Care", *Medical Care Research and Review*, Vol. 67, No. 3, pp. 251-274.

Graf, C., T. Elkeles and W. Kirschner (2009), "Is there a Selection Bias in Disease Management Programmes for Diabetes Care? Results of a National Insurance Survey Regarding DMP-participants and Non-participants", *Zeitschrift für Allgemeinmedizin*, Vol. 85, pp. 74-81.

Ham, C. (2008), "Incentives, Priorities and Clinical Integration in the NHS", *The Lancet*, Vol. 371, pp. 98-100.

Havens P.L., B.E. Cuene, J.R. Hand *et al.* (1997), "Effectiveness of Intensive Nurse Case Management in Decreasing Vertical Transmission of Human Immunodeficiency Virus Infection in Wisconsin", *Pediatr Infect Dis*, Vol. 16, pp. 871-875.

Hibbard, J.H., J. Stockard, E.R. Mahoney and M. Tusler (2004), "Development of the Patient Activation Measure (PAM): Conceptualizing and Measuring Activation in Patients and Consumers", *Health Services Research*, Vol. 39, pp. 1005-1026.

Hofmarcher, M.M., H. Oxley and E. Rusticelli (2007), "Improved Health System Performance through Better Care Coordination", OECD Health Working Paper, No. 30, OECD Publishing, Paris.

IGAS (2006), "Améliorer la prise en charge des malades chroniques : les enseignements des expériences étrangères de 'disease management'", Report presented by Pierre Louis Bras, Gilles Duhamel and Etienne Grass, Inspection Générale des Affaires Sociales, Paris.

IMAI/IMCI publications, available at *www.who.int/hiv/pub/imai/en/index.html*.

Kassenärztliche Bundesvereinigung (2009), *Qualitätsbericht Ausgabe*.

Katz, M.H., W.E. Cunningham, J.A. Fleishman *et al.* (2001), "Effect of Case Management on Unmet Needs and Utilization of Medical Care and Medications among HIV-infected Persons", *Ann Intern Med*, Vol. 135, pp. 557-565.

Kushel M. B., G. Colfax, K. Ragland *et al.* (2006), "Case Management is Associated with Improved Antiretroviral Adherence and CD4+ Cell Counts in Homeless and Marginally Housed Individuals with HIV Infection", *Clin Infect Dis*, Vol. 43, pp. 234-242.

Leichsenring, K. *et al.* (2004), "Moments of Truth. An Overview of Pathways to Integration and Better Quality", in J. Billings and K. Leichsenring (eds.), *Long-term Care in Integrating Health and Social Care Services for Older Persons, Evidence from Nine European Countries*, European Centre, Ashgate, Vienna.

Lewis, G. (2010), "Impactability Models: Identifying Subgroups of High Risk Patients Most Amenable to Hospital Avoidance Programs", *Milbank Memorial Fund Quarterly*, Vol. 88, No. 2

London, A.S., A.J. LeBlanc and C.S. Aneshensel (1998), "The Integration of Informal Care, Case Management and Community-based Services for Persons with HIV/AIDS", *AIDS Care*, Vol. 10, pp. 481-503.

Miksch, A., G. Laux, D. Ose, S. Joos, S. Campbell, B. Riens and J. Szecsenyi (2010), "Is There a Survival Benefit Within a German Primary Care-based Disease Management Program?", *American Journal of Managed Care*, Vol. 16, No. 1, pp. 49-54.

Morrison, S.P. et al. (2008), "Cost Savings Associated with US Hospital Palliative Care Consultation Programs", *Archives of Internal Medicine*, Vol. 168, No. 16, pp. 1783-1790.

Nolte, E., C. Knai, M. McKee (2009), "Managing Chronic Conditions: Experience in Eight Countries", EURO Nonserial Publication Series, Vol. 15, Observatory Studies Series, WHO Regional Office, Europe.

Ose, D., M. Wensing, J. Szecsenyi et al. (2009), "Impact of Primary Care-based Disease Management on the Health-related Quality of Life in Patients with Type 2 Diabetes and Co-morbidity", *Diabetes Care*, Vol. 32, No. 9, pp. 1594-1596.

Payne, F.J., C.S. Sharrett, D.N. Poretz et al. (1992), "Community-based Case Management of HIV Disease", *Am J Public Health*, Vol. 82, pp. 893-894.

Piette, J., J.A. Fleishman, V. Mor and B. Thompson (1992), "The Structure and Process of AIDS Case Management", *Health Soc Work*, Vol. 17, pp. 47-56.

Praag, E.V. and D. Tarantola (2001), "Evaluating Care Programs for People Living with HIV/AIDS", *Family Health International*, available at *www.fhi.org/NR/rdonlyres/ez7svgsmatlnljiupck35ipxkbfwqr43tmid spsesufm2ptudeudeiithei2ufzwfbcsebjiilt4ca/31776textR1enhv.pdf*.

Remonnay, R et al. (2005), "Cancer Treatment at Home or in the Hospital: What Are the Costs for French Public Health Insurance? Findings of a Comprehensive-cancer Centre", *Health Policy*, Vol. 72, No. 2, pp. 141-148.

Shortell, S.M., R.R. Gillies, D.A. Anderson (2000), *Remaking Healthcare in America: The Evolution of Organized Delivery Systems*, 2nd ed., San Francisco.

Schoen, C., R. Osborn, S.K.H. How, M.M. Doty and J. Peugh (2008), "In Chronic Condition: Experiences of Patients with Complex Health Care Needs, in Eight Countries", *Health Affairs*, Web Exclusive, w1-w16 (available at *http://content.healthaffairs.org/cgi/content/abstract/ hlthaff.28.1.w1?ijkey=cOSQSi1j6fDlo&keytype=ref&siteid=healthaff*).

Sherer, R., K. Stieglitz, J. Narra et al. (2002), "HIV Multidisciplinary Teams Work: Support Services Improves Access to and Retention in HIV Primary Care", *AIDS Care*, Vol. 14, pp. 31-44.

Singh, D. and C. Ham (2006), "Improving Care for People with Long-term Conditions: A Review of UK and International Frameworks", Health Services Management Centre, available at *www.improvingchroniccare.org/downloads/review_of_international_frameworks__chris_hamm.pdf*.

Smith, T.J. and J.B. Cassel (2009), "Cost and Non-clinical Outcomes of Palliative Care", *Journal of Pain and Symptom Management*, Vol. 38, No. 1, pp. 32-44.

Sönnichsen, A., A. Rinnerberger, M. Url, H. Winkler, P. Kowatsch, G. Klima, B. Furthauer and R. Weitgasser (2008), "Effectiveness of the Austrian Disease-management Programme for Type 2 Diabetes: Study Protocol of a Cluster Randomised Controlled Trial", *Trials Journal*, Vol. 9, pp. 38-45.

Twyman, D.M. and M.K. Libbus (1994), "Case Management of AIDS Clients as a Predictor of Total In-patient Hospital Days", *Public Health Nurs*, Vol. 11, pp. 406-411.

UNAIDS (2000), "AIDS Palliative Care", UNAIDS Technical Update, available at *www.hospicecare.com/ resources/pdf-docs/unaids-pallcare-aids.pdf*.

Vargas, R.B. and W.E. Cunningham (2007), "Evolving Trends in Medical Care-coordination for Patients with HIV and AIDS", *Current HIV/AIDS Reports*, Vol. 3, No. 4.

Wagner, E.H., B.T. Austin and M. Von Korff (1996), "Organizing Care for Patients with Chronic Illness", *The Milbank Quarterly*, Vol. 74, No. 4, pp. 511-544.

Wagner, E.H., B.T. Austin, C. Davis, M. Hindmarsh, J. Schaefer and A. Bonomi (2001), "Improving Chronic Illness Care: Translating Evidence Into Action", *Health Affairs*, Vol. 20, No. 6.

Weber, C. and K. Neeser (2006), "Using Individualized Predictive Disease Modeling to Identify Patients with the Potential to Benefit from a Disease Management Program for Diabetes Mellitus", *Disease Management*, Vol. 9, No. 4, pp. 242-256.

WHO (2004), "World Health Report – Changing History", World Health Organisation, Geneva.

World Health Organisation, Regional Office for Europe (WHO Europe) (2006), *Gaining Health. The European Strategy for the Prevention and Control of Noncommunicable Diseases*, WHO, Copenhagen.

Chapter 6

Drawing all the Benefits from Pharmaceutical Spending

OECD countries' pharmaceutical policies generally focus on three main objectives: making medicines accessible and affordable to patients; containing public spending growth, and providing incentives for future innovation. This chapter provides a brief review of current pharmaceutical reimbursement and pricing policies in OECD countries, as well as short-term measures adopted in response to the economic crisis. It then focuses in particular on two important issues: decisions pertaining to the coverage of new products with high costs and/or uncertain benefits, and the development of generic markets.

1. Introduction

OECD countries' pharmaceutical policies seek to balance three broad objectives: make medicines accessible and affordable to patients; contain public spending growth, and provide incentives for future innovation.

Countries have adopted different approaches to reconciling these objectives, in line with the general organisation of their health systems. The vast majority of OECD countries regulate pharmaceutical coverage at the central level to offer a standardised drug benefit package to their population, as for other health benefits. They also regulate the prices (or reimbursement prices) of pharmaceutical products covered by public schemes. In other countries, individual private or public insurers design drug cost reimbursement packages for their enrolees, in a more or less regulated environment. In all circumstances, payers have to make decisions about which drug should be covered, and at what price (for the insurer and for the patient).

To foster innovation in the pharmaceutical sector, countries use a range of policies, such as public investments in basic R&D, tax credits for private R&D expenditures, education and training of a high-skilled workforce and protection of intellectual property rights. As discussed in the OECD Innovation Strategy (OECD, 2010b), countries could do more to strengthen innovation, which is an essential contributor to economic growth and societies' well-being. This chapter, however, does not address innovation policies *per se* and concentrates on reimbursement and pricing policies.

The main goal of this chapter is to present recent trends in pharmaceutical policies. Section 1 provides updated data on pharmaceutical spending, and funding sources. Section 2 provides an overview of pharmaceutical reimbursement and pricing policies in OECD countries. Section 3 looks at recent experiences with innovative pricing agreements and Section 4 presents recent policy initiatives aiming to get more value for money from off-patent markets.

2. Pharmaceutical spending in OECD countries

Pharmaceutical spending[1] accounts for 17% of total health spending and 1.5% of GDP on average in OECD countries (Figure 6.1). However, the dispersion around these averages is high: pharmaceutical spending accounts for only 8% of total health expenditures in Norway, while it absorbs 32% of health spending in Hungary, and more than 25% in Turkey, the Slovak Republic and Mexico. Per capita spending (in USD PPPs) ranges from 132 in Chile to 897 in the United States, reflecting large differences in the volume and prices of pharmaceuticals (Figure 6.2; and OECD, 2008).

Expenditures for out-patient pharmaceuticals are predominantly financed by public schemes in all countries but seven (Italy, Iceland, Estonia, Canada, Poland, the United States and Mexico). Public funding accounts for more than three-quarter of pharmaceutical spending in a few countries: Germany, Greece, the Netherlands, the United Kingdom and Luxembourg (see Figure 6.3). Private health insurance plays a significant role in the financing of out-patient medicines in the United States (30%), Canada (30%),

Figure 6.1. **Pharmaceutical spending as a share of total health expenditure and GDP, 2008**

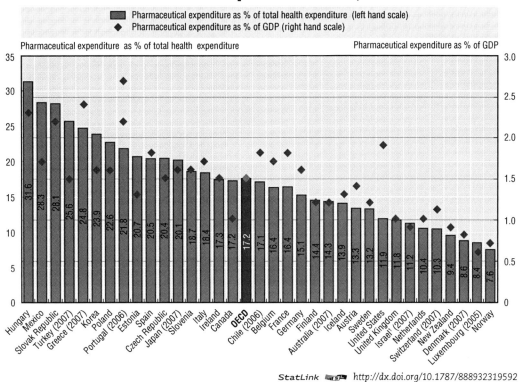

StatLink ⬛️ http://dx.doi.org/10.1787/888932319592

Figure 6.2. **Per capita pharmaceutical spending 2008**

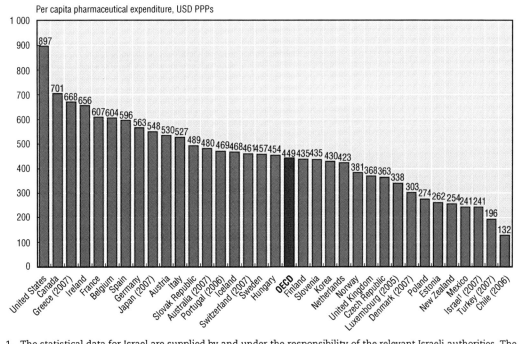

1. The statistical data for Israel are supplied by and under the responsibility of the relevant Israeli authorities. The use of such data by the OECD is without prejudice to the status of the Golan Heights, East Jerusalem and Israeli settlements in the West Bank under the terms of international law.

Source: OECD (2010a), *WHO-NHA Database* and OECD Secretariat's estimates.

StatLink ⬛️ http://dx.doi.org/10.1787/888932319497

Figure 6.3. **Pharmaceutical spending, by funding sources, 2007**

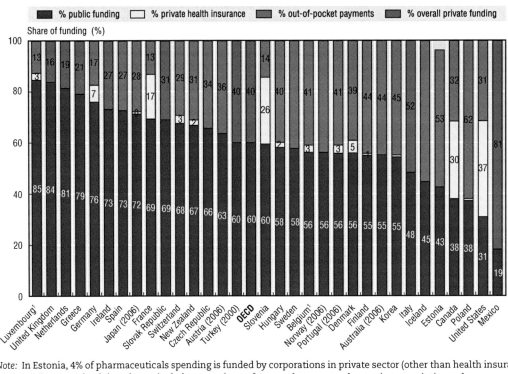

Note: In Estonia, 4% of pharmaceuticals spending is funded by corporations in private sector (other than health insurance).
1. Luxembourg and Belgium do not include any estimate for over-the-counter drugs – i.e. prescription only.
Source: System of Health Accounts 2009, OECD (2010a) and OECD Secretariat's estimates.

StatLink ═══ http://dx.doi.org/10.1787/888932319611

Slovenia (26%) and France (17%) through different mechanisms though. In the United States and Canada, private health insurance offers primary coverage for drug consumption to a significant share of the population (see Box 6.2), while in France, it only covers co-payments left after coverage by social health insurance.

In the past, pharmaceutical spending has risen at a faster pace than total health spending in developed countries. This trend has now reversed: between 2003 and 2008, real pharmaceutical expenditure has grown by 3.1% per year on average in OECD countries, while total health spending has increased by 4.5% (see Figure 6.4). Over this period, growth in pharmaceutical spending surpassed growth in total heath expenditure in only nine OECD countries: Greece, Ireland, Mexico, Japan, Australia, Portugal, and Germany. In Norway, Luxembourg, Italy and Chile, real growth of pharmaceutical spending was even negative.

The economic crisis that hit the world in 2008 has already affected pharmaceutical markets. IMS data on market trends, monitored quarter by quarter from Q1 2008 to Q4 2009 for the World Health Organisation[2] show that a few countries have experienced a significant decline in consumption (ranging from 12% to 25%) in at least one quarter (by comparison with the same quarter in the previous year): the Czech Republic, Estonia, Slovenia, and public schemes in Russia. However, decline in consumption cannot be unambiguously attributed to the crisis. In the Czech Republic for instance, the decline is likely due to changes in pharmaceutical policies which preceded the recession.

Some governments confronted with high fiscal pressure have adopted drastic measures to curb pharmaceutical expenditure growth in 2009 or 2010. In Ireland and Greece, for

Figure 6.4. **Pharmaceutical spending growth, 2003 to 2008**

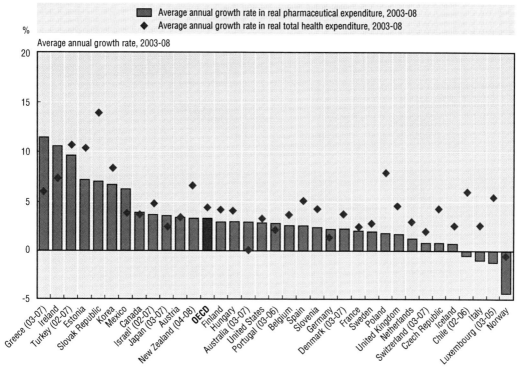

1. The statistical data for Israel are supplied by and under the responsibility of the relevant Israeli authorities. The use of such data by the OECD is without prejudice to the status of the Golan Heights, East Jerusalem and Israeli settlements in the West Bank under the terms of international law.

Note: Spending is deflated using an economy-wide (GDP) price index.

Source: OECD (2010a), *WHO-NHA Database* and OECD Secretariat's estimates.

StatLink ⬛🖵 *http://dx.doi.org/10.1787/888932319573*

instance, where pharmaceutical spending was growing at a very rapid pace, governments enforced emergency measures – mainly sharp price reductions – and announced the implementation of more structural policies (see Box 6.1). In other countries, such as France, Germany or the United Kingdom, price reductions or rebates on pharmaceuticals have often been used as adjustment variables to contain health spending growth (France), tackle health insurance funds deficits (Germany) or cap profits made by companies on NHS sales (the United Kingdom).

On the other hand, some countries reacted to the crisis by adopting measures to ensure access to health care and medicines. For instance, Austria cut the VAT rate on pharmaceuticals from 20 to 10% and Italy distributed social vouchers to vulnerable people (EUR 40 per month) for the purchase of primary goods or pharmaceuticals (Council of the European Union, 2009).

Beyond short-term policies, OECD countries will continue to pursue long-term goals of obtaining good value for money without discouraging innovation. The following paragraphs describe briefly current reimbursement and pricing policies and present recent developments.

3. Reimbursement and pricing policies in OECD countries

In the majority of OECD countries, the entire population is either entitled to coverage for health risks (tax-funded systems) or covered by compulsory health insurance (social

Box 6.1. **Examples of recent pharmaceutical pricing developments**

In the **Czech Republic**, prices and reimbursement were reduced by 7% in 2009 for all drugs not affected by revisions that occurred in 2008.

In **Germany**, the Minister of Health announced a bundle of short-term and structural measures in April 2010. Manufacturers' rebates on pharmaceutical prices (for drugs not subject to reference prices) were increased from 6% to 16% and prices frozen until December 2013. From 2011, pharmaceutical companies will be required to provide information to the Joint Federation of physicians and health insurance funds (G-BA) on the therapeutic benefit of new products, through comparison with existing competitors. The G-BA will assess the product, assisted by the Institute for Quality and Efficiency in Health Care (IQWiG) if needed. If the product has no added therapeutic value, it will be clustered in a group of reference prices. If the product has an added-value, the manufacturer will be invited to negotiate a rebate with the umbrella organisation of health insurance funds. If the two parties cannot reach an agreement, a central authority will set a rebate, using international price benchmarking. Health insurer funds are allowed to negotiate further rebates with the manufacturer, individually or in group.

In **Greece**, prices of pharmaceuticals were reduced in March 2010 anywhere from 3 to 27%, depending on their initial price. Beyond this emergency measure, Greece is revising its reimbursement and pricing policy: a positive list will be established; the three lowest prices in the European Union will be used as benchmark for price at market entry; "dynamic pricing" will be used after market entry (annual increase in sales exceeding 5% will lead to a 2.5% price reduction); and a stepped-price model will be used for generic pricing.

In **Ireland**, the government and the Irish Pharmaceutical Health Care Association (representing international research-based companies) agreed on price cuts of 40% on nearly 300 widely prescribed medicines, as well as an increase in the annual rebate paid by manufacturers to the Health Service Executive on sales under public schemes (from 3.53 to 4%, raised on a wider base). The government decided to introduce a prescription charge (EUR 0.50 per prescription, capped at EUR 10 per month and per family) and announced the implementation of reference prices (maximum reimbursement amounts for clusters of products) and right of pharmacists to substitute cheaper but equivalent products where possible.

In **Spain**, the government has proposed two modifications of the Guarantees Act for Medicines (Ley 29/2006) in order to modify the price of pharmaceuticals. First, the price of generic medicines will be reduced by 25%. Second, a general 7.5% rebate is applicable since July 2010 for all medicines prescribed by NHS physicians and to pharmaceutical inputs bought by NHS hospitals.

In **Switzerland**, the prices of reimbursed medicines was re-examined to be in line with six comparator countries (Austria, Denmark, France, Germany, the Netherlands and the United Kingdom), with a 4% tolerance margin in order to compensate for shifts in currency changes. This change is expected to save about CHF 400 million. Measures recently implemented include a periodic re-examination of prices every 3 years as well as a systematic review of the price of products for which a new indication has been approved by the Swiss Drug Agency.

In **the United Kingdom**, the new Pharmaceutical Pricing Regulation Scheme (PPRS) signed in December 2008 for five years aims to introduce value-based pricing for drugs purchased by the NHS. The government and the industry have agreed on the principle of "flexible pricing", which means that companies will be allowed to increase the price of their products after market entry, if new evidence has been produced about the benefits of their drug (as assessed by NICE, see Section 4 of this chapter). The NHS has implemented "patient access schemes" to provide access to drugs not judged cost-effective by NICE. In the meantime, the PPRS imposed price cuts of 3.9% in 2009 and 1.9% in 2010, as well as measures to increase the use of generics.

Box 6.1. **Examples of recent pharmaceutical pricing developments** *(cont.)*

In the **United States**, the health reform introduced several measures to expand coverage of pharmaceuticals and to contain related costs. A set of measures aims to progressively abolish the coverage Gap[1] for enrollees in Medicare Part D drug plans with standard benefits by 2020. Since January 2010, beneficiaries falling in the coverage gap have received a rebate of USD 250 from their insurer, and from July 2010, they should get a 50% mandatory discounts on the costs of their medications from manufacturers who want their products to be listed in Medicare Part D drug plans. The Medicaid drug rebate percentage increased to 23.1% of average manufacturer price for brand name drugs, to 17.1% for clotting factors and drugs approved exclusively for pediatric use, and to 13% for non-innovator, multiple source drugs. The reform also imposes an annual fee on manufacturers and importers of branded pharmaceuticals. The fee was set at USD 2.5 billion for 2010 and is shared between companies according to their volume of sales. It is planned to increase up to USD 4.1 in 2018 and decrease afterwards.

1. In standard Medicare drug benefits, beyond a certain level of out-of-pocket payments – USD 2 850 in 2010 –, patients have to pay the full cost of prescription drugs until their out-of-pocket payments reach USD 4 550. Then, they are entitled to catastrophic coverage.

Source: Communication from national authorities; Germany: *www.bmg.bund.de* (Press release of 28 April 2010); Greece: *www.sfee.gr/en/price-determination*; United States: *www.kff.org/healthreform/upload/8061.pdf*; Ireland: *http://debates.oireachtas.ie/DDebate.aspx?F=DAL20100119.xml&Node=3052#N3052*, consulted on 29 June 2010; United Kingdom: *www.dh.gov.uk/en/Publicationsandstatistics/Publications/DH_091825*.

insurance-based systems). In these cases, entitlements to health benefits are most often defined at the central level with different degrees of explicitness and detail (Paris *et al.*, 2010). Out-patient pharmaceuticals are most often included in the standard benefit package covered by public or social schemes.[3] In a few countries, patients obtain out-patient drug coverage through a variety of schemes, with possible variations in the range of benefits covered (see Box 6.2).

Countries with universal and uniform entitlements generally establish a list of drugs eligible for reimbursement or public funding ("positive list") at the national level, with the exception of Germany[4] and the United Kingdom, where "negative lists" are established instead; and Greece, where a positive list is in preparation. Pharmaceutical coverage generally entails user charges, with exemptions for some segments of the population and/or categories of drugs.

All OECD countries employ some form of price regulation for at least some market segments

In terms of pharmaceutical price regulation, two general rules apply to the majority of OECD countries. First, in general, countries do not regulate the prices of over-the-counter (OTC) medicines not covered by health insurance, either because they do not consider OTC drugs as merit goods, to which access should be guaranteed for all residents, or because they rely on consumer demand price sensitivity to drive price competition. Second, by contrast, most OECD countries regulate the price or reimbursement price of out-patient prescription drugs covered by health insurance to address well-known market failures.[5, 6]

There are however several exceptions to these general rules. Canada and Mexico, for instance, regulate the prices of *all* patented medicines (whether covered or not) to protect consumers from potential abuse of monopoly power of sellers and ensure that the price of patented drugs are not excessive: Canada sets maximum ex-factory prices, though purchasing

> ## Box 6.2. **Countries with pluralistic systems for pharmaceutical coverage**
>
> In a few OECD countries, out-patient pharmaceuticals are covered by multiple schemes and the range of benefits covered is not uniform: Canada, Chile, Mexico, Turkey and the United States.
>
> In **Canada**, while drugs administered in hospitals are fully covered through the universal, publicly financed Medicare programme, out-patient prescription drugs are not included among the insured benefits guaranteed by the *Health Canadian Act*. Provinces and territories and the federal government provide coverage to about one-third of Canadian residents through publicly financed programmes targeting some populations (seniors, social assistance beneficiaries, indigenous persons, veterans, etc.). Provinces and territories and the federal government make coverage decisions and establish formularies for each of the public plan they manage. About two-third of Canadian residents are covered for prescription drugs by private insurance (employer-based or individual contracts). Private plans establish their own formularies and tend to be more inclusive than public plans though some of them mirror public plans coverage. In Québec, all plans are required to offer coverage at least equal to the public formulary (Paris and Docteur, 2006).
>
> In **Mexico**, more than half of the population is covered through social security; 20% by the Seguro Popular, a publicly-subsidised voluntary scheme targeting the population without access to social security, and 1% by voluntary private coverage. All these schemes provide coverage for out-patient prescription drugs, often with cost sharing. The uninsured can obtain health care services through the Ministry of Health or state health authorities. Social security agencies and public authorities purchase medicines using two formularies (one for primary care and one for secondary and tertiary levels), defined at the central level (Moïse and Docteur, 2007).
>
> In the **United States**, people obtain drug coverage from a variety of sources. In 2008, 58% of American residents obtained prescription drug coverage through employer-sponsored private plans, 9% through individually-purchased private plans, Another 9% are enrolled in *Medicare Part D* plans, a voluntary programme for seniors, subsidised by the federal government and run by private health insurers. About 20% of the population is covered by *Medicaid*, the joint federal-state programme for low-income people. Private health insurers may offer a choice between several drug plans, with different formularies, cost sharing and premiums. Only Medicare Part D drug plans are somewhat constrained by law in terms of formulary design. In Medicaid, prescription drug is an optional service but all state programmes cover drugs, with big interstate differences in formularies, co-payments and limits in the number of prescriptions which can be filled (Kaiser Family Foundation, 2010).

prices can be further negotiated by purchasers, while Mexico limits the retail prices paid by consumers who purchase drugs in pharmacies without social insurance coverage.

Also, a few countries allow manufacturers to set their prices at market entry for out-patient prescription pharmaceuticals: Denmark, Germany, the United Kingdom and the United States. In Denmark, manufacturers can freely set their prices at market entry. However, the price of a product, in relation with its therapeutic value, is a major criterion in coverage decision making (PPRI, 2008a).

In Germany, pharmaceutical companies have been free to set their prices at market entry until recent reforms, even for drugs reimbursed by social health insurance. A broad system of reference prices (see below) puts downward pressure on prices when therapeutic alternatives exist since even new patented products can be clustered with low-priced products, including generics. Until now, health insurance funds have, however, essentially been "price-takers" for truly innovative drugs. The 2007 reform has therefore mandated the Institute for Quality and Efficiency in Health Care (IQWiG) to assess the cost effectiveness of new innovative products to help health insurance funds to set maximum reimbursement prices. This measure will be applicable from 2011.

In the United Kingdom, pharmaceutical companies can freely set entry prices for their products, including those covered by the National Health Service. However, they face some constraints: first, the Pharmaceutical Pricing Regulation Scheme (PPRS) imposes an annual cap on profits made by companies on NHS sales and companies are required to modulate the price of their products to not exceed this cap. Second, price increases are subject to authorisation and must be justified. Third, the National Institute for Health and Clinical Excellence (NICE) assesses the cost effectiveness of medicines with high costs or high budget impact and/or uncertain or low benefits to decide whether the product should or not be funded by the NHS. Though this last feature is not direct price regulation, it can however put some pressure on prices, especially when therapeutic alternatives are available.

In the United States, pharmaceutical prices are not subject to direct price regulation. Pharmaceutical companies can set the price of their drugs at market entry. In the private sector, Pharmacy Benefit Management companies and health insurance plans use formulary management tools to negotiate prices with manufacturers. When therapeutic alternatives are available, third-party payers are able to obtain price discounts or rebates from manufacturers in exchange for listing or status of "preferred drug" (lower co-payment) in their plan's formulary. In other cases, their purchasing power is weaker. Prices of drugs purchased by federal authorities (e.g. the Veterans Health Administration) or for Medicaid programmes are more regulated. For instance, manufacturers are required to enter in national rebate agreements with federal authorities if they want their product to be listed in Medicaid formularies. The price they charge to Medicaid cannot exceed the average manufacturer price (price paid to the manufacturer for the drug in all states by wholesalers for drugs sold in pharmacies, after discounts) reduced by a rebate percentage, recently increased to 23% for on-patent drugs.

OECD countries which regulate the price or reimbursement prices of out-patient pharmaceuticals use three main instruments: international benchmarking, therapeutic benchmarking and economic assessment. Some of them actually use a mix of these instruments, applying to different market segments (e.g. Canada, France and Switzerland use both international and therapeutic benchmarking though for different purposes). The OECD report on pharmaceutical pricing policies, published in 2008, described in more detail the policies employed by member countries and shed light on their impact on prices and availability of pharmaceuticals (OECD, 2008).

International benchmarking

Twenty-four OECD countries use international benchmarking to define the price (or a maximum price) of pharmaceuticals: they look at prices paid by a set of comparator countries to determine a maximum price for a new drug.

The list of "comparator countries" is obviously a key element of this policy tool. Members of the European Union typically refer to each other, and usually select a subset of countries with a similar income level. For instance, the Czech Republic refers to Estonia, France, Greece, Hungary, Italy, Lithuania, Portugal and Spain, while France refers to Germany, Italy, Spain and the United Kingdom. In Canada, the federal Patented Medicine Prices Review Board (PMPRB) uses international benchmarking as one means to ensure that the prices of patented medicines are not excessive (whether reimbursed or not). The PMPRB refers to a set of comparator countries that were selected in part for their perceived commitment to promote pharmaceutical innovation (France, Germany, Italy, Sweden, Switzerland, the United Kingdom and the United States), with the idea that Canada should make a "fair contribution" to global R&D costs. Mexico refers to the prices paid in the six countries with the highest market shares for the product considered.

In general, international benchmarking takes place during the pricing and reimbursement process, before market entry. This is not the case in Canada, however, where the PMPRB regulate *a posteriori* the ex-factory prices of patented medicines, often limiting them to the median price of the comparator countries. In addition, the PMPRB ensures that the price of each patented product does not exceed the highest international price of the comparator countries. If the domestic price is considered excessive, the Board may order the patentee to offset the excess revenue accumulated, by reducing the price of the drug or the price of another drug, or by making payments to the federal government. Some countries define strictly in the regulation that the price must be "equal to the lowest price" in comparator countries or something similar (*e.g.* the Slovak Republic sets its price cap 10% above the average price of the three lowest-price countries among those referenced), while other countries are less prescriptive (in France, the price must be "consistent" with prices observed in comparator countries).

International benchmarking has several drawbacks. First, it is likely to influence companies launch strategies and subsequently delay or even compromise launch in low-price countries (to avoid any reference to them). Second, it has encouraged a disconnection between "list prices" and actual prices paid by third-party payers, often obtained through rebates consented in confidential agreements with manufacturers. This fact is in turn likely to blur price comparisons and benchmarking. Economists and policy makers generally agree on the fact that cross-country price discrimination for patented pharmaceuticals is a win-win situation in which companies earn the revenues they need to invest in R&D while people in lower-income countries access the medicines they would not access at a high price. From the payer's point of view, medicines may have different value, depending on the ability and willingness to pay, the epidemiological context of the country and the costs of other inputs. However, international benchmarking, by itself, does not guarantee that the price set will reflects the country-specific value of a pharmaceutical product.

In fact, several countries use international benchmarking for a limited market segment – the most innovative products – and prefer therapeutic referencing for other parts of the market.

Internal or therapeutic referencing

When using therapeutic referencing, countries regulate the price of new entrants by comparison with the prices of competing drugs in the market. They first assess the therapeutic advantage of the new drug over existing competitors and then determine a "price premium" in relation to the level of innovativeness of the new product. Under this policy, a product with no added therapeutic value will be priced at the same level or at a lower level than existing competitors. This practice mirrors pricing strategies employed by companies in markets with free pricing, where non-innovative products are priced at a lower level than competitor products at market entry in order to gain market shares.

Canada, Belgium, France, Italy, Japan and Switzerland use therapeutic referencing for products which are not "breakthrough" innovations. The assessment of the therapeutic "added value" of the new entrant is, however, applied in different ways: while in France, a Transparency Committee assesses the added therapeutic value on a 1 to 5 scale, Switzerland has a less formalised process leaving more room to negotiation. In Italy, an algorithm was established to evaluate the innovativeness of a product. In all cases, the price premium is set or negotiated on a case-by-case basis with no predefined rules, and often takes other parameters into account, such as expected volumes of sales.

"*Reference price*" policies, which set maximum reimbursement prices for clusters of products with identical properties, can be seen as a variant of therapeutic referencing, with one crucial difference: under such policies, the product's price – either freely set by the company or negotiated – can remain above the maximum reimbursement price, if patients are ready to pay for its "added value" even if this is merely brand loyalty. Reference price policies have been adopted by more than one-third of OECD countries but the scope of such policies varies enormously (Habl *et al.*, 2008). Most countries define clusters of bio-equivalent products (with the same active ingredient or combination of active ingredient, administered in the same way) but a few countries define wider groups of "therapeutically equivalent" products (Germany, the Czech Republic, the Netherlands, New Zealand and the Slovak Republic). As a result, the market share subject to maximum reimbursement prices varies widely, ranging from 5% of total pharmaceutical market in France to 60% in Germany (by volume).

With therapeutic referencing, the price of a new entrant very much depends on the value attached by regulating authorities to incremental innovation (the "added value" of the new product). Experience has shown that the criteria adopted to assess the advantages of a new drug are very different across countries. In addition, the price of the new product is based on the prices set for competitors in the past, not always revised to reflect the current value of therapeutic products. Finally, although therapeutic referencing ensures price consistency *within* therapeutic classes, it does not guarantee price consistency *across* therapeutic classes. Economic tools may help to achieve this, and are discussed in the next section.

Pharmaco-economic assessment

More than half of OECD countries take into account pharmaco-economic assessment (PEA) to make reimbursement decisions given the price proposed by the manufacturer. PEA is thus not directly used to regulate prices but can provide incentives for manufacturers to lower their price in order to meet the requirements for reimbursement. Only a few countries systematically use PEA for all products applying for inclusion in the positive list: Australia, the Netherlands, New Zealand and Sweden. In the United Kingdom, only products with high costs, high budget impact and/or a high level of uncertainty on clinical effectiveness are evaluated to determine whether they should be funded by the NHS or not. In Canada, the intergovernmental Common Drug Review, part of the Canadian Agency for Drugs and Technologies in Health, systematically assesses the cost effectiveness of products with new active substances to inform coverage decisions of public drug schemes. In Italy, PEA is used in the negotiation process in order to support pricing and reimbursement decisions. In Germany and France, new provisions (in 2007 and 2008) state that new innovative pharmaceuticals should undergo economic assessment but how this will be done is still being determined. Korea recently introduced PEA in coverage decision making.

Most often, agencies responsible for economic assessment compute an incremental cost-effectiveness ratio (ICER) to measure added costs per QALY (quality-adjusted life year) gained, by comparison with therapeutic alternatives. They usually adopt a public payer perspective, which means that they consider only costs and potential savings for the public coverage schemes. By contrast, Sweden and Norway have adopted a societal perspective, in which both benefits and costs are estimated at the society level (for third-party payers, but also for patients, their family, employers and the government). ICER thresholds (beyond which a drug is unlikely to be funded) are generally not explicitly defined but can be inferred from past decisions.

Pharmaco-economic assessment is, in many ways, the most rational tool to make reimbursement decisions since it guarantees that costs to society of a new medicine are proportionate to its clinical benefits. It also sends signals to the industry about the type of benefits which are the more valued and payers' willingness to pay. On the other hand, performing such assessments requires expertise and means which are not available in all OECD countries. Moreover, it is not widely accepted by the public, the industry, nor the medical profession, especially when it is perceived as a rationing tool rather that an instrument to improve efficiency of pharmaceutical spending. Finally, countries using ICER thresholds have already been confronted with ethical questions raised by expensive end-of-life medicines or orphan drugs[7] (less likely to meet the cost-effectiveness thresholds) and have adapted their policy to take into account the specificities of those products.

Beside the three main instruments described above, OECD countries use a variety of other instruments to regulate pharmaceutical prices. For instance, Italy negotiates prices as well as individual caps for each pharmaceutical company on revenues drawn from NHS sales, beyond which companies will have to pay rebates. Spain uses a cost-plus regulation; the United Kingdom caps the profit of pharmaceutical companies; and several countries have developed product-specific pricing agreements. These agreements have gained attention of policy makers as interesting tools to promote efficiency in pharmaceutical spending. They are reviewed in the Section 4 of this chapter.

Price regulation and price levels

The discussion above describes briefly the benefits and possible drawbacks of the main policy instruments used by OECD countries to regulate pharmaceutical prices. However, an important conclusion has to be emphasised: price regulation does not necessarily lead to low prices (OECD, 2008). Retail prices of pharmaceuticals ranged from 68% below to 185% above the OECD average in 2005 and some countries with price regulation had high prices (Switzerland, Canada), while countries without direct price regulation at market entry, such as the United Kingdom, had relatively low prices. Pharmaceutical prices are partly related to GDP per capita, though variations in income were found to explain only one-fifth of variations in retail prices; and to economy-wide price levels (variations in which explain more than half of the variations in drug prices). This should not be surprising: in fact, regulators do not always try to obtain the cheapest price and do not exhaust their purchasing power. Their efforts to improve static efficiency of pharmaceutical spending are counterbalanced by their wish to maintain incentives for R&D investments and future innovation (dynamic efficiency). Moreover, the price is not the whole story: efficiency of pharmaceutical spending also depends on appropriate prescription and use of pharmaceuticals and an efficient distribution chain.

This conclusion is not to say that current pharmaceutical pricing policies are ideal and ensure value-for-money for pharmaceutical spending. Efforts have to be made to better link the price of pharmaceuticals to their "value" and some countries have already taken steps to get more value-for-money. Recent initiatives are reviewed below.

4. Recent developments in reimbursement and pricing policies

Policy makers sometimes have to make hard decisions, especially when manufacturers propose new high-priced products for the treatment of fatal or disabling diseases. Confronted with constrained financial resources, they have to weigh the costs and benefits of the new treatment against the benefits of other health care services to be forgone to fund it.

Media coverage of negative reimbursement decisions – for example NICE decisions in England and Wales – indicates how sensitive the population is to "treatment denial". Opponents to the recent US health reform actively raised the spectre of rationing, though the current situation in the United States is far from ensuring access to high cost medicines to anyone who need them (Faden *et al.*, 2009). In the past, England, Australia and New Zealand have often found it to be politically difficult to refuse funding for drugs with poor cost effectiveness and have been forced to find ways to circumvent their own cost-effectiveness thresholds (Raftery, 2008).

Indeed, policy makers face a real dilemma. Cost-effectiveness studies provide scientific information about the benefits and costs (including opportunity costs) of new treatments. However, the general public does not always find appeals to rationality convincing. Treatments which fail to meet efficiency thresholds may be seen as desirable because they extend life or relieve severe symptoms. Apparently in some cases, "rational choices", as defined by economists, do not seem to coincide with collective preferences.

It could be argued that citizens are not well informed about the real costs and benefits of treatments, potential adverse effects, uncertainty, and opportunity costs. Or that the same citizens who oppose rationing are not necessarily ready to increase their contributions to the health care system or to lose current benefits. How then to arrive at a good compromise on what treatments to fund?

Medicines with small population targets, such as orphan drugs and end-of-life medicines, are the most likely to raise this type of problems: manufacturers have a very high reservation price (to compensate for small volumes) and policy makers, on their side, do not like to deny treatments for economic reasons while they do want to provide incentives to develop drugs for small population groups with severe diseases.

In an attempt to respond to all these concerns, policy makers have adapted some of their policy instruments and criteria for decision making. The paragraphs below describe some of these adaptations. This discussion mainly focuses on public policies, since almost all OECD countries regulate the reimbursement and prices of medicines covered by public schemes at the central level. However, other systems are not immune to problems raised by high-cost medicines. In the United States, for instance, strategies have been adopted by public and private payers to cope with high-priced medicines (Box 6.3).

Box 6.3. **Strategies used by private insurers in the United States
to cope with high-price medicines**

In the United States, some public and private insurers have been using pharmaco-
economic assessment (PEA) to design pharmaceutical benefits. Most often, PEA has been
used to compare alternative treatments in order to negotiate prices with manufacturers, to
incentivise the use of cheaper alternative through differential co-payments or, more rarely,
to exclude drugs from coverage in the more restricted formularies. Many insurers, however,
do not exclude treatments without alternative from their formularies. The funding of new
expensive treatments is thus provided by increasing premiums or cost shifting to patients.

Some private health plans have recently introduced a fourth tier for co-payments.
Traditionally, private plans have used three-tiered co-payments to promote the use of the
cheapest drugs: monthly co-payment typically ranges from USD 5 to USD 10 for generic drugs,
USD 20 to USD 30 for brand-name medicines with moderate prices and USD 50 for high priced
brand-name drugs. To respond to cost-pressure imposed by costly medicines, private plans
have introduced a "fourth tier" under the form of a 20% to 30% co-insurance. Tier 4 systems
have been introduced into 86% of Medicare drug plans and 10% of commercial drug plans with
drug benefits (Lee and Emanuel, 2008). For drugs whose price can exceed USD 50 000 a year, co-
insurance represents out-of-pocket payments of more than USD 10 000.

Source: Lee and Emanuel (2008); Faden et al. (2009).

Economic evaluation and drugs with poor cost effectiveness

In many OECD countries, clinical effectiveness is an essential criterion considered
when deciding whether there should be public funding. Even high-cost new drugs usually
end up being reimbursed by public programmes, so long as effectiveness is proven and
benefits are high, though sometimes with severe restrictions and/or prior authorisation
required to limit budget impact. In Australia, for instance, the Pharmaceutical Benefits
Advisory Committee may recommend the use of medications within special programmes,
with access restricted to patients with the greatest capacities to benefit from treatments
(Nikolentzos et al., 2008).

In general, price regulations and rules for reimbursement are lighter for drugs used in
hospital settings than for drugs used in out-patient care. In most cases, drugs are
purchased by hospitals and funded through payments made by third-party payers and
patients. Hospitals are usually under budget constraints and payment schemes will
determine the capacity to use high-cost drugs. Global budgets and payments per case,
which are now widely used in OECD countries, provide few incentives to use new high-cost
medicines, especially when their costs are not yet included in standard average costs per
case which serve to establish prices. To overcome this difficulty, several countries have
introduced special programmes to fund high-cost drugs on top of payments per case (e.g.
Germany, France). In other countries, access to in-patient expensive drugs is unequal and
linked to the ability and willingness of hospitals to pay.

Countries which consider cost effectiveness to make reimbursement decisions have
tried to provide explicit answers to trade-offs between results of economic evaluations and
population expectations. First of all, a common feature of coverage decisions based on cost
effectiveness is that no country has defined an explicit and definitive ICER threshold
beyond which a new drug has no chance to be funded. Instead, countries accept that other

criteria need to be taken into account, and use flexible thresholds, beyond which a drug is simply less likely to be funded.

Sweden made explicit the criteria to be taken into account beyond cost effectiveness in coverage decisions. The "need and solidarity principle" states that serious diseases must be given a higher level of priority when making decisions (Box 6.3). To comply with this requirement, the Pharmaceutical Benefits Board use different cost-effectiveness thresholds, linked to the severity of the treated ailment. As a result, it has in the past funded treatments with costs per QALY exceeding EUR 90 000 (Garau and Mestre-Ferrandiz, 2009). In addition, in Sweden, the consideration of "budget impact" in the assessment process plays in favour of high-cost medicines with small target population, such as orphan drugs: decision makers are more likely to fund medicines with high cost per QALY when expected budget impact remains reasonable.

In the United Kingdom, institutes in charge of economic appraisal have adapted their guidance to take into account these problems. In England and Wales, NICE revised its guidance for the appraisal of life-extending and end-of-life treatments in July 2009 (see Box 6.4). Similarly, in Scotland, the Scottish Medicines Consortium takes other criteria than

---

Box 6.4. **Social values and economic assessment**

The incremental cost-effectiveness ratio (ICER) is widely used to assess the value of a new product and recommend or make coverage decisions. However, ICER are generally not considered in isolation from "social values".

Social values and criteria for coverage decisions in Sweden

The Pharmaceutical Benefits Board[1] makes coverage decisions for medicines used in out-patient care. Decisions are based on three criteria:

- The *human value principle*: equality of human beings and the integrity of every individual should be respected. Coverage decision should not discriminate between people because of their age, sex, race, etc.

- The *need and solidarity principle*: those in greatest need take precedence for reimbursement decisions, i.e. people with more severe diseases are prioritised over people with less severe conditions.

- The *cost-effectiveness principle*: the costs of using a medicine should be reasonable from a medical, humanitarian and socio-economic perspective.

In Sweden, cost effectiveness is assessed with a societal perspective, which means that all costs and benefits are considered, regardless of who pays (third-party payers and patients) and who benefits from health gains (patients, employers, central or local governments).

NICE's new guidance for the appraisal of life-extending, end-of-life treatment

Since 1999, the National Institute for Health and Clinical Excellence (NICE) has been assessing the cost effectiveness of health strategies to recommend their use or otherwise in the England and Wales National Health Systems. In 2008, NICE published a report on the consideration of social values in its appraisal process and explicitly excluded the "rule of rescue"[2] as a relevant decision criteria (NICE, 2008). More recently, however, NICE revised its guidance for the appraisal of life-extending, end-of-life treatments to allow funding of such treatments whose ICER is above the usual GBP 30 000/QALY threshold. The supplementary guidance applies to the following:

- Treatments indicated for patients with a *short life expectancy*, normally less than 24 months.

Box 6.4. Social values and economic assessment *(cont.)*

● There is sufficient evidence that the treatment offers an extension to life, normally *at least three additional months*, compared to current NHS treatments;

● The treatment is licensed or otherwise indicated, for *small patient population*.

In these circumstances, the appraisal committee is expected to consider the impact of giving greater weight to QALYs achieved in the later stages of terminal diseases in the ICER and to assess the magnitude of the additional weight needed to fall within the current threshold range. Any guidance produced using this supplementary advice should be reviewed within two years.

1. Created in 2002, the Pharmaceutical Benefit Board (LFN) is now part of the Dental and Pharmaceutical Benefits Agency (Swedish acronym TLV).
2. The "rule of rescue" refers to the fact that any available means should be employed to attempt to save someone from a severe threat, at any cost (like is done for people lost in mountains). This rule is mentioned by some analysts to justify the unrestricted use of high-cost medicines for serious conditions.

Source: LFN (2007); Mason and Drummond (2009); NICE (2008, 2009).

ICER into account to make decisions, such as whether the drugs treats a life-threatening disease, substantially increases life expectancy or quality of life, or bridges a gap to a "definitive" therapy (Garau and Mestre-Ferrandiz, 2009).

Beyond adaptations of criteria for decision making, these countries have been using product-specific agreements for drugs with poor cost-effectiveness ratio or high budget impact.

Product-specific pricing agreements

Payers and pharmaceutical companies have developed product-specific *pricing agreements* to enhance access to medicines with high costs or high budget impact (IMS, 2009; Carlson *et al.*, 2010). These agreements between third-party payers and pharmaceutical companies, either seek to link the "value" brought by a new product in terms of health gain, to the unit price or, more basically, to limit budget impact. Several typologies have already been developed to classify these agreements (IMS, 2008; Carlson *et al.*, 2010). An alternative typology is used here, which distinguishes agreements according to their objectives: to extract a share of companies' rent beyond an agreed level of revenues; to limit impact on public budgets; to improve the evidence about effectiveness or cost effectiveness, or to share the risks of uncertain benefits (see Figure 6.5).

In *volume-price agreements*, the unit price of a product is linked to volumes sold, so that it declines when volumes increase. It is consistent with the idea that a seller is willing to reduce its reservation price in exchange for higher volumes. Price reductions most often take the form of confidential discounts or rebates, agreed between manufacturers and third-party payers. Volume-price agreements have been widely used by private insurers and Pharmacy Benefit Managers in the United States, who used to negotiate discounts or rebates in exchange for formulary listing or listing with a "preferred drug" status (*i.e.* a lower prescription charge for consumers). In France, volume-price agreements are signed by the regulating authority when there is a risk of inappropriate use likely to generate volumes greater than those expected at the time of price negotiation. Australia also uses two types of agreements with the same logic, with price reductions beyond an agreed volume of sales or manufacturers' rebates beyond an expenditure cap. Volume-price

Figure 6.5. **Typology of product-specific reimbursement and pricing agreements**

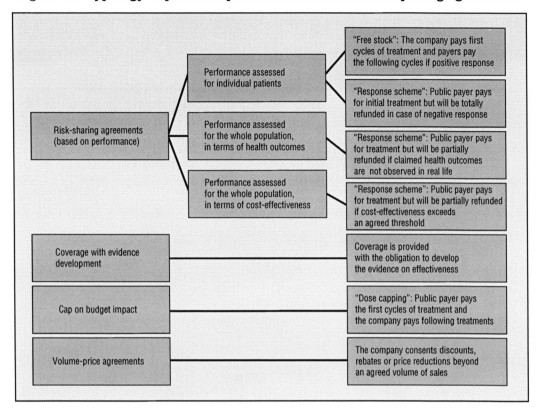

Source: OECD Secretariat.

agreements do not really allow third-party payers to control spending but just to extract a share of companies' rent.

Agreements to limit budget impact simply preclude public payers from spending more than a fixed amount per patient. Such agreements have been concluded between NICE and pharmaceutical companies in "dose capping" Patient Access Schemes (see Box 6.4). For instance, the NHS agreed to pay for the first two years of multiple myeloma treatment by lenalidomide provided that costs after two years will be borne by the manufacturer.

Coverage with evidence development (CED) schemes have been adopted in Italy, the United Kingdom, the United States, and Sweden (Carlson *et al.*, 2010) and will be used in certain circumstances in Australia from 2011. They link coverage to data collection by the company to inform payers about health outcomes achieved either in new clinical trials or in "real life". CED schemes are adopted when there is a high level of uncertainty in the clinical evidence produced by the manufacturer in its application for funding. Typically, in the United Kingdom, CED schemes provide coverage only for patients included in clinical trials. In Sweden, these schemes provide coverage in exchange for information on the actual use of the product (*e.g.* obesity treatments), on long-term effects on morbidity and mortality (*e.g.* cholesterol products), on quality of life (*e.g.* insulin detemir), and/or on cost effectiveness (*e.g.* treatment for Parkinson's disease, vaccine for cervical cancer). In Italy, web-based "Registries" have been developed, for instance for innovative oncologic and orphan drugs, with the aim to collect information about rational and appropriate use of specific medicines in a single database; to monitor the related consumption and expenditure; and to provide information needed for risk-sharing agreements. The overall objective of CED schemes is thus to improve knowledge about the product's impact on health.

Risk-sharing agreements are also signed when there is a high level of uncertainty about the benefits claimed by the manufacturer. When health benefits are potentially high, the third-party payer agrees to fund the new treatment but will ask to be (at least partly) refunded by the company if claimed benefits are not observed in the real life. The agreement signed by the English NHS with several manufacturers in 2002 for multiple sclerosis treatments is the most famous example.

Risk-sharing agreements can take several forms. Outcomes to be assessed can be defined in terms of *clinical benefits* (*e.g.* clinical response, improvement in quality of life) or in terms of *cost effectiveness* (the cost/QALY gained should not exceed a certain threshold). The outcomes can be assessed at the *individual level* (*i.e.* for each patient treated), or at the *aggregate level*, considering the whole population treated. For instance, in Germany, a health insurance fund signed an agreement with Novartis to obtain a refund of a patient's treatment for osteoporosis if an osteoporosis-related fracture occurs. In England, Janssen Cilag agreed to refund treatment of multiple myelomia for patients who do not respond positively after four cycles of treatments. In England also, companies producing treatments for multiple sclerosis agreed to reduce the price of their products in order to maintain an average cost/QALY at GBP 36 000 (IMS, 2009). In France, the coverage of a treatment for schizophrenia claimed to improve compliance was approved under the condition that the company monitors compliance in real life and will refund a part of social security spending if compliance targets are not met. In Italy, two types of agreements exist: in so-called "risk-sharing" agreements, manufacturers are required to pay back a percentage of NHS spending for patients not responding to the treatment, while in "payment by results", manufacturers will pay back all costs for patients that do not respond to the treatment.

Many of these agreements are too recent to be evaluated. In terms of process, they are likely to increase administration costs and R&D costs (not least, the costs incurred by generating evidence) but their benefits are expected to offset their costs. Carlson *et al.* (2010) reviewed the available evidence on CED and performance-based agreements concluded in the past decade. They found that several drugs initially funded under CED agreements were successfully approved for general or restricted coverage after the CED period, though this was not always the case. They found only two studies which evaluated risk-sharing agreements. In England, an agreement between Pfizer and the North Staffordshire region's health authority on an anti-cholesterol product ended with positive health outcomes (the population treated met cholesterol level targets) and no refund from the company. The results of the UK NHS agreement on multiple sclerosis are more mixed: in spite of positive health outcomes, the cost effectiveness of the treatment could not be assessed with certainty.

Product-specific agreements could well prove to be a useful new instrument in promoting patient access to innovative treatments while linking public funding to therapeutic value. However, as yet, there is insufficient evidence to be confident in their utility. As these agreements are developing quickly in OECD countries, their results in terms of benefits and costs need to be assessed. The assessment should focus on their design (are all agreements workable?) as well as on their final outcomes.

> **Box 6.5. Patient Access Schemes in the United Kingdom**
>
> The 2009 Pharmaceutical Price Regulation Scheme introduced Patient Access Schemes (PAS) in order to enhance access to innovative treatments whose cost effectiveness was too high to meet NICE standards for NHS funding. PAS take several forms:
>
> - Under *free stock* agreements, the company provides the first cycles of treatments for free and the NHS bears the costs of following cycles if the clinical response to first cycles is positive. For instance, UCB agreed to provide at no cost the first 12 weeks of its treatment for moderate to severe rheumatoid arthritis (certolizumab pegol) and the NHS will continue to fund the treatment if the clinical response is positive.
>
> - Under *dose capping* agreements, the NHS pays for the first cycles of treatments and the company bears the costs of following treatments. For instance, the NHS pays for the first 14 doses (per eye) of treatment for acute wet-macular degeneration by ranibizumab and Novartis will cover following injections, up to three years.
>
> - *Discount* agreements provide a simple minimum discount to the NHS (which can be further negotiated by local purchasers), which differs from usual confidential agreements concluded between pharmaceutical companies and public or private payers in other OECD countries in that it is public and, in some circumstances, caps the cost of the whole treatment for an individual. For instance, Roche has agreed to discount by 14.5% the price of its treatment for non-small cell lung cancer (erlotinib) in order to equalise its price to a cheaper competitor until definitive results of head-to-head clinical trials are available and a new NICE appraisal.
>
> A recent survey on PAS implementation in the United Kingdom concluded that refunds received by hospitals according to two of these schemes were not passed on to Primary Care Trusts, who ultimately pay for health services delivered to their patients. In addition, hospitals complained about the lack of staff to manage PAS and recuperate funds from companies. The new NICE's PAS Liaison Unit is likely to facilitate implementation, which would also benefit from the production of standard templates for local PAS (Williamson, 2010).
>
> *Source:* NICE website; Williamson (2010), Pharmaceutical Price Regulation Scheme, 2009 (*www.dh.gov.uk/en/Publicationsandstatistics/Publications/DH_091825*).

5. Efforts to develop generic markets

All OECD countries see the development of generic markets as a good opportunity to increase efficiency in pharmaceutical spending, by offering cheaper products than on-patent drugs and allowing a reallocation of scarce funds to innovative medicines. Most OECD countries have implemented policies to promote generic use (see Table 6.1). However, generic market shares in pharmaceutical sales show wide variations across OECD countries (Figure 6.6).

Since generic entry often entails a dramatic fall in revenues for original products, pharmaceutical companies have developed a set of strategies aimed at maximising the period of market exclusivity for their product and/or countering generic entry (OECD, 2008). In a huge inquiry on practices used by pharmaceutical companies to delay generic entry in 27 EU countries between 2000 and 2007, the European Commission identified legitimate and less legitimate strategies, among which: patent filing strategies (multiply sequential patents related to a single product to increase uncertainty about patent expiry); undue patent litigation; and settlements with generic companies to restrict or delay market entry

Table 6.1. **Policies to promote the use of generic drugs**

	Prescription in INN			Generic substitution			Incentives to prescribe/ dispense/ purchase generics (or cheap drugs)			Pricing and reimbursement policy	
	Not allowed	Allowed	Mandatory	Not allowed	Allowed	Mandatory	Incentives for pharmacists	Incentives for patients	Incentives for physicians	Reference price system	Price linkage (discount for 1st generic entrant/ originator's price)
Australia		X			X		F	F	–	Y	−12.5%[1]
Austria	X			X			N	n.a.	NF	N	−48%,−15%+S
Belgium		X		X			NF	F	F&NF	Y	−30%
Canada[2]		X[2]	X[2]		X[2]	X[2]	F[2]	F[2]	[2]	Y/N[2]	[2]
Chile			X[3]		X		N	F	NF[3]	N	N
Czech Republic	X				X		n.a.	F	F	Y	−20%
Denmark	X					X	NF	F	NF	Y	N
Finland		X				X	NF	F	NF	Y	−40%
France		X			X		NF	F	NF&F	Y	−55%+S
Germany		X				X	NF	F	F	Y	N
Greece	X			X			N	F	N	Y	−20%+S
Hungary		X			X		NF	F	N	Y	−30%,-10%,−10%
Iceland					X		n.a.	F	n.a.	Y	n.a.
Ireland		X			X[4]		N	F	NF	Y[4]	S
Italy		X			X		F	F	NF	Y	−20%
Japan		X			X		F	F	[5]	n.a.	−30%[5]
Korea		X			X		F	F	n.a.	n.a.	−32%,−15%
Luxembourg		X		X			n.a.	n.a.	NF	N	n.a.
Mexico			X		X			F	NF	N	N
Netherlands		X			X		F	F	n.a.	Y	N
New Zealand		X			X[6]		F	F	NF	n.a.	n.a.
Norway		X			X		F	F	NF	N	S
Poland		X			X		NF	F	N	Y	−25%, −25%
Portugal			X		X		N	F	N	Y	−35%
Slovak Republic		X				X	NF	F	NF	Y	N
Spain		X				X	NF&F[7]	F	NF&F[7]	Y	−30%
Sweden		X				X	NF&F	F	NF	N	N
Switzerland		X			X		F	F	N	N	−20% to −50%[8]
Turkey	X				X			F	–	Y	−20%
United Kingdom		X		X			F	N	NF	N	N
United States[9]							F[9]	F[9]	N	N	N

Note: INN= International Non-proprietary Name; F= Financial incentive; N= No; n.a.= not available; NF= Non financial incentives; S= Stepped price model (prices of both originators and generics are reduced after an initial period); Y= Yes. For pharmacists, this table only considers incentives provided by drug coverage schemes. Market incentives (such as rebates from manufacturers, vertical integration, etc.) are not reported. Price linkage: pricing policy linking the (maximum) price of the first generic entrant (and followers in some cases) to the price of the original drug. Pricing dynamics may differ across countries afterwards.

1. The price reduction applies to the generic and the originator product.
2. In Canada, the regulation of prescription and generic substitution differs across provinces and territories. Incentives for doctors, pharmacists and patients vary across drug plans. Reference prices are only used by some drug plans.
3. Only in the public sector.
4. To be implemented.
5. In Japan, there is no direct incentive for physicians, but an incentive for medical institutions exists. Generic prices are revised after market entry.
6. If the pharmacist has a substitution arrangement with the prescriber.
7. In some regions.
8. Depending on originator's market sales.
9. Legislation on prescription in INN and substitution is not uniform across states. Incentives for pharmacists, patients and doctors vary across drug plans. Patients' co-payments are generally lower for generics.

Source: Various sources, including PPRI country profiles (http://ppri.oebig.at, in press) and personal communications.

StatLink http://dx.doi.org/10.1787/888932319839

Figure 6.6. **Generic drug market shares in 2008**

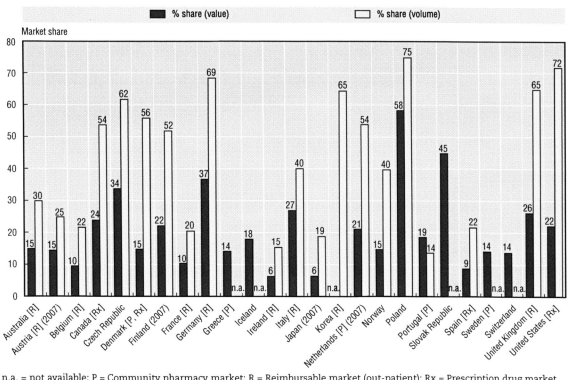

n.a. = not available; P = Community pharmacy market; R = Reimbursable market (out-patient); Rx = Prescription drug market. Otherwise: total market.

Source: National sources and EFPIA (2010).

StatLink ᴍᴤᴘ *http://dx.doi.org/10.1787/888932319630*

(European Commission, 2008). The European Commission concluded that compliance with Competition Law needed to be more closely scrutinised and that the European Union would benefit from the creation of Community patents and a unified litigation system.

However, it would be wrong to conclude that it is primarily the actions of the pharmaceutical industry which alone are holding back the development of generic markets. Many public policies continue to hinder their development too. "Patent linkage", for instance, may impose undue delays to generic entry: according to this rule, the authority in charge of marketing authorisation is expected to check whether a patent has expired before granting marketing authorisation. Most OECD countries have adopted a "Bolar type" provision allowing drug agencies to assess generic applications and deliver market authorisations before patent expiry[8, 9] so that generics can enter the market as soon as the patent expires. However, a few countries continue to link the delivery of marketing authorisation to patent expiry (*e.g.* the Slovak Republic, Mexico).

In addition, in many countries, pricing and reimbursement processes impose further delays to generic entry. With regards to the specificity of generic products, procedures could certainly be shortened or accelerated to speed up generic penetration (EGA, 2009; European Commission, 2008). In Australia, for instance, the recent agreement between the government and the major pharmaceutical industry association plans for a parallel assessment of new products by authorities in charge of marketing authorisation and reimbursement policy from 2011. On top of marketing authorisation and reimbursement and pricing procedures, some countries add another step to restrict substitution opportunities by defining groups of "interchangeable products" which can be substituted for each other by pharmacists. Countries may consider the costs and benefits of this procedure and see whether it could be replaced by a general procedure setting the rules for interchangeability and substitution at a more general level once and for all and letting pharmacists decide for product-specific cases.

Reference price policies and "price linkage" may reduce generic price competition in some circumstances. In reference price policies, payers set a maximum reimbursement price (MRP) for clusters of products, most often by reference to the price(s) of the cheapest generic(s). Consumers have to pay any difference between the price and this reimbursement amount. This policy does not provide much incentive for generic manufacturers or pharmacists to sell generic drugs below the MRP and may well reduce price competition in the long run, especially if reference prices are not frequently updated. On the other side, reference price policies unambiguously favour generic penetration of the pharmaceutical market, which is still a high priority for several countries.

Many countries regulate the prices of generics in relation to the originator's price, with a fixed discount – a practice known as "price linkage". In France, generic prices are set 55% below the originator's price (see Table 6.1). For third-party payers, this policy does not guarantee good "value-for-money": once a patent has expired, there is no reason for them to pay a higher price for a brand-name drug than for bio-equivalent products. A unique reimbursement price for the cluster offers better value-for-money to third-party payers, with the possibility for individual providers to set prices above this amount if they can benefit from brand loyalty. In addition, price linkage may reduce dynamic price competition in generic markets: in markets with free pricing, generic prices will likely decrease when the number of competitors increases. Some countries have introduced "stepped pricing models", in which prices of originators (and sometimes generics) are reduced after an initial period with the wish to mirror off-patent market dynamics (e.g. Austria, France, Norway). However, this approach does not guarantee that generic prices will be as low as they could be in a freer market.

A majority of OECD countries have allowed physicians to prescribe in International Non-proprietary Names (INN) and/or pharmacists to substitute (cheaper) equivalent medicines to brand-name prescribed products[10] (see Table 6.1). However, professional behaviour is not only shaped by laws. If 80% of prescriptions are written in INN in the United Kingdom, this is only the case of 12% of prescriptions in France (PPRI, 2008b). Similarly, pharmacists may be allowed to substitute generics for brand-name drugs, without doing it in practice. A few countries still do not allow prescription in INN or generic substitution in pharmacies, including Greece, where the generic market share is exceptionally low. In another small number of countries, generic substitution by the pharmacist is mandatory (e.g. Denmark, Sweden). However, this does not seem to be a necessary condition to ensure high generic penetration, since generics have high market shares in several countries without mandatory substitution (see Figure 6.6), including Poland and the United Kingdom.

Financial incentives for physicians, pharmacists and patients have been created to foster the development of generic markets. Physicians have been provided financial incentives to prescribe cheaper alternatives in different ways: they may receive per capita funding for their patients and be allowed to keep any savings achieved through economic prescribing, as it was the case for some physician groups in the United States in the 1990s or GP fundholders in the United Kingdom. They may be financially rewarded by extra payments if they reach targets in terms of generic prescription, as defined in pay-for-performance schemes. For instance, the French Contracts for improvements of individual practices (CAPIs), signed on a voluntary basis by primary care doctors, link bonus payments to targets in the share of generic prescription for a few generic groups (see Chapter 4). On the contrary, they can be penalised if they have average prescription costs above the average of a peer group. This option has been used in Germany. Though it proved very difficult to penalise physicians, the incentive encouraged the prescription of cheaper medicines.

Incentives for patients depend on out-of-pocket payments. The way user charges are designed is likely to influence generic take-up, when patients have a choice. Patients have a financial interest to choose cheaper drugs when the co-payment is a co-insurance rate (expressed as a percentage of the price), when fixed co-payments are lower for generics ("tiered" co-payments) or in "reference price" systems. Some countries have supplemented existing incentives to further encourage generic use. For instance, in 2006 Switzerland increased the co-insurance rate for brand-name drugs for which cheaper interchangeable generics are available from 10 to 20%. France decided in 2008 that patients had to pay in advance for their drugs and be reimbursed later when they refuse generic substitution (while the usual rule is direct payment of the pharmacist by third-party payer).

Incentives for pharmacists generally consist in correcting the disincentive inherent in pharmacists' remuneration schemes in the vast majority of OECD countries: pharmacists margins are set in relation to the price of medicines and are therefore higher (in absolute terms) for more expensive products. With such an incentive, pharmacists are penalised when they substitute a generic for a more expensive drug. Several countries have reversed or at least neutralised this incentive (e.g. France). Other countries have created positive incentives: in Switzerland for instance, pharmacists receive a fee for generic substitution. In several countries (e.g. Hungary, Norway, Poland), pharmacists have the obligation to inform patients about the possibility of a cheaper alternative, which acts as a non-financial incentive to encourage generic substitution.

Another important feature of the distribution chain is the ability of manufacturers to negotiate rebates and discounts with wholesalers and/or pharmacists in order to gain market shares over generic competitors. Since pharmacists are generally free to pick up any generic when they substitute a generic for an original drug, generic manufacturers are ready to negotiate high rebates or discounts on their products to gain market shares. Fierce competition has led to big rebates in some countries, enhancing pharmacists' revenues. However, a common concern for countries with regulated prices or maximum reimbursement prices for generics is that third-party payers and consumers do not benefit from generic price competition that occurs at the pharmacy level. In Canada, for instance, rebates and allowances given by manufacturers to pharmacies were estimated at 40% of payers' generic drug costs (Competition Bureau Canada, 2008).

To ensure that payers benefit from these rebates, OECD countries have adopted different strategies. Some countries have capped manufacturers' rebates (France, the Canadian Province of Ontario for its public drug benefit).

In 2007, Australia commenced implementing a new policy of "price disclosure". Under this new arrangement, the "weighted average disclosed price (WADP)" is computed on a regular basis for drugs subsidised by the Pharmaceutical Benefits Scheme (PBS) across all products with the same active ingredient(s) and the same mode of administration, for a period of 12 months, taking into account manufacturers' discounts. When the gap between the current PBS ex-factory price and the WADP is 10% or more, the PBS price is adjusted to the new calculated price. In Japan, the drug prices are regularly (usually biennially) revised to be brought closer to actual market prices as measured by the government's drug price survey. With such arrangements, payers and consumers can benefit from generic price competition.

Other countries have developed direct contracting between health insurers and manufacturers. The discussion below presents these recent developments, as well as the evidence on their impact.

Contracting, tendering, procurement and competition in generic markets

Contracting, tendering and public procurement policies have been used for decades in some market segments in OECD countries. In the past four years, several countries developed contracting opportunities to extend those practices with the aim to foster generic price competition in the out-patient sector. Though huge price reductions have been obtained in some cases, the long-term impact on generic markets is unclear, and could even prove harmful according to recent studies. Careful design is needed to use contracting to achieve better value-for-money in pharmaceutical spending.

In the United States, health insurers and pharmacy benefit managers have been contracting with pharmaceutical companies since the 1980s. They have obtained substantial discounts or confidential rebates from manufacturers in exchange for "listing", "preferred drug status", or even "exclusive listing"[11] in their formularies for both patented and off-patent drugs sold to out-patients (US Federal Trade Commission, 2005). New Zealand introduced competitive tendering for generic drugs subsidised by the public drug plan for out-patients in 1997. The tendering process resulted in significant price reductions: 40% on average in 1997/98 and 60% in 1999/2000. For some products, price reductions reached 84% to 96% in five years (OXERA, 2001). In other countries, contracting has mainly been used in the hospital sector, as well as for the purchase by public authorities of specific medicines (mainly vaccines) and has only recently been developed in the out-patient sector in a small number of countries (Leopold et al., 2008; Kanavos, 2009).

In the Netherlands, health insurers are allowed to select one or more products, within a cluster of products with the same active ingredient, to be eligible for reimbursement. They contract with pharmaceutical companies to obtain discounts or rebates on prices in exchange for the exclusivity of the reimbursement status, for a given period of time. Under this policy, patients have to pay out-of-pocket the price of non-selected products, unless a doctor has confirmed a medical need for a specific product.

Dutch health insurers have been using both collective and individual tendering. In 2005, seven private health insurers in the Netherlands, covering about 70% of the population, decided to tender jointly for the purchase of three high-selling off-patent active ingredients (simvastatin, pravastatin and omeprazole). Manufacturers offering the lowest price (or no more than 5% above) were selected and their drugs were supplied to patients free of charge, while other drugs were not reimbursed at all. Following an agreement between the Health Insurance Board, the generic association and the pharmacists' association for 2007-08, collective tendering has not been extended to other active ingredients. However, 33 substances were listed for potential tenders, led by individual health insurers. Insurers can use additional incentives: one insurer decided for instance to exempt patients who use preferred drugs from the annual deductible for out-patient pharmaceuticals (Maarse, 2009; Kanavos, 2009).

The total initial savings of the tendering practices in the Netherlands were substantial (EUR 355 million): price reduction reached 90% in some cases and generic substitution increased. However, pharmacies experienced a dramatic loss of the revenues they previously earned from the discounts granted by generic manufacturers which were not passed on to health insurers, threatening the financial sustainability of many of them. To compensate this loss, the dispensing fee for pharmacists was increased from EUR 6 to EUR 8.25, which generated an additional income of EUR 200 million for pharmacists but also offset part of the savings achieved by health insurance funds (Kanavos, 2009).

However, according to generic manufacturers, the current tendering practice puts excessive price pressure on the generic market, and compromises the generic market in the long term, as companies may be tempted to leave the Dutch market.

In Germany, the 2007 Health Insurance Competition Enhancing Act designed a set of incentives to foster health insurance funds' contracting opportunities. According to the new law, when health insurance funds contract with a pharmaceutical company (in practice mainly generic companies) to obtain price reductions, pharmacists are obliged to substitute the "preferred" drug for the initial prescription, unless a doctor has formally excluded substitution.[12] Health insurance funds tender for two types of contracts: contracts for the purchase of a specific active ingredient or contracts for a product portfolio.

These provisions were challenged by pharmaceutical companies with the German antitrust agency and examined by the European Court of Justice, who finally ruled that German health insurance companies have to comply with European regulations for public procurement (Kanavos, 2009).

In Canada, British Columbia, Ontario and Saskatchewan issue tenders for the purchase of a small number of top-selling molecules by their public plans. The winner is the company offering the highest confidential rebate and receives exclusive listing for a set period of time. The size of confidential rebates gained through this practice is not known. However, in one case, the government of Ontario dropped a tender process for a drug (ranitidine) because the brand manufacturer reduced its formulary price by 75%, which suggests that potential price reductions are likely to be of this magnitude (Competition Bureau Canada, 2008; Hollis, 2009).

All these experiences show that tendering processes allow short-term savings, obtained both by drastic price reductions and, in some cases, by an increase in generic market penetration. However, they also tend to increase market concentration, with the risk of lower price competition in the longer term if some generic providers decide to exit the market. In some cases, bid winners also failed to supply the market and countries experienced shortages.[13] A careful design of tendering processes is therefore needed to guarantee both that winning companies will be able to supply adequately the market or otherwise risk enforceable penalties, and prevent competing companies from abandoning national markets.

6. Conclusions

Policy makers have continuously adapted pharmaceutical policies to respond to new challenges posed by market dynamics and medical progress, with the objectives of ensuring access to affordable medicines to their citizens, containing spending growth and sustaining R&D efforts. The impact of these policies on national markets and innovation capacities need to be monitored in order to make adjustments when necessary.

To cope with the economic crisis and address unprecedented budget deficits, several OECD countries have recently implemented drastic policies to cut pharmaceutical spending or, at least, contain their growth. Several countries are trying to make decisions about the pricing of new pharmaceutical products more "rational" in order to maximise the value-for-money of pharmaceutical spending. Cost-effectiveness and/or budgetary impact are sometimes taken into account explicitly when making decisions about coverage of new drugs. Restricting coverage is unpopular and decision makers are torn between "economic rationality" (to maximise the efficiency of public spending) and the pressure to respond to people's expectations.

To deal with this dilemma, some countries have amended the criteria to be taken into account for coverage decisions. Other countries have developed innovative pricing agreements linking public spending to health outcomes obtained. Although the jury is still out until more evidence has been collected, it appears that some of these arrangements may well be useful new policy tools for payers of health services in their attempt to get good value-for-money without taking on too great financial risk.

Another strategy for increasing value-for-money in pharmaceutical spending is to expand the market for generic drugs. OECD countries have implemented policies to promote generic uptake: physicians have been given the possibility to prescribe in INN, and pharmacists the right to substitute generics for brand-name products in almost all countries. However, in several OECD countries, generic markets remain underdeveloped, suggesting that appropriate economic incentives for providers, physicians, pharmacists and patients are lacking. Moreover, in several countries, price competition has been weak or has not benefitted consumers and third-party payers. More aggressive use of tendering processes, for instance in Germany and the Netherlands, has led to immediate and sometimes huge price reductions. However, the approach is not without risks: experience shows that calls for tender need to be carefully designed in order to avoid the problem of supply shortages and excessive market concentration in the longer term.

Notes

1. In the system of health accounts, "pharmaceutical expenditure" refers to expenditures for pharmaceuticals and other medical non-durables dispensed to out-patients. It includes prescribed medicines, over-the-counter medicines, as well as a range of medical nondurables such as bandages, elastic stockings, incontinence articles, condoms and other mechanical contraceptive devices. It does not include spending for pharmaceuticals dispensed in in-patient care. The latter accounts for 5% to 15% of total spending on pharmaceuticals in countries for which data are available.

2. *www.who.int/medicines/areas/policy/imsreport/en/index.html*, accessed on 18 May 2010.

3. Drugs used in hospitals are generally covered by public and social schemes through "hospital benefits".

4. In Germany, 10% of residents are covered by private health insurance. Though private health insurers have some latitude to define their benefit package, they most often cover the same pharmaceutical products than statutory health insurers.

5. The main market failures in the market for out-patient prescription drugs are the following: low consumer price sensitivity (due to insurance coverage); manufacturers' monopoly position for on-patent drugs, especially when there is no therapeutic alternative; and separation of the decision to

purchase (by the doctor, generally not sensitive to price) from the responsibility to bear the cost (patients and third-party payers). In countries where drug insurance is mainly provided by social or public schemes, the need to contain health spending growth and spend efficiently is another justification for the regulation of reimbursement prices.

6. There is no clear trend regarding price regulation for medicines used in hospitals: many countries set maximum list prices while others do not regulate prices at all. The common feature is that purchasing processes generally allow price negotiations. Hospitals under budget constraint are sensitive to price and use their purchasing power to negotiate prices whenever possible.

7. "Orphan drugs" basically refer to medicines developed for rare conditions. Countries use different thresholds to consider that a disease is rare: "rare conditions" are those which affect less than one in 1 500 people in the United States, less than one in 2 000 people in the European Union and less than one in 2 500 people in Japan. The United States and the European Union have implemented policies to encourage private investments in R&D for rare diseases (*e.g.* increased market exclusivity) and have consequently defined criteria to be met by a medicine to be granted an "orphan drug status". In the European Union, those criteria are: the severity of the disease; the fact that it serves an unmet need; and either prevalence below one in 2 000 or a negative expected return on investment.

8. Drug agencies cannot assess generic application before the end of the "data exclusivity period", which lasts 5 years in the United States and 8 to 11 years in the European Union.

9. "Patent expiry" is used in this text as a synonym for expiry of patents and supplementary protection certificates which exist in many OECD countries.

10. "Substitution rights" are useless or implicit when doctors prescribe in INN.

11. "Listing" means that the drug is covered by the plan. Under "preferred drug" status, a drug benefits from lower co-payments than its competitors. "Exclusive listing" means that the drug is the only product covered by the drug plan in its therapeutic class or for a given molecule.

12. To ensure consistency with policies aiming to encourage efficient prescription by physicians, "preferred drugs" are excluded from statistics used to monitor physicians' prescription targets and impose financial penalties when necessary.

13. According to Carradinha (2009), both Netherlands and New Zealand experienced shortages because the bid winner was unable to fulfil its commitment. In both cases, a solution was found because competitors were ready to supply the product.

Bibliography

Carlson, J.J. *et al.* (2010), "Linking Payment to Health Outcomes: A Taxonomy and Examination of Performance-based Reimbursement Schemes Between Health Care Payers and Manufacturers", *Health Policy*, in press.

Carradinha, H. (2009), "Tendering Short-term Pricing Policies and the Impact on Patients, Governments and the Sustainability of the Generic Industry", *Journal of Generic Medicines*, Vol. 6, No. 4, pp. 351-361.

Competition Bureau Canada (2008), *Benefiting from Generic Drug Competition in Canada: The Way Forward*, Competition Bureau Canada, Ottawa.

Council of the European Union (2009), "Second Joint Assessment by the Social Protection Committee and the European Commission of the Social Impact of the Economic Crisis and of Policy Responses", Council of European Union, Brussels.

EFPIA – European Federation of Pharmaceutical Industries and Associations (2010), *The Pharmaceutical Industry in Figures – Edition 2010*, EFPIA, Brussels.

EGA (2009), *How to Increase Patient Access to Generic Medicines in European Health Care Systems*, European Generic Medicines Association, Brussels.

European Commission (2008), *Executive summary of the Pharmaceutical Sector Inquiry Report*, Communication from the Commission, Brussels.

Faden, R. *et al.* (2009), "Expansive Cancer Drugs: A Comparison between the United States and the United Kingdom", *The Milbank Quarterly*, Vol. 87, No. 4, pp. 789-819.

Garau, M. and J. Mestre-Ferrandiz (2009), "Access Mechanisms for Orphan Drugs: A Comparative Study of Selected European Countries", *OHE Briefing*, No. 52, Office of Health Economics, London.

Habl, C. *et al.* (2008), *Referenzpreissysteme in Europa*, ÖBIG Forschungs- und Planungsgesellschaft mbH, Vienna.

Hollis A. (2009), *Generic Drug Pricing and Procurement: A Policy for Alberta*, SPS Research Papers – The Health Series, Vol. 2, No. 1, University of Calgary, Calgary.

IMS (2008), "Defining Risk Sharing", *Pharma Pricing and Reimbursement*, No. 2, IMS, Norwalk, CT, pp. 78-80.

IMS (2009), "Innovative Pricing Agreements to Enhance Access Prospects", *Pharma Pricing and Reimbursement*, Vol. 14, No. 8, IMS, Norwalk, CT, pp. 238-243.

Kaiser Family Foundation (2010), "Prescription Drug Trends – May 2010 Fact Sheet", Kaiser Family Foundation, Washington.

Kanavos, P. (2009), *Tender Systems for Outpatient Pharmaceuticals in the European Union: Evidence from the Netherlands, Germany and Belgium*, London Schools of Economics, London.

Lee, T.H. and E.J. Emanuel (2008), "Tier 4 Drugs and the Fraying of the Social Impact", *The New England Journal of Medicine*, Vol. 359, No. 4, pp. 333-335.

Leopold, C., C. Habl and S. Vogler (2008), *Tendering of Pharmaceuticals in EU Member States and EEA Countries*, ÖBIG Forschungs- und Planungsgesellschaft mbH, Vienna.

LFN – Swedish Pharmaceucitcal Benefits Board (2007), *The Swedish Pharmaceutical Reimbursement System*, LFN, Solna.

Maarse, H. (2009), "Drug Preference Policy", *Health Policy Monitor*, October 2009, available at: *www.hpm.org/en/Surveys/BEOZ_Maastricht_-_Netherlands/14/Drug_preference_policy.html*.

Mason, A. and M. Drummond (2009), "Public Funding of Cancer Drugs: Is NICE Getting Nastier?", *European Journal of Cancer*, Vol. 45, pp. 1188-1192.

Moïse P. and E. Docteur (2007), "Pharmaceutical Pricing and Reimbursement in Mexico", OECD Health Working Paper, No. 25, OECD Publishing, Paris.

NICE (2008), *Social Value Judgements: Principles for the Development of NICE Guidance*, NICE, London.

NICE (2009), *Appraising Life-extending, end-of-life Treatments*, NICE, London.

Nikolentzos, A., E. Nolte and N. Mays (2008), *Paying for (Expensive) Drugs in the Statutory System: An Overview of experiences in 13 Countries*, London School of Hygiene and Tropical Medicine, London.

OECD (2008), *Pharmaceutical Pricing Policies in a Global Market*, OECD Publishing, Paris.

OECD (2010a), *OECD Health Data*, OECD Publishing, Paris.

OECD (2010b), *The OECD Innovation Strategy: Getting a Head Start on Tomorrow*, OECD Publishing, Paris.

OXERA (2001), *Fundamental Review of the Generic Drugs Market*, A report prepared for the Department of Health, OXERA, Oxford.

Paris, V. and E. Docteur (2006), "Pharmaceutical Pricing and Reimbursement in Canada", OECD Health Working Paper, No. 24, OECD Publishing, Paris.

Paris, V. and E. Docteur (2008), "Pharmaceutical Pricing and Reimbursement in Germany", OECD Health Working Paper, No. 39, OECD Publishing, Paris.

Paris, V., M. Devaux and L. Wei (2010), "Health Systems Institutional Characteristics: A Survey of 29 OECD Countries", OECD Health Working Paper, No. 50, OECD Publishing, Paris.

PPRI Participants (2007), *The United Kingdom Pharma Profile*, Publications/country reports, ÖBIG, Vienna, available at *http://ppri.oebig.at*.

PPRI Participants (2008a), *Denmark Pharma Profile*, Publications/country reports, ÖBIG, Vienna, available at *http://ppri.oebig.at*.

PPRI Participants (2008b), *France Pharma Profile*, Publications/country reports, ÖBIG, Vienna, available at *http://ppri.oebig.at*.

Raftery, J. (2008), "Paying for Costly Pharmaceuticals: Regulation of New Drugs in Australia, England and New-Zealand", *The Medical Journal of Australia*, Vol. 188, No. 1, pp. 26-28.

US Federal Trade Commission (2005), *Pharmacy Benefit Managers: Ownership of Mail-order Pharmacies*, US FTC.

Vogler, S., J. Espin and C. Habl (2009), "Pharmaceutical Pricing and Reimbursement Information (PPRI) – New PPRI Analysis Including Spain", *Pharmaceuticals Policy and Law*, Vol. 11, pp. 213-234.

Vogler, S. *et al.* (2007), "PPRI (Pharmaceutical Pricing and Reimbursement Information) Report", GOG-ÖBIG, Vienna, available at *http://ppri.oebig.at*.

Williamson, S. (2010), "Patient Access Schemes for High-cost Cancer Medicines", *The Lancet Oncology*, Vol. 11, pp. 111-112.

Chapter 7

Redesigning Health Systems
with the Support of ICTs

Evidence suggests that information and communication technologies (ICTs) can make significant improvements in health care delivery – reducing medical errors, improving clinical care through adherence to evidence-based guidelines, and preventing duplication and inefficiency for complex care pathways. ICT has great potential to increase value for money in health, yet the health sector lags far behind other parts of the economy in exploiting the productivity benefits of ICT. This chapter looks at the increasingly use of ICT to redesign health systems to achieve better performance.

1. Introduction

Information and communication technologies (ICT) are enabling technologies that have changed practically every sector of the modern economy, from on-line retailing, to just-in-time manufacturing, to computerised inventory management. They are changing health care too, and many of the lessons learned about how to make the most of the new opportunities opened up by ICT apply to health sector as well.

Evidence suggests that ICT can make significant improvements in health care delivery – reducing medical errors, improving clinical care through adherence to evidence-based guidelines, and preventing duplication and inefficiency for complex care pathways. ICT has great potential to increase value for money in health, yet the health sector lags far behind other parts of the economy in exploiting the productivity benefits of ICT.

Information technology contributes little to gains in productivity and service quality on its own. The value of ICT lies not just in its technical capacity to generate, store, analyse and transmit data, but in enabling new ways of working, such as enabling a clinician to review a radiograph taken at another hospital; a physician directly submitting a prescription to a pharmacy; expert systems aiding clinicians to choose the right drug; or carry out a consultation in a rural area through a video-conference. The possibilities of improving clinical care through ICT technology are almost endless. Perhaps the most immediately promising applications are improving the co-ordination of care for managing chronic disease where health professionals could share information to manage complex diseases, and enabling patients to have more involvement in their own care.

Introducing new work practices in a system as complex as health care provision takes time. Structures, organisation and skill sets have to be redefined, at the cost of considerable investment in training and equipment, disruption and possibly less satisfactory outcomes, while various new components start working efficiently together. Health care is particularly complicated in this respect, since it involves so many actors, many of whom may be unused to co-operating with each other. Health systems remain like "cottage industries" – small-scale producers with limited economies of scale and scope contrasting with large scale transformations that have spurred technological diffusion of ICT in other sectors.

This chapter looks at how a more comprehensive use of ICT can improve value for money in health care in a number of ways. It examines the barriers to getting the maximum benefit from ICT, such as privacy concerns and the lack of common standards and co-ordination across systems, as well as the reasons why the implementation of electronic health records is slow in most countries.* Finally, we look at how better use of

---

* This chapter draws upon a more extensive report published in 2010 by the OECD: *Improving Health Sector Efficiency: The Role of Information and Communication Technologies*. This report was based on an in-depth review of six OECD countries (Australia, Canada, the Netherlands, Spain, Sweden and the United States). The OECD has been in the forefront of developing common definitions and data for the adoption of ICT in health in the OECD.

ICT can form the basis for improving health performance, making shared, intelligible data a foundation for efficient, quality health care delivery.

2. What ICT can (and cannot) do for health care

An extensive study completed by the OECD in 2009 (*Improving Health Sector Efficiency: The Role of Information and Communication Technologies,* see footnote p. 186) identifies the range of potential interrelated benefits from ICT implementation including: increased quality and efficiency of care; reduced operating costs; reduced administrative costs; and supports to new modes of care.

As discussed in Chapter 5, chronic care has gained significant attention. The treatment of complex chronic diseases requires input across many different health care professions and multiple health care providers, thereby creating a complex set of data that the various people in the care process need to understand and use. Sharing information across providers is essential to improve clinical outcomes and also to prevent unnecessary duplications. The increasing importance of chronic disease and the new emphasis on co-ordination of care have been one of the drivers for increased use of ICT in health, where there is much greater scope for greater co-ordination and integration of clinical information systems and clinical care.

The chapter shows that there is increasing evidence that ICT can help improve the quality of health care. The effect of ICTs on costs is more equivocal and in only a few cases have investments in ICT led to lowering health care costs. For example, in health insurance systems, there is evidence to suggest that computerisation of billing can lower administrative costs. The use of Picture Archiving and Communications Systems (PACS) has led to lower number of x-rays, improved turnaround time, and some cost savings. Generally, however, cost savings have been demonstrated in small scale pilots but have proven difficult to realise at scale.

The importance of ICT is that it provides the necessary foundation to improve integration of care for chronic diseases. It also provides the information needed for incentive programmes such as pay for performance. ICT therefore plays a critical facilitative role, but is not alone sufficient to reform the health systems. When it is part of a broader strategy to improve health system performance, however, it can have a dramatic effect on results.

3. How can ICT improve value for money in health care

Improving patient safety

In recent years, a substantial body of evidence has documented the high rate of medical errors which the US Institute of Medicine estimates kills more people than traffic accidents (IOM, 2001). To date, the largest contribution that ICTs play is reducing medical errors and improving patient safety. Three types of medical errors are common: errors due to forgetfulness or inattention, errors of judgement or planning (rule-based errors), and errors resulting from a lack of knowledge. ICT can prevent these types of errors by making it easier for health care professionals to acquire and share information.

One common medical error is taking the wrong medications, leading to an adverse drug reaction (ADR). Adverse drug reactions have been estimated to be one of the leading causes of death in the United States (estimated between 4th and 6th highest cause). When drug prescriptions are computerised, an expert system can check for adverse drug reactions.

Box 7.1. **ICTs in health care**

Information and communication technologies (ICTs) in health care cover a variety of systems with different levels of complexity and potential, ranging from simple systems for electronic claim processing to more sophisticated systems allowing providers to share clinical information across different providers. The following is a list of common components of ICT in health (Jha, 2006; Blumenthal, 2006).

Electronic Medical Record (EMR) is an electronic version of a medical record and refers to electronic documentation of providers' notes, electronic viewing of laboratory and radiology results and electronic prescribing (CPOE) e-prescription: electronic prescribing of medication orders.

Electronic Health Record (EHR) is evolving concept but refers to subset of data from different Electronic Medical Records to create a linked record across multiple providers for care co-ordination.

Computerised Physician Order Entry (CPOE) consists in the entry of medication and other care orders, as well as ancillary services, directly into a computer.

Picture Archiving and Communication System (PACS) is computers or networks dedicated to the storage, retrieval, distribution and presentation of laboratory test results and radiology procedure result reports.

Telemedicine/electronic communication tools include: integrated health records, e-mail and web messaging – for use among health care team members, between physicians, laboratories, radiology and pharmacies and with patients; telemedicine or electronic communications between providers and patients who reside in remote areas; home telemonitoring for the elderly or others with chronic diseases.

	Basic system	Fully functional system
Health information and data: five functions		
Patient demographics	x	x
Patient problem lists	x	x
Electronic lists of medication taken by patients	x	x
Clinical notes	x	x
Notes including medical history and follow-up		x
Order-entry management: five functions		
Orders for prescriptions	x	x
Orders for laboratory tests		x
Orders for radiology tests		x
Prescriptions sent electronically		x
Orders sent electronically		x
Results management: three functions		
Viewing laboratory results	x	x
Viewing imaging results	x	x
Electronic images returned		x
Clinical decision support: three functions		
Warning of drugs interactions or contraindications provided		x
Out-of-range test levels highlighted		x
Reminders regarding guideline-based interventions or screening		x

Source: DesRoches *et al.* (2008).

DesRoches *et al.* (2008), using a Delphi process, defined the key functions that constitute an effective out-patient EHR. The functions that should be present to qualify a system as "fully functional" consist of four domains : recording patients' clinical and demographic data, viewing and managing results of laboratory tests and imaging, managing order entry (including electronic prescriptions), and supporting clinical decisions (including warnings about drug interactions or contra-indications).

It flags possible ADRs for patients taking multiple drugs, as well as contra-indications for drugs, such as patient age. It also generally contains patient information on history of reactions such as allergies to penicillin or sulfa drugs and provides a warning if these drugs are being prescribed. Studies have shown that ICT systems (including e-prescribing) reduce medication errors and decrease adverse drug reactions (Chaudry, 2006). The *Cochrane Review* has shown that electronic prescribing improves quality, but is equivocal on its cost effectiveness (Durieux, 2008).

Clinical decision support: compliance with evidence-based guidelines

A large body of literature has recently emerged providing evidence that following evidence-based clinical guidelines improve quality of care and patient outcomes. IT can play an important role in increasing compliance with guidelines – or protocol-based care, particularly in the management of chronic diseases such as asthma, diabetes or heart failure. In particular, IT systems are important in increasing the uptake of preventive services like screening tests for cancer. See Chapter 3 for more detailed discussions of evidence-based guidelines and Chapter 5 on Disease Management Programmes (DMPs).

Telemedicine for rural populations

ICT offers the possibility of improving access to quality care for those who live far away from health facilities. For example, in rural Western Australia, remoteness and low population density make it difficult to provide health services. ICTs (*e.g.*, through telemedicine) provide access to services to remote populations through shared EHRs and electronic messaging. In British Columbia the introduction of telemedicine has allowed thoracic surgery patients in rural areas to be assessed closer to where they live. Figure 7.1 shows how the number of patients who were seen increased significantly after telemedicine was introduced in 2003. It also shows how just one year post implementation, telemedicine gradually became the preferred mode of service delivery for both patients and doctors.

Efficiency gains

Given the productivity gains in other sectors, many hope that adoption of ICTs in health will improve productivity and reduce health spending in the long run. As discussed above, there are many possible areas where the introduction of ICT could lead to efficiency gains. Some of the gains could be through allocative efficiency by decreasing the use of health services – particularly expensive hospital care – through better co-ordination between primary and secondary care. There is also scope for improvements in technical efficiency such as preventing duplication of laboratory and diagnostic tests and preventing medical errors that can be extremely costly. Furthermore technical efficiency gains in administration may be possible particularly for insurance systems with complex financial accounting systems including premium collection and billing.

There is some evidence that ICTs can reduce costs. The most frequently cited positive effects are generally attributed to *reduced utilisation of health care services*. More effective information sharing, such as rapid electronic delivery of hospital discharge reports or the use of computerised provider order-entry systems can reduce the uptake of laboratory and radiology tests – sometimes by as much as 24% (Chaudry *et al.*, 2006). In most cases, clinical decision support features can also influence prescribing behaviour, and save money by informing physicians about "comparative effectiveness" of alternative medical treatments.

Figure 7.1. **The effects of telemedicine**

Thoracic surgery patients seen at outreach clinics in British Columbia (1998-2005)

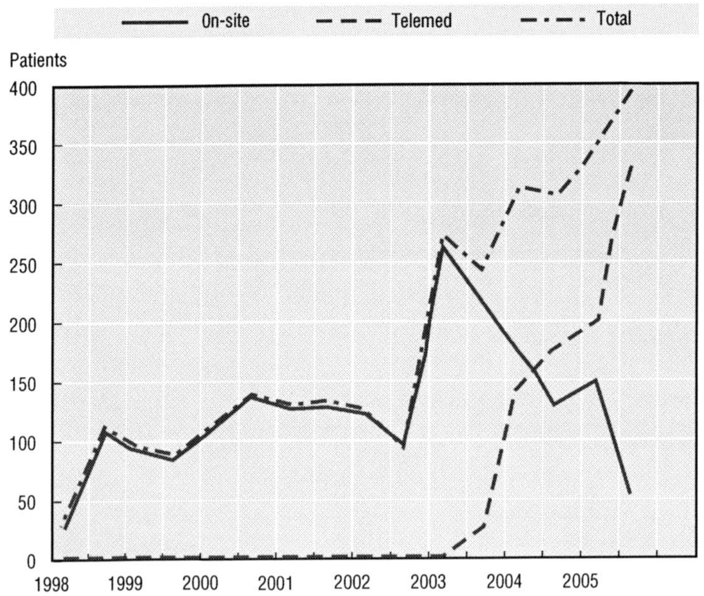

Source: Humer et al. (2006).

Administrative processes such as billing represent a prime opportunity for savings in most countries. OECD (2010) reports staggering administrative cost savings as a result of introducing electronic claims processing through the New England Healthcare Electronic Data Interchange Network (NEHEN). Claims that cost USD 5.00 to submit in labour costs per paper transaction were processed electronically at 15 cents per transaction after the introduction of NEHEN. Between July 1998 and February 2000, in less than two years, NEHEN was able to reduce annual members' costs per million transactions from USD 10.4 million to USD 1.4 million. This 90% savings was driven in large part by reductions in the amount of time needed to manually process billing and claims-related information.

In theory, ICTs can reduce costs of clinical services by *saving time of clinicians*. In British Columbia, where Picture Archiving and Communication Systems (PACS) have been widely adopted, 87% of radiologists reported improvements in their reporting and consultation efficiency, and 93.6% indicated it had reduced the time spent locating radiological examinations for reviews. However, in the OECD review of ICT in six OECD countries (Australia, Canada, the Netherlands, Spain, Sweden and the United States) GPs rarely reported a reduced workload as a result of using electronic medical records, with only Swedish physicians mentioning savings of approximately thirty minutes a day as a result of using e-prescription (OECD, 2010). Allied health professionals in Western Australia also reported a gain, indicating that using electronic messaging saved them time in a range of activities. They related this improvement to easier access to patient data, faster communication, and the availability of higher quality and more complete data.

ICTs reduce costly medical errors. Medication errors account for a significant number of additional hospital admissions and consultations in primary care. A UK study estimated adverse drug reactions due to medication errors at GBP 466. ICTs have the potential to *improve co-ordination of care for chronic diseases.* In British Columbia, Canada, the cost of the management of diabetes care dropped between 2001/02 and 2004/05 from an average of CAD 4 400 (Canadian dollars) to CAD 3 966 per patient after the measures described in Box 7.2 were implemented. There is limited evidence that ICT saves money, except in more narrow areas like PACS and administrative billing. There is however evidence that ICTs as a component of broader disease management programmes improve quality of care and often at price which is cost effective, but that these programmes rarely save money (see Chapter 5 on care co-ordination).

Box 7.2. Chronic disease management toolkit in British Columbia, Canada

In 2002, the Health Department of British Columbia identified problems with management of chronic diseases. This included low adherence to clinical guidelines for diabetes, with only 39% regularly having their blood sugar monitored through HbA1c, and low uptake of preventive measures. British Columbia developed a Chronic Disease Management (CDM) toolkit, a web-based information system for diabetes, congestive heart failure, and depression. CDM incorporates clinical practice guidelines into flow sheets and includes other features that allow health professionals to monitor care for chronic disease. The CDM tool increased the proportion of people with diabetes who had HbA1c, blood pressure and lipid tests from 21.8% in 2001/02 to 48.6% in 2004/05.

High upfront cost of ICTs with delayed benefits

Health ICT investments costs are difficult to determine. Costs estimates provided to the OECD were rough estimates and it can be difficult to separate health ICT costs within overarching budgets. In some cases, national and local projects are phased and only the budgets for the first phase (feasibility study) can be estimated. The actual budgets clearly depend on the final scope of the projects. The sums indicated may be a mix of capital or operational expenditure and may or may not include purchase and implementation costs such as training. Notwithstanding these difficulties, Table 7.1 below provides estimates of current budgets (2008-09) of three major national ICT agencies funded by government. Government funding is in the range of 0.1% to 0.3% of total expenditure on health in the three countries with investment per capita varying from USD 7 to 14. Australia's per capita investment has risen as a result of its 2010-11 budget announcements in eHealth.

Protti (2007) reported a rough assessment of total investment costs per capita that ranged from an estimated USD 129 in Canada to USD 552 per enrolee in Kaiser Permanente (United States) with the level depending on the degree of sophistication of the systems. Anderson et al. (2006), developed similar estimates for six countries including Canada and the United Kingdom. Striking in both the Protti and Anderson estimates as well as those of the OECD (see Table 7.2) is the relatively large per capita health ICT investment in the United Kingdom. Although well within the range of the per capita being spent by Kaiser Permanente, it stands out in comparison with other countries.

This high figure may in part be explained by the fact that the total costs reported for the UK programme run through 2015. In addition, the total includes central costs paid and recorded by "NHS Connecting for Health", as well as estimates of the local costs incurred in deploying the systems. Although a recent UK NAO (2008) suggests that local costs are

Table 7.1. **Current budget for ICT initiatives in three OECD countries**

Agency/Initiative	United States	Canada	Australia
	Office of the National Co-ordinator	Canada Health Infoway	Australian Government Department of Heath and Ageing
Total expenditure on health (million USD at exchange rate) and % of GDP[1]	2 198 764[2] 16.0% of GDP	154 329 [3] 10.6% of GDP	90 243[4] 9.1% of GDP
Current budget for ICT initiatives (million USD at exchange rate)	2 061[5]	455[6, 7]	268[8, 9]
Current investment per capita (USD)[10]	6.83	13.8	11.96

1. *OECD Health Data 2009.*
2. 2007. The figures in Table 7.1 and Table 7.2 do not include provincial/territorial investments in eHealth initiatives, made on their own, or in collaboration with Canada Health Infoway (Infoway). Infoway projects are cost-shared with the provinces/territories (typically Infoway: 75%, provinces/territories: 25%).
3. 2008.
4. 2007-08, *Australia's Health 2010*, Chap. 8, pp. 406 onwards.
5. *Source:* HHS, FY 2010, Congressional Justification for Departmental Management, includes ARRA funds.
6. *Source:* Canada Health Infoway, "Building a Healthy Legacy Together, *Annual Report 2008/2009*".
7. 2009, exchange rate: USD 1 = CAD 1.10.
8. *Source:* Personal communication – E-health-Policy and Future Directions, Department of Health and Ageing, Australia – and updated information provided in July 2010.
9. 2009-10, exchange rate: USD 1 = AUD 1.1476.
10. *OECD Population Data, 2007.*
Source: Protti (2007); Anderson (2006).

StatLink ⟪ *http://dx.doi.org/10.1787/888932319858*

underestimated, it appears that – unlike many other countries – both the United Kingdom and the United States may have more realistic estimates of total health ICT costs given the top down and centralised nature of their programmes.

Table 7.2. **Total budget allocated by national government in two OECD countries**

Agency/Initiative	Canada	United Kingdom
	Canada Health Infoway (2001-2010)	NHS Connecting for Health Programme (2002-2015)
Total expenditure on health (million USD at exchange rate) and % of GDP[1]	154 329 10.6% of GDP	235 816 8.4% of GDP
Total budget allocated (million USD at exchange rate)	1 430[2]	20 633[3]
Total investment per capita (USD)	35.81	338.38

1. *OECD Health Data 2009.*
2. Through March 2010, exchange rate: USD 1 = CAD 1.10.
3. NAO, through December 2015, exchange rate: USD 1 = GBP 0.61.
Source: Protti (2007); Anderson (2006).

StatLink ⟪ *http://dx.doi.org/10.1787/888932319877*

The costs in implementing health ICT solutions are incurred up front, and the benefits, both financial and clinical, are not always immediately realised. It takes a long time to reach a level of functionality needed to truly serve the needs of clinicians and purchasers. A review of Canadian investments into ICT, "Pan Canadian EHR: Projected Costs and Benefits", reported that cost/benefit analysis was still negative after ten years. However, after 20 years the savings would be substantial.

4. Use of electronic health records is slow with a few exceptions

The OECD recently undertook a study on how ten OECD countries were monitoring and evaluating adoption and use of ICTs in the health sector. The study looked at:

● Policy needs and information requirements.

Box 7.3. **Stages of ICT diffusion**

In the early 1990s, the OECD developed a conceptual framework for the diffusion of information technology. This framework recognises that measuring ICT is a "moving target". Countries follow an S-shaped curve that begins with increasing access. Once IT reaches a critical stage of diffusion, policy interest shifts from access to quality of data and its impact on performance.

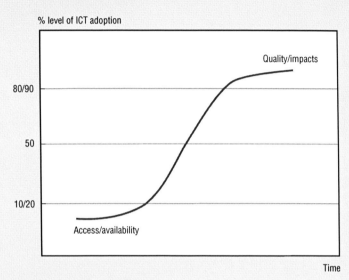

Source: OECD (2010, p. 115).

When ICT is at a low level, there is interest in indicators concerning availability and access to infrastructure or the readiness to adopt ICTs. As ICT use progresses, countries place greater emphasis on the purpose and level of ICT use (intensity). In the United States, where use is low, the most important question is increasing adoption rates. In the Scandinavian countries, where electronic health records are widespread, the constraints are linking up different components of the system and concerns about privacy.

- Common or leading-edge practices which might be further developed and implemented.
- A framework for the selection of internationally comparable indicators.
- Areas for international action and future research.

The study found that most OECD countries are only taking their first steps in ICT implementation. In particular, integration of ICT across health providers, where data was shared for care co-ordination, was at an early stage in almost all OECD countries.

The implementation of ICTs in clinical care has proven to be a difficult and risky undertaking, in spite of the promise they offer. Adoption across OECD countries has remained remarkably uneven. In the United States, a 2008 survey shows an uptake of only 13% of the most basic functions of EHRs by primary care physicians. In Australia, the United Kingdom, as in many Scandinavian countries, EHRs are almost ubiquitous in primary care, but uptake of the most advanced features has been slow and exchanging health information with other parts of the system remains often largely paper-based. For example, Finland has nearly 100% adoption of EHRs in hospitals and nearly the same in primary care. However, electronic exchange of key documents such as referrals and discharge letters between these settings has lagged (Figure 7.2).

Figure 7.2. **Use of Electronic Health Records in Finland, Norway and the United States (2007)**

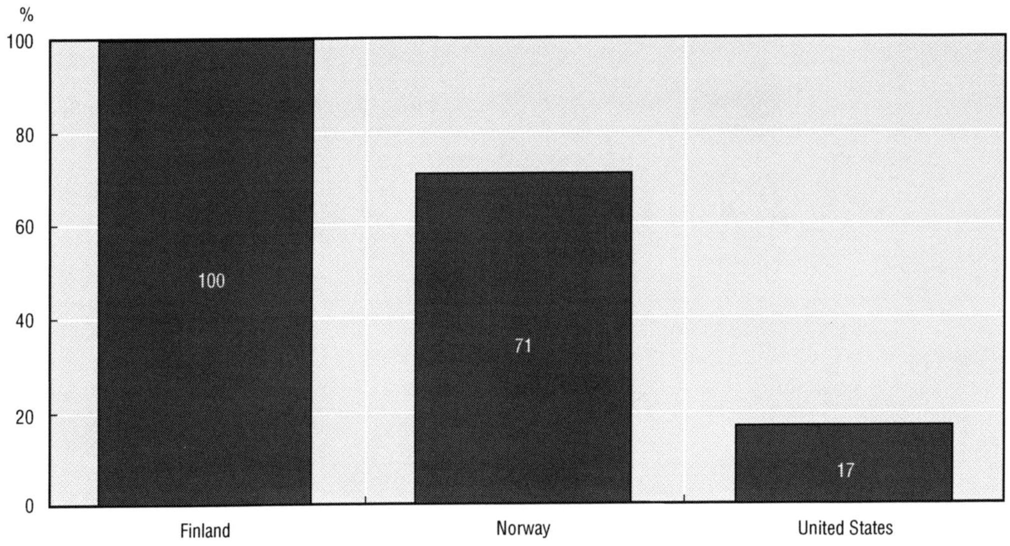

Source: Finn Telemedicum and STAKES; Office of the Auditor General of Norway; DesRoches *et al.* (2008).

StatLink ⊞⊑⊒ *http://dx.doi.org/10.1787/888932319649*

There is very limited monitoring of ICTs across the OECD. Generally, statistical offices (with exception of Canada, the United States and the Czech Republic) do not collect information on ICT use in the health sector in spite of the fact that there is growing interest in measuring ICT penetration across the economy. Most surveys are conducted on an *ad hoc* basis, and most focus on the primary care sector.

5. More widespread adoption requires overcoming several challenges

Understanding the challenges to adoption and use of ICTs is critical to achieving more widespread penetration. The following section discusses the major issues that need to be addressed to realise the potential of ICT in the health sector.

Incentives should be aligned, benefits and costs fairly allocated

Building a business case for ICT adoption is difficult because so far most evidence shows improvement in patient quality of care without clear evidence of cost savings. Health care organisations may be reluctant to take on the cost of implementation and maintenance of ICTs like EHRs, if better quality is not accompanied by better payment or at least some compensation. Another problem inhibiting the uptake of ICTs is how costs are distributed. Those who benefit from greater use of ICT are often not those who bear the costs of adoption.

The way providers are paid plays a critical role in how they behave – incentives matter. They are not the only factor determining behavior, but financial incentives do play an important role in the decisions that providers like hospitals and primary care providers make. Unfortunately, in most health systems there is no incentive for providers to invest in new information systems. Payment systems often do not pay extra to providers for providing electronic information. Often, electronic record systems do not generate the necessary information needed by purchasers. It is therefore not very surprising that there is low uptake in ICT in health care.

If one looks at traditional payment systems for hospitals, there is no additional payment for having electronic patient records. Even a sophisticated system like Diagnosis Related Groups (DRGs) to pay hospitals does not require a hospital electronic medical record. This explains how the United States, with its low penetration of EHRs, could still support some of the most sophisticated hospital payment systems in the world. In primary care, the traditional payment systems are fee-for-service (FFS) and capitation. In FFS, there are usually no special payments received for having electronic medical records, e-prescribing, clinical decision support systems. Similarly, with capitated payments, this does not require using electronic health records as evidenced by its use in UK general practice before the large IT programme.

Therefore, payment systems need to encourage the uptake of ICTs. This has been a central plank of many successful programmes to improve uptake of ICTs. It is important to note that the investments in IT are often part of a wider strategy to improve primary care and hospital performance and are linked with broader incentive regimes that pay for performance and reforms to improve chronic care such as disease management. Often pay-for-performance schemes begin with paying for reporting which provides financial incentives for ICT adoption and providing data on the quality of care in regular electronic form. Pay for reporting is a necessary prelude to a more full scale pay-for-performance scheme.

There is a need for new business model for ICT which allocates funds from those who benefit from ICTs to those to have to bear the costs. In the current environment, providers bear most if not all of the costs and yet receive little benefit which is mainly improved patients outcomes.

Broader governance agenda to align ICT objectives with health system objectives

One of the issues that emerged from the OECD case studies on ICT adoption in health is the broader issue of "governance" or "stewardship". When embarking on the implementation of complex ICT programmes, often the underlying health goals can be lost in myriad technical details such as standards for interoperability. It is important to keep sight of the underlying health system goals that these systems are supposed to help health professionals do their job better and to give patients access to their own health information.

Broader governance also calls for commonly-defined and consistently-implemented standards. While health care organisations have access to an ever increasing number of information technology products, their systems often cannot speak to each other, thus preventing the gains from sharing information. "Linkages" remain a serious problem. EHR systems must be interoperable, clinical information must still be meaningful once transferred, both between systems and between versions of the same software. It must also be gathered consistently if secondary analysis is ever to be performed effectively.

The development of standards to enable exchange of information continues to be a political and logistical challenge. Standards development must be considered in the context of technical, societal and commercial needs, both locally and globally. The problem has been now widely recognised as a market failure, and governments need to intervene.

Box 7.4. **Interoperability and legacy systems**

Different computer systems are said to be interoperable, when they can exchange data with and use data from other systems. Simply converting data from a paper format to a digital format is not enough to ensure interoperability. This requires standard rules specifying how to send information back and forth using a standard language of machine readable codes for things like diagnosis, procedures, drugs, laboratory and radiological tests, etc.

Legacy systems refer to systems already in place. Problems can arise in trying to link up legacy systems to other IT functions. Currently, many providers are already using proprietary systems for electronic health records and other applications. These systems are difficult to change because users are familiar with them and learning a new system can be disruptive. The Netherlands faced this problem in 2005, when there were many different vendors creating and supporting electronic health records. Most of the systems were not interoperable. Subsequently, the Netherlands implemented a new programme that created standards for interoperability of electronic health records.

Four stage taxonomy of interoperability

The Center for Information Technology leadership has developed a classification system for understanding interoperability based on three factors: the amount of human involvement, the sophistication of the ICT, and the adoption of standards.

Level 1. Non-electronic data. ICT not used to share information. Information shared orally or written. Common examples: postal mail and phone.

Level 2. Machine transportable data. Transmission of non-standard information via basic ICT. Information within document cannot be electronically manipulated. No computerised data processing or logic can be applied. Common examples: email of free text; exchange of scanned documents, faxing, pictures, PDFs.

Level 3. Machine organisable data. Transmission of structured messages containing non-standardised data. This often results in incompatible data because different organisations are using different definitions and there is no common data dictionary. Common examples: secure email of free text; incompatible /proprietary file formats, HL-7 messages.

Level 4. Machine interpretable data. Transmission of structured messages containing standardised and coded data. This is the ideal situation in which all systems exchange information using the same formats and vocabularies. All content can be extracted and converted electronically in each filed and no longer requires human intervention. Examples: automated exchange of coded drugs for e-prescription, lists of diagnosis for PACS, diagnosis and procedure coding for DRGs.

Table 7.3. **Measures to address lack of interoperability by country**

Area of focus	Australia	Canada	Netherlands	Spain	Sweden	United States
Certification of products	NO	YES	YES	YES	YES	YES
Standards-setting activities	YES	YES	YES	YES	YES	YES
Vendor conformance and usability requirements	YES	YES	(YES) In proof of concept stage	NO	NO	NO

Source: Center for Information Technology Leadership; Walker *et al.* (2005).

To move interoperability forward, many governments have set up specific bodies or agencies to co-ordinate standard-setting and have developed strategies at a national level. Under pressure from vendors and users, as well as international standards organisations, countries have started to collaborate more openly in the development and refinement of standards.

The main constraint to implementing ICTs in health is the governance challenge of orchestrating all of the different elements and diverse stakeholders. ICTs only realise their potential when all parts of the system work. ICTs projects are notoriously difficult to manage as evidenced by the experience of United Kingdom's major ICT programme which has suffered many delays and unforeseen technical difficulties that have delayed implementation (NAO, 2006).

Getting privacy and confidentiality right at the beginning is key to future success in ICT

Although the OECD (2010) revealed that many countries have achieved great success in implementing a variety of health IT solutions, security/privacy issues have remained one of the biggest challenges. Health information can be extremely sensitive particularly for stigmatised diseases like sexually transmitted diseases, AIDS and mental disorders including substance abuse. Electronic health records sometimes contain information about personal behaviour such as smoking, alcohol use and information on sexual preferences. There is concern that information could have detrimental effects on employment, be used by health insurance companies to deny coverage or increase premiums, to harm social integration in the community. Numerous surveys have shown that the public is very concerned about the privacy of personal medical information.

Most countries cited legislative impediments as a significant issue in implementing EHRs (OECD, 2010). There are for instance many legal issues involved in the sharing of medical information. In many countries, the information belongs to the patient and consent is required for the release and use of information. In some systems reviewed by the OECD, patient consent is presumed (patients have the right to opt-out of disclosure). In other systems, consent is required up-front (opt-in). As in other domains like pensions, behavioural economics has repeatedly shown that opt-out provisions – where the default is participation – will lead to higher rates of use compared to systems where people must choose to participate (Thaler, 2009).

Privacy issues are viewed by many as the main "road block" to creating a co-ordinated information system for patient care and wider sharing of health information across different parts of the system. Even in Sweden, which enjoys country-wide e-prescribing, GPs are currently unable to access the full list of medications that their patients have been prescribed because of legal restrictions.

It is important to deal with privacy issues at the beginning of the long journey up the diffusion curve. Appropriate privacy protection should be incorporated into the design of new ICT systems and policies from the outset. Lack of clarity in the purpose and scope for privacy may have unintended consequences. If privacy protections prevent the sharing of information then potentially large gains in quality of care for patients will be diminished.

6. ICT is the foundation for a wider approach to improving health system performance

ICT can be a significant tool for improving health care quality and enhancing value for money. Information sharing is essential for a value-driven health system. Electronic medical records provide the most hope for improved assessment of clinical quality in the future. ICTs are central to efforts to reorganise clinical care to face the new challenges of chronic disease management, allowing greater integration between primary and secondary care, but also between health and social care.

Evidence to date suggests that to improve performance requires more than just investment in ICT. It also requires aligning incentives, re-designing service delivery, and integrating providers into a common culture committed to quality of care, where ICT objectives are aligned with broader health system goals. When all of these components are in place, it is possible to find real gains in performance such as improved outcomes at lower costs (few hospitalisations with shorter lengths of stay).

As in other sectors, investing in ICTs does not automatically boost productivity growth. There is a "productivity paradox" first described by Solow in 1987: computer technology can be found everywhere but in the productivity data. It was almost impossible to disentangle how much improved economic performance was due to the enabling technologies and how much was due to the transformation in how businesses managed their internal operations and their relationships with customers, competitors, and suppliers. The "productivity paradox" was resolved a decade later, when accumulating evidence showed that IT-intensive industries had greater productive growth than less IT-intensive industries (Colecchia and Shreyer, 2002). The delay in productivity gains from IT investment was due in part to the learning process inherent in the use of the new technologies.

In the health ICTs, there is also a productivity paradox. To date, there is very limited evidence that ICTs are leading to significant increases in productivity. There are exceptions like the use of PCRs and for administrative billing. However, evidence from high performing systems show what is possible once all the pieces are in place. ICT is an important building block in many promising areas for improved health performance, such as pay for performance and foundations for disease management programmes and therefore a critical component in improving value for money in health systems.

7. Conclusions

ICT has great potential to increase value for money in health – reducing medical errors, improving clinical care through adherence to evidence-based guidelines, and preventing duplication and inefficiency for complex care pathways. Getting the maximum benefit from ICT requires addressing privacy concerns and the lack of common standards and co-ordination across systems.

The most promising applications are improving the co-ordination of care for managing chronic disease where health professionals could share information to manage complex diseases; and enabling patients to have more involvement in their own care. IT can play an important role in increasing compliance with guideline – or protocol-based care, particularly in the management of chronic diseases such as asthma, diabetes or heart failure. In particular, IT systems are important in increasing the uptake of preventive services like screening tests for cancer.

In terms of productivity gains and cost savings, IT can achieve improvements in technical efficiency such as preventing duplication of laboratory and diagnostic tests and preventing medical errors that can be extremely costly. Furthermore, technical efficiency gains in administration may be possible particularly for insurance systems with complex financial accounting systems including premium collection and billing.

Broader governance calls for commonly-defined and consistently-implemented standards. While health care organisations have access to an ever increasing number of information technology products, their systems often cannot speak to each other, thus preventing the gains from sharing information. Electronic health record systems must be interoperable, and clinical information must still be meaningful once transferred, both between systems and between versions of the same software.

Furthermore, payment systems need to encourage the uptake of ICTs. It is important to note that the investments in IT are often part of a wider strategy to improve primary care and hospital performance and are linked with broader incentive regimes. Finally, there is a need for new business model for ICT which allocates funds from those who benefit from ICTs to those to have to bear the costs. In the current environment, providers bear most if not all of the costs and yet receive little benefit which is mainly improved patients outcomes.

Bibliography

Anderson, G.F., B.K. Frogner, R.A. Johns and U.E. Reainhardt (2006), "Health Care Spending and Use of Information Technology in OECD Countries", *Health Affairs*, Vol. 25, No. 3, pp. 819-831.

Australian Health Information Council (2007), "E-health and Future Directions", Department of Health and Ageing, Australia.

Blumenthal, D., C. DesRoches, K. Donelan *et al.* (2006), "Health Information Technology in the United States: The Information Base for Progress", Robert Wood Johnson Foundation, Princeton, NJ.

Canada Health Infoway (2009), "Building a Healthy Legacy Together", *Annual Report 2008/2009*.

Chaudhry, B. *et al.* (2006), "Systematic Review: Impact of Health Information Technology on Quality, Efficiency and Costs of Medical Care", *Annals of Internal Medicine*, Vol. 144, pp. E-12-E-22.

Colecchia, A. and P. Schreyer (2002), "ICT Investment and Economic Growth in the 1990s: Is the United States a Unique Case? A Comparative Study of Nine OECD Countries", *Review of Economic Dynamics*, Vol. 5, No. 2, pp. 408-442.

Halamka, J.D. (2000), "New England Healthcare EDI Network – The New England Approach to HIPAA", available at: *www.ehcca.com/presentations/HIPAA2/106.pdf*.

HHS – US Department of Health and Human Services (2010), "Congressional Justification for Departmental Management".

Humer, M., A. Luoma and B. Nelems (2006), "Distant Thoracic Surgical Patient Assessment in Rural British Columbia: The Evolution from On-site Clinics to Telemedicine Clinics, 1985-2005", *BC Medical Journal*, Vol. 48, No. 6, pp. 279-284.

Jha, A., T.G. Ferris, K. Donelan, C. DesRoches, A. Shields, S. Rosenbaum and D. Blumenthal (2006), "How Common Are Electronic Health Records in the United States? A Summary of the Evidence", *Health Affairs*, Vol. 25, pp. 496-507.

NAO – UK National Audit Office (2006), "The National Programme for IT in the NHS: Progress since 2006", Report by the Auditor general.

OECD (2007), *OECD Population Data 2007*, OECD Publishing, Paris.

OECD (2009), *OECD Health Data 2009 – Statistics and Indicators for 30 Countries*, OECD Publishing, Paris.

OECD (2010), *Improving Health Sector Efficiency: The Role of Information and Communication Technologies*, OECD Health Policy Studies, OECD Publishing, Paris.

Protti, D. (2007), "Canada's EHR Journey: Pragmatic Progress and Promising Potential", Powerpoint presentation to OECD Expert Meeting on ICT in the Health Sector, Paris.

Pyra Management Consulting Services Inc. (2008), "Emerging Trends in Diabetes Care and Management".

Solow, R.M. (1987), "We'd Better Watch Out", *New York Times Book Review*, 12 July.

Thaler, R.H. and C. Sunstein (2008), *Nudge: Improving Decisions about Health, Wealth, and Happiness*, Yale University Press.

Wagner, E.H. (1998), "Chronic Disease Management: What Will it Take to Improve Care for Chronic Illness?", *Effective Clinical Practice*, Vol. 1, pp. 2-4.

Walker, J. *et al.* (2005), "The Value of Health Care Information Exchange and Interoperability", *Health Affairs*, Supplement Web Exclusive: W5-10–W5-18.

OECD PUBLISHING, 2, rue André-Pascal, 75775 PARIS CEDEX 16
PRINTED IN FRANCE
(81 2010 14 1 P) ISBN 978-92-64-08880-1 – No. 57473 2010